Experience of the Sacred

EXPERIENCE OF THE SACRED

Readings in the Phenomenology of Religion

Sumner B. Twiss and Walter H. Conser, Jr.

EDITORS

BROWN UNIVERSITY PRESS

Published by University Press of New England / Hanover & London

Brown University Press
Published by University Press of New England, Hanover, NH 03755
© 1992 by the Trustees of Brown University
All rights reserved
Printed in the United States of America   5   4   3   2   1
CIP data appear at the end of the book

Acknowledgments begin on page 293

For
ELLEN P. PRESTON
and
BEATRICE R. REYNOLDS
—SBT

To
EMILY, DAVID, AND MEGAN
—WHC

Contents

LEVELS OF MEANING IN THE
RELIGIOUS LIFE-WORLD
(*Existential-Hermeneutical Phenomenology of Religion*)

Preface

Phenomenology of religion denotes a family of related types of inquiry into religion that has developed over the past ninety years. In order to understand and appreciate fully the phenomenology of religion, it is necessary to become acquainted with the range and scope of its activities. Unfortunately, few teaching materials are expressly designed to familiarize students of religion with the wealth of work done and results achieved under the name of phenomenology of religion. To remedy this deficiency and to improve students' access to phenomenology of religion, we have designed a sourcebook that illustrates the range, type, and results of significant twentieth-century investigations in this area. Naturally, we cannot hope to be exhaustive in our selections. Rather our goal is to provide a collection of accessible and representative readings for use in the variety of courses that assign and study such materials.

In selecting the readings for this volume, we included materials regarded as classics in the field, for example, selections from Otto, Scheler, Eliade, and Ricoeur. We also made a special effort to include contemporary selections which, while using the "classics" as touchstones, attempt to forge new ground in a clear, rigorous, and provocative manner, for example, selections from Kristensen, Bynum, Smith, and Westphal. Finally, we have incorporated selections representing phenomenological inquiry into non-Western and prehistoric religious traditions as well as women's religious experience, for example, selections from Sekida, Kitagawa, Arthur, and Christ.

Following the introduction, the remainder of the book is divided into three sections plus a selected bibliography. Each of these sections examines a distinctive mode of phenomenology of religion—essential, historical-typological, and existential-hemeneutical phenomenology—through readings illustrating representative materials, for example, accounts of numinous, mystical, and feminist religious experience; forms of the sacred such as sacred words or sacred places; and themes in the religious life-world such as guilt, hope, and freedom.

Finally, we have demonstrated phenomenology's interdisciplinary use and relevance by including at the end of each section a selection from one of the three principal disciplines employing and contributing to the phenomenology of religion—philosophy (Dupré), anthropology and history of religions (Hultkrantz), and psychology (Pruyser). Our goal throughout the volume has been to provide an anthology of accessible readings that highlight the phenomenology of religion in action.

It is our very great pleasure to acknowledge the assistance of various colleagues in the preparation of this volume. For their critical and constructive comments on our introductory essay and the volume as a whole, we are deeply indebted to Professors Wendell S. Dietrich and John P. Reeder, Jr., of Brown's Department of Religious Studies, Professor Ernest Sosa of Brown's Department of Philosophy, and University Press of New England's anonymous external readers. For their valuable counsel on the volume's reprinted selections, we thank J. Keith Green, a doctoral candidate in Brown's Department of Religious Studies, and Professor Pierre Saint-Amand of Brown's Department of French. For their material help in the logistics of gaining permissions for the reprinted selections, we thank Bonnie Buzzell and Dominique Coulombe of Brown's Rockefeller Library, Gail Tetreault, Academic Office Coordinator of the Department of Religious Studies, and Katherine Langhaugh, undergraduate student assistant to the Department. For her expert word-processing as well as her ability to master and use new computer technologies for the volume's preparation, we thank Jane Simmons, manuscripts secretary of Brown's Department of Religious Studies. For timely support from Brown's Faculty Research Fund, we thank Bryan Shepp, Dean of the Faculty. And for his ongoing general support of our enterprise, we thank Professor John P. Kenney of Reed College's Department of Religion.

Note: In order to simplify the production of this volume, we have eliminated all nonsubstantive footnotes from the reprinted selections. Readers interested in seeing these footnotes may consult the original sources.

S.B.T.
W.H.C., Jr.

Experience of the Sacred

Introduction

The phenomenology of religion is a method of investigation in the academic study of religion, that broad humanistic exploration of religion which has emerged so forcefully in American colleges and universities. As the academic study of religion (or religious studies as it is often called) has consolidated its position within the curricular offerings of American institutions of higher education, two important developments have become clear.[1] First, the academic study of religion has clearly established its independence from the theological study of religion. As more and more departments and programs of religious studies have appeared in state universities and private colleges, they have repeatedly demonstrated their distance from the presuppositions and assumptions associated with seminaries and divinity schools. Second, as the field of religious studies has matured, its course offerings and institutional profile have increasingly become that of a multidisciplinary and humanistic field in the academy. Religious studies has grown from its origins in textual criticism and philological investigation to incorporate the scholarship from historical, literary, philosophical, and social scientific fields of inquiry.

The phenomenological study of religion has contributed to both of these developments. For, as these introductory remarks will more amply demonstrate, phenomenology typically brackets or lays aside metaphysical questions of the real existence of the sacred or the divine. In this way it, too, distances itself from traditional theological inquiry and demonstrates the fruitfulness of an academic approach to the study of religion. Beyond that, as the tradition of the phenomenological analysis of religion has developed, it likewise has incorporated many of the insights and creatively responded to the challenges contained in the findings of other fields of research into religion.

The history of the phenomenology of religion is a complex one. It might be compared to a musical composition that contains three separate but related voices—the essential, the historical-typological, and the existential-hermeneutical phenomenology of religion. Schematically, the first voice begins with the publication of Rudolf Otto's *The Idea of the Holy*, which establishes the direction and overall tone of the composition.[2] Subsequently, in the work of Gerardus van der Leeuw and others, the second voice appears, embellishing upon the first voice yet clearly projecting its own distinctive sound.[3] Though receding somewhat into the background, the first voice continues to be heard, and in fact enriches the composition through its interplay with the now dominant second voice. Finally, the third voice, that of the existential phenomenology of religion, enters, and new elements as well as established themes are audible.[4] In this way the three voices interact with one another, shaping the overall melody and contrapuntally contributing their parts to the resonance and power of the composition as a whole. This phenomenological composition has a certain unfinished character to it. For it not only continues in the present, it also influences such established traditions outside itself as philosophy, history, and psychology as well as such fresh new postmodern modes of criticism as deconstruction and the hermeneutics of gender.

As the musical image suggests, there has been both unity and creativity in the history of the phenomenology of religion. The first use of the phrase "phenomenology of religion" occurred in the 1887 edition of the *Manual of the Science of Religion* by the Dutch scholar, P. D. Chantepie de la Saussaye (1848–1920).[5] However, Chantepie de la Saussaye conceived of phenomenological analysis as little more than a cataloging of the forms of religion, and his views had little impact on the later development of phenomenology of religion; indeed, the whole section on phenomenology was dropped from the next edition of the *Manual*.

Far more influential for the subsequent history of the phenomenological analysis of religion has been the work of Edmund Husserl (1859–1938) and Wilhelm Dilthey (1833–1911). While there were significant differences between the two, particularly in terms of philosophical style and approach, these German philosophers developed methodological and conceptual insights that reverberated throughout the history of the phenomenological study of religion.

Edmund Husserl's proposals for a philosophical phenomenology amounted to a call for a fresh start in philosophy.[6] In what has become a motto for the phenomenological movement, Husserl called for a "return to the things themselves." By this phrase Husserl sought to free philosophy from prior dogmatic claims about the nature of knowledge, the world, and ourselves, claims that he felt lacked any ultimate philosophical justification. Suspicious of theoretical preconceptions that shape and form the experience we are trying to describe before that description has even begun, Husserl sought to develop a philosophy without presuppositions. For example, regarding epistemological inquiry he emphasized that phenomenology must not initially take over informal metaphors, such as "stream of consciousness," nor adopt explicit theoretical constructs, such as the rigid distinction between mind and body, for both of these distort our attempt to describe the experience. Instead, phenomenology must limit itself to descriptions and analyses of experience, inquiries that are open to further revision and improvements.

In his writings, Husserl expanded this insight into a distinctive procedure for examining the nature of human experience. This procedure divides into roughly four major phases: (1) bracketing commonsense beliefs, (2) focusing reflectively on the phenomena of experience, (3) analyzing the traits of these phenomena and their implications, and (4) reporting the results to others for further confirmation or disconfirmation. These phases constituted the core of Husserl's phenomenology, yet they would seem to raise an immediate question: is it not disingenuous of Husserl to decry previous theory builders, only to devise one of his own? At one level, the answer is yes, and Husserl stands in a long line of distinguished thinkers who argue that their predecessors erred and we have to start over again. Yet, at another level, this criticism misunderstands an important point of Husserl's project. For while the characteristics of his procedure do distinguish phenomenology from other philosophical approaches, Husserl contends that phenomenology is not a conceptual imposition upon experience and further that the importance of the procedure is attested by the accuracy and fruitfulness of the method itself. As Robert Solomon has pointed out, for Husserl there is no distinction between method and result in phenomenology.[7] And as Husserl himself demonstrates in his own work, this procedure does not remain privileged and unchallenged, but rather constitutes methods continuously questioned and sharpened in the doing of phenomenology.

The first phase of bracketing (also called by Husserl epoché and the phenomenological reduction) involved suspending all commonsense beliefs and judgments about the existence, value, or truth of the objects encountered in experience. Such a step is so thoroughgoing as to include suspending belief in, and philosophical concern with, the existence of the external world. Here again, we find Husserl's concern to see our experience without the presupposition of theory, interpretation, or assumption imposing upon and shaping what we see. The forest we see from the window of our study, for example, is not an interdependent ecosystem of flora and fauna in competition for survival and threatened by pollution. Rather, it is a vista of variegated colors, shapes, sounds, and scents. Phenomenological analysis does not contradict either the existence of the object or the scientific analysis of the world, but it does bracket them so that we can directly describe what we see.

The first step positions the inquirer for the next which involves viewing the experience reflectively, and seeing how in his experience he is conscious of or related to the objects of his experience. In this second step, for example, the inquirer sees himself (reflectively) in his own act of seeing an object (perceptually); that is, he focuses in a second-order reflective way on his first-order conscious act of perceiving an object. The image is: looking at himself looking at some object; the "looking at object" is ordinary perception, while the "looking at self" is an intellectual act of reflection (discernment, intuition). As Husserl would say, the inquirer becomes the "disinterested spectator" of himself and his conscious experience. This step in turn positions the inquirer to reflect on the intrinsic features of conscious experience, its phenomena and acts.

Husserl always maintained that phenomenology was concerned with the essence and not simply the incidental aspects of experience. For him this third phase of essential examination (he also called it eidetic reduction) sought to analyze the basic traits and types of objects, to figure out the implications and possible interconnections of the experiences under review. Phenomenologists often call this technique "free imaginative variation." It seeks to peel away the extraneous attributes, to lay bare the object that is before one. Thus phenomenological analysis of the experience of friendship, of solving a mathematical theorem, or of the holy produces the essential qualities of that experience. Establishing the relation between the circumference and radius of a circle, for example, tells us something significant about the necessary aspects of all possible circles. We can distinguish between our experience of the circle and all other types of geometric figures. We can reflect imaginatively about other properties and relations pertaining to a circle. When we have completed our analysis of the circle, we know something about the essence of all possible circles. Husserl insists that these qualities are not essential merely because we happen to believe that they are essential. Nor are they essential but only in some confined sphere correlated to our position in an economic class or cultural setting. Rather, Husserl insists that phenomenological analysis produces apodictic knowledge, knowledge not relative to time and place.

The final phase or step involves communicating phenomenological discoveries to a broader audience so that the findings may be verified or disconfirmed. Husserl called himself a "perpetual beginner" and in this characterization he again signalled his opposition to dogmatic philosophizing. One must always be willing to go back to the beginning, back to the experience itself, to see more directly and analyze more completely. Beyond that, Husserl believed that phenomenological findings, like all scientific claims, must be subject to independent testing and verification. Yet such verification was more than simply checking for syllogistic fallacies or misplaced premises. Indeed, as the phenomenologist, Max Scheler, cautioned, "one must read a phenomenological book with a completely *different attitude*." [8] For Scheler notes that phenomenological discussions often appear indirect and roundabout. They possess these qualities precisely because they are designed to report discoveries in an active rather than inert manner, attempting to lead others to see and verify for themselves what phenomenologists claim to discern. Phenomenological discussions are expressly designed to engage the reader's active intellect; they are complex communicative acts designed to position readers to see the essential nature of phenomena for themselves.

One final observation is appropriate at this point. Husserl maintained that the phenomenological method demonstrated the intentionality of human consciousness. By this phrase Husserl meant that consciousness is always consciousness of something, it always has an object. My experience of anger, of faith, of love always has an object toward which it is directed. This object, Husserl points out, can be a real or material object, such as another person, or it can be an unreal or ideal object such as the Fountain of Youth or a geometric proof. Beyond this, Husserl argues that analysis of the intentional nature of consciousness points to the distinction between the *act* of consciousness (noesis), for example, doubting, worshipping, loving, and the intentional *object* of consciousness (noema). The act of consciousness is clearly related to the intentional object of consciousness; however, they are analytically separable. Thus, on Husserl's account, the phenomenological description of our experience investigates either the act of consciousness, the intentional object of consciousness, or both. This object may or may not exist; however, following the phenomenological reduction, the question of the metaphysical existence of the intentional object of experience, apart from my experiencing of it, is bracketed.

Sometimes called a philosopher of life or a philosopher of the human studies, Wilhelm Dilthey spent his scholarly career exploring the distinctive nature of human experience. [9] Four themes in Dilthey's work were influential in the later development of the phenomenological analysis of religion. First, much like Husserl, Dilthey emphasized the need to focus upon human experience and to analyze it without preconceived ideas, reductionist theories, or philosophical commitments. Moreover, though he did not use the specific vocabulary of intentionality, Dilthey joined Husserl in underscoring the purposive nature of human consciousness and experience. Where Husserl noted that consciousness always has an object toward which it is directed, Dilthey made the related observation that the expressions of human consciousness always point beyond themselves to something else.

Second, Dilthey repeatedly emphasized that recognition of the purposive dimensions of human experience entailed that such expressions are meaningful in some fundamental sense. In making a gesture or travelling to a foreign university as a guest professor, it is not the physiology of the gesture nor the task of making travel arrangements that is important for comprehending the experience. Rather it is the tacit significations of the gesture, the ensemble of anticipated opportunities contained in the offer of a new professional circumstance that need to be comprehended. In this way, Dilthey emphasized that there was an inner life to human experience, one that found expression in any number of areas, such as religion and the arts, but also in nonlinguistic and nonverbal aspects of everyday life. Any adequate examination of human experience must account for and make intelligible these dimensions as well.

Third, the methodology appropriate to discern human meanings was what Dilthey called the process of understanding (*Verstehen*). To understand something, whether it be a linguistic text, the performance of a ritual, or the affirmation of a set of doctrinal beliefs, is to interpret it. The process of interpretation, or hermeneutics as it is often called, involves placing the item to be interpreted in an appropriate context of known past references, present lived experiences, and possible future expectations. Thus, for Dilthey, the process of understanding involved the challenge of correctly discerning the meaning of human experience. It involved grasping what people meant in speech and action, discerning the significance of the complex symbolic dimensions of human expression, and finally, entering into the minds of human agents in ways ranging from appreciating their intentions to identifying with and even incorporating their meanings into one's own experience.

Finally, Dilthey often called for the use of typologies in the human studies and is well known for his own typology of human worldviews. In making this point about the usefulness of typologies, Dilthey reminded his readers that such typologies are always generalizations of historically determined human experiences, comparisons, in other words, of concrete social historical reality. Dilthey recognized the epistemological and scientific value of comparative analysis. In the process of gaining knowledge and understanding of our world, we are always engaged in implicit and explicit comparisons. We recognize the color blue in part by comparing it with a spectrum of other colors, and we assess the greetings of a friend as enthusiastic or cool by provisionally comparing them with other such greetings.

Moreover, in scientific inquiry, typologies, comparisons, and generalizations play an important role. For while the results of a specific scientific experiment or historical event can be important, their true significance is established by comparing them with other experiments and events, by placing them within a larger context of similar and dissimilar items. In stressing the utility of comparative typologies, Dilthey insisted that they were primarily heuristic aids, which always needed to be scrupulously checked against the specific data of empirical evidence and historical case study. Typological comparisons, then, were not lifeless apparitions existing apart from the real world. Rather, they reflected concrete historical reality, at the same time that they both embodied something larger and provided a basis for classificatory assessments of similarity and difference.

Any further orientation to the phenomenology of religion requires explicit delineation of its three principal voices. So let us now turn to these, beginning with that earliest voice which so decisively shaped the direction and contours of the field as a whole.

First Voice: Essential Phenomenology of Religion

The first voice in the phenomenology of religion is what we call, following Max Scheler, the essential phenomenology of religion.[10] "Essential" here means a basic concern with the essence or true nature of the religious consciousness of the believing soul—the defining traits of his or her religious apprehensions, emotional states, and motivations for religious activities (what, in a nicely turned phrase, Rudolph Otto calls the distinctively religious "states of the soul").[11] This voice in phenomenology of religion is well represented by the researches of Rudolph Otto and Max Scheler, who are often regarded as the founding fathers of this voice, as well as the writing of others, such as Louis Dupré and William Earle, who follow in their path. The thinkers who represent this voice possess both distinctive aims and a reasonably unified method of inquiry, though, of course, as with all scholars, they differ in emphasis and nuance about some issues.

Aims

The aim shared by all essential phenomenologists of religion is to describe and analyze those experiences and concepts uniquely characteristic
of religious consciousness. That is, all scholars working within this voice
want to clarify for themselves as well as others those apprehensions, emotions, motivations, and activities distinctive to the believing soul who
claims to live his or her life in full recognition of a transcendent or sacred
dimension of human experience. What, asks the essentialist, defines the
consciousness of this sort of person (or community of persons)? In what
way does this consciousness differ from nonreligious perspectives on the
world? How does the believing soul think, feel, and act, and what does
he or she "see" that nonreligious others do not? Questions such as these
shape the researches of those working within the essential voice, and they
suggest immediately the propriety of employing a method of inquiry that
is able to explore sensitively and without bias the committed subjectivity
of faithful believers. Before, however, turning to the details of that
method, we should ask whether our essentialists share any other aims or
goals.

Digging a little deeper into this matter reveals a surprising result. All
of our researchers do in fact have other aims, but many of these are not
shared. With respect to the essentialists represented in this book, for example, one can discern a number of discrete aims. Otto is interested finally in putting his description of numinous consciousness in service of
the broader theological aim of showing that knowledge of the Christian
God can be advanced by careful attention to religious experience. Scheler
seeks the less theological aim of grounding in a rigorous way a new science of religions. Earle wants to show that at least one type of distinctive
religious experience—mystical experience—is continuous with ordinary
self-awareness, thus demonstrating to contemporary philosophers that
the apparently "irrational" claims of religion have something to contribute to the rational researches into the philosophy of the self. Sekida offers
his phenomenology of samadhi as a way of communicating Eastern religious consciousness to the broader audience of the Western world. Christ
is concerned to recover the true nature of women's religious consciousness in order to advance the cause of a feminist critique of male-domi-
nated theology and religious thought. And Dupré wants to use essential
phenomenology of religion to debunk a myopic vision of philosophy of
religion as answerable only to autonomous norms of rationality. So, as it
turns out, many essentialists have deeper (and somewhat hidden) agenda
governed by normative aims of one sort or another. Being aware of these

deeper aims is important, for it puts us in a position to ask whether they have any bearing on the shared aim of the elucidation of religious consciousness.

What we need to do at this point is to draw a distinction between the phenomenological aim of scholars working within the essential voice, and their broader normative aims since after completing their phenomenological investigations they often go on to use their results in other non-phenomenological programs of inquiry—whether theological, philosophical, or social-cultural. Drawing this distinction has two advantages. It permits us to see the relatively unified integrity of essential phenomenological research (in its descriptive aim and method) and it alerts us to a potential problem in this research—namely, that its descriptive aim and method might at times be affected by a researcher's larger project. Being thus alerted, we are in a better position to assess critically whether a particular piece of phenomenological research is true to its intrinsic phenomenological aim. Let us now turn to the question of what method unifies our essential phenomenologists.

Method

Besides sharing the descriptive and analytical aim suggested above, researchers within the essential voice also share a relatively unified method of inquiry. This method follows (with some variations) the Husserlian program of adopting the "phenomenological attitude" as a way of gaining insight (intuition) into what makes religious consciousness what it is. Thus, with Husserl, all of our researchers hold that religious consciousness, in its various states and manifestations, is consciousness of something and is structured in a bipolar way involving the correlation of an active "subject" pole (noesis) and an "object" pole (noema). They agree on the importance and propriety of adopting the phenomenological attitude (or epoché) toward their subject-matter—the phenomena or states of religious consciousness—bracketing or suspending judgment about whether religion is true or valuable, about whether the objects of religious experience are real or not, about whether religious consciousness can be explained in some sort of causal way by the human sciences, and so on. They also agree on the utility of employing "sympathy" or "empathy" in gaining access to the content of religious consciousness—temporarily reenacting or reexperiencing within their methodical or tutored consciousness the intentions, experiences, beliefs of the believing soul and then intuitively "observing" and reflectively probing these contents to see what makes them tick, so to speak. They agree that in order to do justice to these contents in conveying them to others, it is crucially important to provide evocative or "warm" descriptions that aim ultimately at getting others to appreciate (or even reexperience in a sympathetic way for themselves) the "moments" of religious consciousness.[12] And they agree that in order to properly elucidate or clarify the consciousness of the believing soul, it is necessary to identify its essential or defining traits (what makes it distinctively religious).

In gaining further understanding of this method, it may be useful to see it in operation, and this is precisely what is supplied by the authors in the first section of the book. Let us glance at a few of these to see how they understand their method. Since Otto, Scheler, and Earle are especially self-conscious about their method of inquiry, they furnish a particularly perspicuous "lens" on the methodological underpinnings of the essential voice. Each seems adept in clarifying one or another aspect of their shared method, and taken together they provide a rather comprehensive picture of the method in action.

Otto is particularly clear in identifying the basic aim of the essential phenomenology of religion. At the very outset of his inquiry, for example, he indicates that he is concerned to probe and analyze the religious "states of the soul," paying attention to "what is unique in them rather than to what they have in common with other similar states." As he so illuminatingly puts it, "to be rapt in worship is one thing; to be morally uplifted by the contemplation of a good deed is another; and it is not to their common features, but to those elements of emotional content peculiar to the first that we would have attention directed as precisely as possible." This states clearly that Otto's aim is to identify, describe, and analyze the essence of religious consciousness, and he goes on to do just that in his famous characterization of the "most fundamental element in all strong and sincerely felt religious emotion" as "mysterium tremendum et fascinans" (i.e., being simultaneously daunted and fascinated by an awe-inspiring, majestic, and overpowering mystery encountered within religious experience).

Both Scheler and Earle, together with all others working within this voice, clearly agree with this aim. Scheler, for his part, claims that the method of his inquiry into the nature of revelation (understood as divine self-disclosure) involves "the phenomenological scrutiny of essence" of revelation. And Earle, for his part in his study of mystical experience (a particular type of religious consciousness), states his aim as the analysis of his "essence of mystical experience" understood as the "experience of the identity of myself with Absolute Reality." Within this agreed upon aim, our three essentialists then go on to speak of the method necessary for describing and analyzing the various aspects of the consciousness of the believing soul.

Earle is straightforward about the fact that this method is fundamentally Husserlian in orientation, though it must also be noted that both Otto and Scheler were fully aware of the relevance of Husserl's researches for their inquiries. (Husserl, by the way, in a letter to Otto, explicitly approved of Otto's work, praising his *Idea of the Holy* as an original contribution to and a "first beginning" in the essential phenomenology of religion.)[13] Earle characterizes the method in the following way:

. . . the attempt to reflect radically upon experience as that experience presents itself to the experiencer. It will be then mind reflecting upon itself, without presupposition, in an effort to discern explicitly what the structure and content of that experience is. This reflection from first to last will try to confine itself to experience as it offers itself without presupposing from the start what reality "must" be, what the ego experiencing "must" be, notions drawn from sources external to that experience itself. In a word, that phenomenological reflection does not begin with any logical, biological, physical or philosophical presuppositions. All of that must be put in brackets; the effort will be to reflect upon the experience itself, to see once again what it is rather than to attempt a critique from supposed truths drawn from elsewhere. Phenomenology thus understood is nothing but an attempt to make clear to oneself the phenomenon of any experience whatsoever just as it offers itself to the mind reflecting.

What seems clear from this characterization is that Earle sees the method as involving the adoption of the "phenomenological attitude," implying that the investigator brackets all distorting assumptions about the truth, value, or reality of religion and focuses precisely on the phenomena of religious consciousness as they appear in that consciousness. Furthermore, Earle evidently adopts the technique of imaginative or sympathetic reenactment within his own consciousness of the experience of the believing soul (in his case, the mystic) precisely in order to gain a purchase on "the structure and content of that experience." Thus does Earle link his method—and the method of essential phenomenology of religion more generally—to those features of Husserlian phenomenology that we earlier identified as "focus on religious phenomena as they appear," "bracketing or epoché," and "sympathetic reexperiencing of phenomena," followed by "intuitive observation of and reflection on reenacted content."

Otto and Scheler, for their part, appear to be entirely in accord with these facets of the phenomenological method. Thus, Otto, for example, though he does not use Husserlian terminology, seeks to describe the elements of the numinous consciousness (another term for "mysterium tremendum et fascinans") as they appear within that consciousness, and he explicitly speaks of the investigator's using "every effort of sympathy and imaginative intuition" and "precise introspection" in so doing. Scheler speaks of the investigator's analyzing the "primal datum" of the religious consciousness understood as consisting of "natural religious acts" that must be respected as they appear in order to be understood properly by the investigator. His acceptance of the method—in its bracketed focus on the contents of religious consciousness as phenomena to be respected as they appear—is evident in his criticism of the psychologist William Wundt, where against Wundt, Scheler contends that the phenomenological method involves "a dialectical intention to redirect the mind's attention to the all-important object . . . to look here and now upon the supraconceptual datum which can only be beheld, to gaze directly upon its pure self-given state." [14] This somewhat hyperbolic way of emphasizing the phenomenological attitude seems clear enough. Though in the present selection Scheler says little about the methodical step of sympathetic reexperiencing, it is apparent from his other phenomenological researches that he embraces an empathetic method. Indeed, this may be inferred even from the present selection in his positive appraisal of Otto's phenomenological method, where he quotes approvingly the following from Otto: "There is only one way to help another to an understanding of it [the category of experienced Holiness]. He must be guided and led on by consideration and discussion of the matter through the ways of his own mind, until he reaches the point at which the numinous in him perforce begins to stir, to start into life and into consciousness." This quotation surely shows Scheler's commitment to the method of sympathetic reenactment.

Both Otto and Scheler—and to a lesser extent Earle—are also clearly committed to those steps of the phenomenological method which we have labeled as "evocative description" and "reflective elucidation" of essential, defining features of the religious consciousness. Otto is particularly vivid in his articulation of the step of evocative description when he writes, "we must once again endeavor, by choosing feelings akin to them for the purpose of analogy or contrast, and by the use of metaphors and symbolic expressions, to make the states of mind we are investigating ring out, as it were of themselves." And his manner of exemplifying this step by getting his reader to reflect upon commonly accessible analogues (e.g., dread of the uncanny, awe before a majestic power) as well as the meaning of metaphoric descriptions (e.g., "Wrath of Yahweh," "feeling like dust and ashes," "The Wholly Other or Alien," and "dizzy intoxication") is a compelling illustration of evocative description within a phenomenological study of religious consciousness. Indeed, Otto has few peers in his ability to evoke within his reader an appreciation for the peculiarities of religious experience—this is precisely why he is so often admired and quoted by other religious scholars (to great effect, we might add). Scheler too shows enormous appreciation for Otto's evocative descriptions of numinous consciousness, but he does more than just admire, for he goes to the trouble of explaining the rationale for this phenomenological practice.

According to Scheler (and here we venture to suggest that Otto would agree), this sort of description constitutes a "negative method of successively peeling away the correlates and contraries that . . . offer progressive indications to the *phenomenon demonstrandum* [the phenomenon to be demonstrated] with the consequent laying bare of the phenomenon and its presence to the inspecting mind." Thus, suggests Scheler, when Otto attempts to bring before his reader's "notice all that can be found in the other regions of the mind, already known and familiar, or again to afford some special contrast to the particular experience" and then adds "this X of ours is not precisely this experience, but akin to this one and the opposite of that other . . . cannot you now realize for yourself what it is?," he is attempting to both point to *and* awaken in the reader's consciousness his or her own sympathetic reexperiencing of the religious phenomenon. Thus the phenomenologist's evocative description turns out to be a type of performative language intimately tied to his method of inquiry: the phenomenologist uses language in a quasi-causal way to evoke or prompt the reader's own empathetic response and appreciation of aspects of religious consciousness. This performative use of language to describe evocatively is indicative of the phenomenologist's respect for showing the phenomenon as it appears in religious consciousness as well as his methodological commitment to experiential understanding of the structures of human consciousness.

Scheler not only agrees with Otto on this step of evocative description but also displays in his own work an ability to employ such performative description to considerable effect. Thus can we appreciate the way he attempts to analogize the revelations (divine self-disclosures) experienced by the believing soul when contemplating the beauty of the natural world or certain sacred objects, places, or events, to such commonly accessible phenomena as a window becoming conspicuous in a series of windows (on the side of a building) when we see someone inside looking out, or the way a mirror reflects to another the image of a person, or the way that an artist's spirit is present in and shows through his work. Suggests Scheler, the divine revelation is like the conspicuous window but not quite, like a reflective mirror but not quite, like an artist's presence but not quite, and so on—all in an attempt to get us to appreciate how divine revelation appears to the believing soul. For his part, Earle too follows in the footsteps of these past masters of evocative description (though he may be somewhat less successful) when, for example he encourages his readers to examine their own self-reflexive awareness, perceptual activity, temporal awareness, and the like, in order to appreciate the mystical religious consciousness's wonder at the ego as well as its expressive claims like "I am God." Whether or not Earle is finally convincing here, the point is that he too attempts to use evocative description to prompt his reader to see and appreciate aspects of mystical consciousness and experience.

Of course, all of this performatively oriented evocative description serves a purpose, and that purpose is contained within the final step of the essential phenomenologist's method—namely, the reflective elucidation of the essential or defining traits of religious consciousness. This final step fulfills the intrinsic aim of the essentialist's enterprise. All phenomenologists working within this voice not only say they are interested in such an aim but also do their utmost to satisfy this aim by indicating what they regard—after due reenactment and reflection—as the essential traits that make religious phenomena what they are. Thus, for example, Otto proposes that the essential traits of religious consciousness are identified by the formula "mysterium tremendum et fascinans" and then goes on to elaborate in precise ways the component of each element of this formula—the "tremendum" is analyzed into sub-traits of awefulness, overpowering majesty, and vital energy; the "mysterium" is analyzed in terms of the wholly other mystery incommensurable with all the known world; and "fascinans" is analyzed as potently charming Dionysiac captivation and intoxication. In this way, Otto hopes to have identified, made comprehensible, and analyzed the necessary and sufficient conditions for recognizing and defining the numinous consciousness—without one or another of these traits, we may have a phenomenon very like the numinous religious consciousness but not that consciousess in all of its essential uniqueness and purity. But we must be careful here, for in offering us this discussion of the "mysterium tremendum et fascinans," Otto does both more and less than articulate a set of necessary and sufficient conditions for the numinous consciousness. He does more and less in the sense that his description and analysis is not simply intended as a definitive analysis of its traits but also designed as a set of pointers or signposts for us (his readers) to come to see or intuit those essential features for ourselves—that is the point of using language in an evocative manner. Otto wants to bring us with him in sympathetically reexamining and then reflectively observing or intuiting the essential features of numinous consciousness—in this way, we are to see for ourselves what the essential traits are.

Similarly, Scheler also tries to identify what he calls the "essential attributes" of the divine in its self-disclosure, identifying such features as "absolute being" and "holiness" and then further analyzing these as constitutively composed of "utterly active," "almighty," "self-subsistent," "pure," "sublime," "ground of all that is," and so on. And though Scheler is perfectly willing to say that the revealed divine "invariably possesses these attributes," it is clear from his discussion that he too means to guide us (his readers) and redirect our attention to behold the datum for ourselves and to intuit for ourselves its essential features. In effect, his discussion (like Otto's) is designed to lay "bare . . . the phenomenon and its presence to the inspecting mind," making possible our own scrutiny of its essence. Earle too is clearly attempting to specify the essential traits of mystical consciousness which he proposes in one traditional formulation as "the experience of the identity of the soul and God" but then in the interests of phenomenologically neutral retranslation rephrases as "the experience of the identity of myself with Absolute Reality." The performative (evocative) function of this retranslation should not go unnoticed, for with it Earle attempts to guide us into a self-aware recognition that we as transcendental egos are able (at least in sympathetic reenactment) to realize how and why the mystical consciousness identifies itself with the absolute. His whole discussion and analysis is structured with this goal in mind—to enable us to see for ourselves what this mystical identification involves in an essential way. Earle's wager is that if we can come to see ourselves as transcendental egos with essential traits of nonspatiality, nontemporality, and absolute freedom, then we will be in a position to appreciate sympathetically as well the mystic's claim that his or her self has "exactly the same structure as the Absolute Reality itself," expressed in the typical formulation of unitary mysticism as "I am God" (meaning I have the same structure as, or am identical with, the divine). Again, our point is, whether or not he is correct in his characterization of mystical consciousness, Earle clearly means to lead us to see for ourselves what he regards as the essential traits of this consciousness.

Issues

Thus far, we have attempted to clarify the aim and method of the essential phenomenology of religion through the eyes or "lens" of representative practitioners. It remains to take this clarification one step farther to gain a more critical purchase on this voice. We need to become aware of some of the problems and issues raised, for in this way we may be better able to understand why other voices have been developed in the phenomenology of religion. This is not to say that the essentialist voice has been superseded—indeed it continues to this day—but rather that other voices which have developed have done so in part because the essentialist voice, while having certain strengths, may also have certain limitations. And it is wise to be aware of these limitations (or at least controversy about them) before proceeding further.

Six possible problems can be cited in connection with the essentialist voice. The first has already been mentioned—namely, the concern over whether hidden agenda (or normative aims) somehow bias or distort the descriptive and analytic aim and results of essential phenomenology of religion. A second problem is whether the phenomenological attitude itself—in its apparent neutrality about truth and value—is able to do justice to religious phenomena of ultimate commitment (faith), which are quite the contrary of neutrality and suspended judgment. A third problem is whether the phenomenological attitude naively assumes the transparency of consciousness to itself—that is, whether it is or can be sufficiently suspicious of and critical about the factors constituting and governing religious intentions and motivations (might not some of these be below the threshold of consciousness?). The fourth problem concerns the status of the process of sympathetic or empathetic reenactment. It is claimed that the exact nature and epistemic value of this process remains somewhat obscure in many phenomenological discussions. The fifth problem concerns a possible anti-historical bias in the emphasis on static "essences" of religious consciousness. The sixth and final problem is whether the essential voice subscribes to an inadequate theory of human experience that fails to acknowledge the embodied nature of human consciousness as well as its radically intersubjective context. Each of these problems may indicate a limitation on the value and legitimacy of the essentialist voice, and though we cannot here fully analyze, much less decisively resolve, these issues, we can try to clarify their significance and indicate how they might prompt and support the development of other approaches both within and outside the phenomenology of religion.

With respect to the first problem—the biasing effects of essentialists' hidden agenda and normative aims—it must be candidly conceded that much work done within this voice tends to be normatively "loaded" toward identifying religious consciousness with the consciousness of a classical Christian theistic believer. This does not necessarily invalidate the adequacy of the phenomenological studies *as studies of a certain kind of theistic religious consciousness*, but it does question whether these studies accurately capture other forms of theistic consciousness (where, for example, the divine is not experienced as a "wholly other" alien power) much less nontheistic forms of religious consciousness (e.g., certain types of Asian religious experience). This is, in part, why we include in our selections and bibliography phenomenological studies of diverse forms of religious consciousness (e.g., Zen Buddhism, women's nontraditional religious experience, Shinto, Native American traditions, etc.). By seeing these other studies we are able both to correct for any theistic bias of some of our investigators and at the same time show that the essentialist voice can be used to clarify other forms of religious experience or consciousness. The student should be especially alert to how both Otto and Scheler, two founding fathers of the essentialist approach, tend to load their work with a theistic emphasis or orientation. Again, this may not invalidate their work as adequate for certain forms of religious consciousness, but it does suggest significant limitations on their broader adequacy. And, of course, one can still appreciate how their method may be usefully applied in studying other forms of religious consciousness that they did not study themselves.

The second problem, however, concerning the possible biasing effect of the phenomenological attitude's detachment, raises a deeper issue regarding possible limitations on the method itself.[15] It needs to be understood from the outset that the phenomenological attitude does not appraise religious consciousness negatively (dismissing its value or truth), but rather suspends all judgment or appraisals (pro or con). Thus, the phenomenological attitude cannot be interpreted as antithetical or hostile to religion. So this issue is not one of hostility to religion, but is rather more subtle. The concern is whether an attitude of detachment (or suspension of judgment about truth and value) can do justice to the depth of commitment (ultimate concern) embedded in the totally committed subjectivity of the believing soul. Can, in a word, detachment understand and represent deep commitment? It is not clear that it cannot, for the phenomenological method while "suspending judgment" also involves "empathetic reenactment" of the religious consciousness, thus enabling it (the method) to understand at a distance, so to speak. Indeed, the suspension of judgment can enhance this empathy because epoché puts "out of play" the investigator's own distorting prejudices and biases, thus enabling him or her to be empathetic to and resonant with the believing soul's experiences from its own standpoint. This contention, though, is subject to the stipulation that empathetic reenactment makes sense and can be defended as a valuable tool of inquiry (more on this below).

The third problem, concerning a possible insufficiency of suspicion on the part of the phenomenologist who may assume the self-transparency of consciousness, raises a much discussed problem that naturally occurs to all in our culture who are aware of the "schools of suspicion" associ-

ated with Freud, Marx, Foucault as well as other post-modern decon-
structionists.[16] In a nutshell the criticism comes down to this: inasmuch
as essentialists by virtue of their method focus principally on the avowed
intentions and motivations of the believing soul, do they not blind themselves to what may really be going on in and behind religious consciousness—for example, unconscious factors in the personality, social forces
of one sort or another, and so on? Are not their descriptions and analyses
relatively superficial, since they have incapacitated themselves from getting at the heart of the matter? These sorts of objections betray a deep
misunderstanding of what essential phenomenology is all about as well
as a deep misunderstanding of the significance of the phenomenological
task. Among the selections in this book, Dupré indicates the proper response to these objections when he writes with reference to psychology
and the Freudian school of suspicion:

> Any claim of psychology to a full understanding of the religious experience, there-
> fore, assumes that the religious act can be explained entirely as a subjective ex-
> perience. Indeed, empirical psychology deals exclusively with the reality of the
> experience (i.e., its subjective, empirical aspect) and does not consider its inten-
> tional, ideal aspect. . . . If psychology ignores this limitation . . . it will interpret
> the religious experience entirely by its genetic process or by the partial elements
> of which the experience is composed. But to do this is to overlook the fact that
> the experience is determined by its objective intentionality. A psychological ex-
> planation may be instructive as regards to building material . . . of the religious
> consciousness, but it never comes to grips with the religious consciousness as
> consciousness, i.e., as a subject ideally related to an object without ever coin-
> ciding with it. To explain the entire religious experience psychologically is to as-
> sume that religion is not more than the sum of some other, simpler experiences.
> Religion is then reduced to the non-religious: it is an experience of fear, a projec-
> tion of the individual's feeling of inferiority with respect to the totality of the
> human race, or a sublimation of man's sexual drive. . . . The psychoanalytic
> interpretation . . . is more sophisticated in that it explains the religious experience
> by means of elements of a different nature (subconscious) rather than subordi-
> nating one conscious experience to another. Yet, even here the fact remains that
> wherever psychoanalysis pretends to possess a full understanding of man's reli-
> gious activity, it dogmatically assumes that this activity can be explained through
> the real elements of the experience (which are different from the experience itself
> rather than through its own ideal intentionality). We should not be surprised to
> learn that with this approach religion turns out to be an illusion.

Dupré's point is a relatively easy one to grasp. The psychoanalytic
approach has its place in the study of religious consciousness, but its
operation depends crucially on the prior constitution of religious consciousness as a religious form of consciousness—in effect the phenomenologist supplies his or her descriptive analysis to other schools of inquiry
such as psychoanalysis, and in order to do this he or she must respect the

conscious intentions and motivations of the believing soul, precisely because doing so constitutes the object of investigation as religious consciousness in the first place. And in order to do this—to reconstruct, as it were, the phenomena and essential traits of religious consciousness—the phenomenologist must bracket (suspend judgment) about the applicability and validity of all theoretical approaches precisely in order to appreciate in an unbiased way the standpoint of the consciousness of the believing soul from that soul's own vantage point. Thus does essential phenomenology provide a distinctively religious subject-matter, which other disciplines may, from their various vantage points, investigate and possibly explain in terms of nonreligious factors. This is the tremendous value and significance of the phenomenological approach: its goal and method must be first in the order of inquiry. Consequently, we suggest that the problem of insufficiency of suspicion is, for phenomenology, a pseudo-problem.

The fourth problem—that of the obscurity of the procedure of sympathetic reenactment—intends to cast doubt on the legitimacy of a crucial step in the phenomenological method. Perhaps the most effective rebuttal of this criticism is to invite the critic to attempt individual sympathetic reenactment to see whether it is both possible and useful; that is, actual practice may be the most effective way to shortcut this objection. However, some may find this sort of rebuttal question-begging, and so we need to say more about this step.[17] Two phenomenologists in particular, Merold Westphal and Ninian Smart, have done a very creditable job in undercutting this objection—by finding analogues to sympathetic reenactment in a variety of humanistic disciplines and arguing that if the process is unproblematic in these areas, then it should be no more problematic in phenomenology.

Westphal identified three such analogues—the detached perception or contemplative regard employed in aesthetic appreciation and understanding in the visual arts (where the viewer suspends prejudgments in order to grasp and then reflect on the meaning of a particular piece of art); the actor's reenactment in sympathetic imagination of the motivations and intentions of a character in a play (where the actor tries to see and feel and display through acting how a given character approaches the world); the good listening engaged in by a psychotherapist in dealing with a client (where the therapist is fully present to the client and listens for what is both said and not said by that client).[18] Westphal suggests that these three activities taken together provide a comprehensive model for the phenomenological step of sympathetic reenactment (or reexperiencing), for the phenomenologist has a detached (bracketed) contemplative regard for the believing soul; he or she reenacts in sympathetic imagination the motivations and intentions of the believing soul, and also is "present to" the conscious avowals of the believing soul and listens for what is expressed (and not expressed) using a technique of gentle probing to ascertain the essential traits of the consciousness that thus expresses itself. Furthermore, Westphal suggests at least implicitly that inasmuch as we can understand and accept the analogues we have identified, then we can, by parity of reasoning, understand and accept as well the phenomenological step of sympathetic reenactment. This is not an implausible claim.

Ninian Smart cites one of the analogues adduced by Westphal—playacting—and offers others in addition—reading and interpreting an novel, and the participant-observation of the social anthropologist in his or her fieldwork.[19] With regard to playacting, Smart is particularly suggestive when he points out that the actor imaginatively rehearses the feelings and beliefs of a given character, while simultaneously bracketing issues of truth, value, and commitment—the actor, after all, does not actually become a character except imaginatively in a kind of epoché (unless, of course, the actor is suffering from some sort of pathological condition). So too the phenomenologist: he or she imaginatively "rehearses" the feelings and beliefs of the believing soul, while simultaneously bracketing questions of truth, value, and commitment. Smart further suggests that, in reading and assimilating a novel, the reader enters into another social world (displayed by the novel) imaginatively without actually accepting the presuppositions of that world—this implies that it is possible for the reader to hold simultaneously mutually conflicting attitudes empathetically understood, precisely because he or she does not actually commit to the truth of the attitudes but only imaginatively entertains them in an empathetic way. So too the phenomenologist is able to enter into the world of a believing soul empathetically and imaginatively without thereby accepting the presuppositions and values of that world. And, for his final analogue, Smart proposes that of participant-observation of the social anthropologist, who in doing fieldwork needs to empathetically understand and appreciate how the native tribe, for example, feels, thinks, acts, and sees the world. Smart perceptively points out that the anthropologist's procedure is not just a process of sympathetic imagination but also involves learning a new language and conceptuality in an effort at transcultural understanding. So too the phenomenologist who, in being empathetic, nonetheless also has to learn how the religious consciousness perceives the world, how that consciousness thinks and acts in a distinctively religious manner.

The point of citing these analogues must by now be apparent: far from being an obscure and unusual procedure, the process of sympathetic re-enactment is quite clear and replete in a variety of contexts and disciplines. The onus, then, is on the objector to show cause why he or she regards it as especially problematic for either phenomenology or any of the other contexts and disciplines mentioned. It seems to be a well-accepted procedure for many types of inquiry.

The fifth problem we must consider is the charge that essential phenomenology of religion is insufficiently historical, that is, fails to acknowledge the important fact that all religious consciousness is embedded in and shaped by the historicity intrinsic to human consciousness and activity. Before considering this objection, we need to clarify what exactly it means. It seems to suggest that essential phenomenology is more concerned with timeless essences rather than historical development and is therefore blind to the fact that all religious consciousness develops over time. Further, it seems to suggest as well that essential phenomenology is relatively oblivious that different forms of religious consciousness exist and can be correlated with different social and historical contexts—for example, the consciousness of an early Christian may be different from that of a modern Christian; the consciousness of a Christian may be different from that of a Buddhist whether or not they live in the same historical period; and so on. There is something right about these criticisms and something misleading as well.

What is right about them is this—essential phenomenologists have in fact often ignored the consideration that different forms of religious consciousness may be correlated with different historical and social-cultural contexts. Furthermore, there is considerable truth in the contention that some have ignored the process of development of a given form of religious consciousness. But there are exceptions here, and both Otto and Scheler are two such exceptions. Otto quite clearly recognizes the fact that religious consciousness develops over time—this is why he so freely speaks of the development of numinous consciousness from primitive to more developed (and pure) forms. Scheler, for his part, acknowledges both such developments of theistic forms of religious consciousness and the fact that different forms of religious consciousness arise in different societies and cultures.[20] So the charge cites at best only a tendency of essential phenomenology of religion to be anti- or more accurately non-historical. At least some phenomenologists appear to escape this charge.

Moreover, in speaking of timeless essences, the charge betrays a serious misunderstanding of what phenomenologists mean by the term "essence" (or "essential traits"). They do not mean "essence" in some platonic sense—timeless essences or forms existing in a perfect and changeless ontological realm. Rather they use "essence" to refer to the characteristic and constitutive traits of a given phenomenon—if this phenomenon happens to change (for whatever reason), then the new or successor phenomenon will have its own constitutive defining traits which may be different from the previous phenomenon. Phenomenology accepts (at least in principle) the possibility of such change, and this means that phenomenologists are not discussing timeless essences in the platonic sense. So in this respect the charge is woefully misguided. Absolutely nothing prevents the essential phenomenologist from using his or her method of inquiry to investigate in a successive way states of religious consciousness as they change and develop over time—in an apt image of this possible use of the method, Ninian Smart speaks, for example, of phenomenology's ability to produce a "moving picture" of successive phases of the development of a given type of religious consciousness (we will return to this point in connection with historical-typological phenomenology of religion).[21] Such a possibility shows that essential phenomenology of religion need not be anti-historical.

The sixth and final problem we need to consider is whether essential phenomenology of religion subscribes to a theory of experience or consciousness that implicitly values mental as contrasted with corporeal phenomena. At first blush, this may seem to be a most implausible problem given that Husserlian phenomenology was originally designed to avoid just such dualisms and valences, and in fact Husserl's thought itself seems to escape this sort of problem inasmuch as it appears to recognize that human consciousness is embodied.[22] Nonetheless, the essential phenomenologists of religion are not Husserl, though they may be influenced by his ideas, and evidence that there may be a real problem here is supplied by one of our representative essentialists—William Earle—when he writes in the context of his study of mystical consciousness that "each now need consider nothing but himself as a thinking self. My own body, other persons, and the physical world of nature are not ingredient in the very essence of that thinking self. The I as it is for myself is only *accidentally* related to its body, to the physical world, to other persons. It may turn its thinking attention to them, but it is not they, or even like them."

This sort of claim seems very problematic from the viewpoint of many non-essentialist phenomenologists and philosophers who would contend that our experience shows itself to be incarnate (bodily) as well as intersubjective. In the words, for example, of Gabriel Marcel, "we are incarnated," and this sort of claim is intimately related to the phenomenological datum that we (or all I's) are irreducibly situated in a world of other embodied consciousnesses.[23] For these thinkers, we do not find consciousness only "accidentally related" to body, world, and other persons, but necessarily so related: we cannot escape our corporeality and other persons, for both are integrally involved in our consciousness. Interestingly, the careful reader will find many essentialists agreeing with this point, inasmuch as they identify "creaturehood" (sense of being a finite creature) as part of religious consciousness. Otto and Scheler are two such essentialists who identify creaturehood as an essential trait of numinous consciousness and the human apprehension of divine self-disclosure.

Nevertheless, even acknowledging such a possible recognition of embodied consciousness, there is a tendency on the part of essentialists to downplay or ignore or—in Earle's case—explicitly deny this feature of human consciousness. And this, in turn, suggests that they may be unconsciously biased against such a datum because they are still unduly influenced by the tenet of Cartesian philosophy that posits a dualism of mind and body and a valence favoring the mind over the body. That the issue is a real one—and that the essential phenomenology of religion is problematic in this respect—is clearly suggested by the fact that another voice—existential phenomenology of religion—defines itself precisely around the clear acknowledgment that we are indissolubly our bodies and are indissolubly bound within an intersubjective world of conscious (and unconscious) relations. And so we have to admit candidly that this failure on the part of at least some essentialists openly and consistently to acknowledge this feature of our consciousness (and of religious consciousness in particular) may well constitute a significant limitation of their approach.

In reviewing these six problems or concerns about the essentialist voice in phenomenology of religion, we have cited some of its strengths and weaknesses. Though we have tended to rebut these concerns—save for the last—we should also be aware that continuing perceptions of these as real and inescapable tensions within the method have had no small role in helping to generate or at least strengthen the resolve of other voices in the field. Thus, for example, the issues of "detached objectivity" and "an inadequate theory of consciousness" have tended to support the development of the voice of existential phenomenology of religion, while the issues of "normative loading" and "anti-historical bias" have tended to support the development of the voice of historical-typological phenomenology of religion. Furthermore, the issue of "transparency of consciousness" has played into the hands of those who would like to supplant phenomenological inquiry with other, more hermeneutical, schools of suspicion. Nonetheless, none of these voices—either inside or outside phenomenology of religion—deny that the essentialist voice has had and continues to play an important and vital role in the study of religious phenomena.

Second Voice: Historical-Typological Phenomenology of Religion

The second voice in the phenomenology of religion is what we call, following Ninian Smart, the "historical-typological phenomenology of religion."[24] The label is particularly apt since this type of inquiry is undertaken primarily by historians of religions interested both in the distinctive ethos and worldviews of particular religious traditions and in persistent or recurrent patterns shared by those traditions. How, in other words, do the participants of a given religious tradition "intend" the world? How do they understand, respond to, feel about, and act in the world from their distinctive standpoint? And further, how does this way of intending the world compare with those ways of being represented by other religious traditions? The pursuit of these questions is bound up with a distinctive set of aims and, once again, a reasonably unified method of inquiry, constituting a distinctive voice in the phenomenology of religion. These aims and method are ably represented by the researches of Arthur, Kristensen, Kitagawa, and Eliade (in this book), in addition to such influential figures as Gerardus van der Leeuw and Smart. Let us examine in some detail these aims and method as well as issues or problems they may pose.

Aims

One aim shared by all historical-typological phenomenologists of religion is to understand in a qualitative manner the particular forms of life within a religious tradition and thereby to recover a picture and a sense of what these elements (e.g., doctrinal beliefs, ritual practices, codes of conduct) *mean* from the viewpoint of the adherents of particular religious traditions. The aim is to see what the "external" facts of a tradition add up to when understood and viewed as expressions of distinctive worldviews and existentially experienced standpoints of life and the world. Following the lead of Wilhelm Dilthey, historical-typologists contend that recovering how religious paticipants see the world—what life means for them in relation to their transcendent focus (e.g., a god or sacred realm)—helps to animate, so to speak, otherwise "inert" knowledge, thereby permitting the scholar to more truly understand the mass of data acquired about religions by other more quantitatively oriented scholarly methods. As Arthur puts it, "what now seems to block understanding in many areas is a glut of information and a methodological insistence on distancing neutrality . . . we cannot dispense with the facts, but it seems that once we have acquainted ourselves with them to a certain level, a further step needs to be taken if our understanding is to advance." Furthermore, historical-typologists are convinced that their more qualitative understanding of participants' intentions and beliefs enables the scholar to draw distinctions between more important and less important religious phenomena—from the participants' standpoint—thereby enhancing appreciation of what may be truly distinctive in a given tradition's approach to the world.

A second aim shared by all historical-typologists is an historically contextualized understanding of a particular tradition's ethos and worldview. Thus, unlike the essentialists, these phenomenologists aim to recover a dynamic picture of how an ethos and worldview develops over time, not simply how these appear at a given time. In the image posed by Ninian Smart, historical-typologists expressly seek a "moving" phenomenological picture of the central religious elements of a particular tradition.[25] In acquiring this moving picture, they may well take static "snapshots" or "frames" of a particular tradition at particular times, but then they put these "frames" together in a more comprehensive picture of the tradition's developmental flow. Thus they seek a qualitative understanding of a tradition's forms of life in a temporally structured manner that reveals the changes that may occur in the participants' own self-understanding of what their tradition is about. It is important to note that this diachronic qualitative understanding is focused primarily on a given tradition's own internal development, for all historical-typologists are wary of the distortions introduced by grand speculative attempts to postulate "ideal" patterns of development between traditions. Unlike internal developmental histories, "ideal" developmental histories are evolutionary visions on a wide scale, often positing that some religious traditions not only precede others temporally but also valuationally so that some traditions are conceived as being more "primitive" and less developed than other "more advanced" and "higher" traditions. From the historical-typologists' perspective, this evolutionary view of religious traditions is quite objectionable because it is often based on scant historical evidence, is a type of reductive analysis, and tends to be "loaded" or governed by covert normative opinions about what is the best and purest form of religion (often taken to be Christianity). This tack, according to our phenomenologists, can only lead to distortion of those traditions considered to be the "lower stages" on a speculative ladder leading to the "ideal" religion.

Though historical-typologists are skeptical of grand synoptic perspectives on the evolution of religious traditions, they nonetheless do engage in carefully controlled comparative inquiry of a certain sort, and this activity represents yet a third aim that they all share: the systematic comparison of the standpoint of one tradition with the standpoints of other traditions. Indeed, though he is careful to "object to [the] kind of classification" involved in evolutionary views of religions, Kristensen, for example, goes so far as to claim that: "phenomenology of religion is the comparative study of the history of religions." Though not all historical-typologists would subscribe to the way that Kristensen chooses to highlight his own interest in comparison, they all would nonetheless concur in his more temperate statement that "phenomenology makes use of comparison only in order to gain a deeper insight into the self-subsistent . . . meaning of each of the historical data . . . to understand the conception of believers themselves, who always ascribe an absolute value to their faith." Here Kristensen signals how historical-typologists share with many non-phenomenological scholars the view that by comparing traditions, they can gain a better understanding of any one tradition. Indeed, many of these researchers have suggested that an inquiry focusing on only one tradition—eschewing any and all comparison whatsoever with others—is severely hampered in its ability to see and appreciate what may be truly distinctive to the tradition under scrutiny, precisely because that inquiry lacks a comparative reference. How can one identify what is truly distinctive to one tradition without knowing (by comparison) where and how it differs from others? Inquiry without a comparative reference is essentially myopic or blind, and so historical-typologists contend that comparison between religions will help them to understand and appreciate the true uniqueness of any one tradition.

Related to this comparative aim—and accounting for the other half of the name of this sort of phenomenological inquiry—is yet a fourth aim on the part of scholars working within this voice: to identify "universal" or at least "recurrent" features common to particular religious traditions—that is, *types* of phenomena shared by traditions. This interest in typology is two-fold. On the one hand, delineating universal features or recurrent patterns of religious forms of life assists that comparison necessary to understanding the worldviews of particular traditions—in this sense, the typological aim is subsumed under the comparative aim. On the other hand, identifying such features or patterns also represents an aim in its own right, since such factors may teach us things about the religious nature of humankind (*homo religiosus*) or the general religious dimension of human existence in the world.

The first aspect of the typological aim—patterns in the service of comparison—is well represented by Kristensen in his contention that "phenomenology has set itself the task of so grouping phenomena [in his case, the phenomena of prayer] that they shed light on one another and lead to a deeper insight into the essence of a whole group of similar phenomena" [again in his case—the case of prayer—"the basic attitude is one of surrender to and trust in the leading of the Spirit, who created and governs man and cosmos"]. Kristensen is careful to indicate that this typology of prayer(s) as a recurrent religious form of life develops a comparison in order to gain a deeper understanding of particular traditions from their (internal) points of view; and so he later states "we must always try in our study to put ourselves in the position of the believer, because it is there alone that the religious reality is to be found which we wish to understand." Kitagawa agrees with this restrained typological aim when he writes:

To be sure, it is the task of the historian of religions to delineate universal structures out of the multitude and variable religious data and to telescope long and complex histories of religions by depicting certain significant events and their persistent characteristics. Yet, his conceptions and abstractions must be constantly re-examined in the light of the integrity and unique cluster of meanings of particular religious systems or phenomena.

And with reference to the subject matter of religious pilgrimage, Kitagawa exemplifies this restraint once again when he writes, "not withstanding these 'universal' features, which are shared by the pilgrimages of various traditions, each one tends to show a unique ethos of its own, which can be understood only within its religious and cultural contexts."

The second aspect of the typological aim—identifying universal types of phenomena in order to explore the general religiosity of humankind—is most vividly represented by the phenomenological researches of Eliade. In the selection included in this book, he argues that the way religious people organize their houses, villages, and cities constitutes a "universal" feature shared by religious traditions, a feature he calls "sacred space":

Indeed, for a religious man, space is not homogeneous; some parts of space are qualitatively different. There is a sacred and hence a strong, significant space; and there are other spaces that are not sacred and so are without structure, form, or meaning. Nor is this all. For a religious man, this spatial nonhomogeneity finds expression in the experience of an opposition between space that is sacred— the only *real* and *really* existing space—and all other spaces, a foremost expanse surrounding it. The religious experience of the nonhomogeneity of space is a primordial experience, comparable to the forming of the world. . . . So it is clear to what a great degree the discovery—that is, the revelation—of a sacred space possesses existential value for a religious man; for nothing can begin, nothing can be *done* without a previous orientation—but any orientation implies acquiring a fixed point. It is for this reason that religious man has always sought to fix his abode at the "center of the world." If the world is to be *lived in* it must be *founded*—and no world can be born in the chaos of the homogeneity and relativity of profane space.

And so, for Eliade, "sacred space" is a universal category or form of religious experience that reveals a general structure of the religious dimension of human existence in the world, and he is able to conclude:

What is relevant for our theme is that we find everywhere the same fundamental conception of the necessity to live in an intelligible and meaningful world, and we find that this conception emerges ultimately from the experience of a sacred space. Now one can ask in what sense such experiences of the sacred space of houses, cities, and lands are still significant for modern desacralized man. Certainly, we know that man has never lived in the space conceived by mathematicians and physicists as being isotropic, that is, space having the same properties in all directions. The space experienced by man is *oriented* and thus anisotropic, for each dimension and direction has a specific value; for instance, along the vertical axis "up" does not have the same value as "down"; along the historical axis, left and right may be differentiated in value. The question is whether the experience of oriented space and other comparable experiences of intentionally structured spaces (for example, the different spaces of art and architecture) have something in common with the sacred space known by *Homo religiosus.*

Though he concludes with a question, it is reasonably clear from the context that the question is rhetorical and intended to suggest that "sacred space" is not only a universal feature of all religious traditions but indeed a universal feature of all human experience in the world—even secular moderns have their "sacred spaces"—whether these be national memorials or sports stadiums.

The historical-typological phenomenology of religion has a nexus of rather distinctive aims (qualitative understanding, historical sensitivity, comparison between traditions, and typology), though it also seems clear that the first two can be construed as the more dominant aims while the second two can be conceived as more subsidiary. It remains to be asked whether historical-typologists, individually or collectively, have more normative aims or agenda comparable to those we discerned for the essentialists. Do they, like the essentialists, put their research into the service of other more ultimate aims, and, if so, are these ultimate aims consonant with their more historically oriented concerns?

Many historical-typologists do, in fact, have more ultimate agenda. One of these is closely connected with the second aspect of the typological aim of identifying universal structures or patterns of religion in order to learn something about the general religiosity of humankind. Those who pursue this aim in a self-conscious way—sometimes making it the dominant aim of their historical-typological research—often have an interest in recovering and making explicit these structures in order to countervail modern tendencies toward secularization which they see as dangerous and debilitating for humankind's self-understanding. So their deeper concern is to call moderns back to a more authentic understanding of themselves as "spiritual" (not just natural) creatures. There is nothing illegitimate or unworthy about this more ultimate aim, but we need to be aware that it has the potential to encourage such researchers to find "universal" structures of religion even if they might not be there in the phenomenological data—because the more universal and dominant the religious structures, the easier it is to make the case for humankind's spiritual nature. Another deeper project pursued by some historical-typologists involves advancing the cause of their own religious commitment to a particular tradition. This theological agendum can have the effect of viewing their own tradition as somehow superior to others they may be investigating, and this, in turn, may have the effect of their highlighting or discounting certain features of a tradition under scrutiny without doing full justice to its ethos and worldview. They might, for example, tend to "read" Christianity into another tradition and thereby highlight certain features of that tradition as being important for that reason (apart from whether the tradition itself considers that feature important). Or they might, for example, tend to discount or devalue a feature of a tradition under scrutiny because that feature is in some sort of tension with an aspect of their personal religious commitments.

Thus one should not overlook the possibility that other non-phenomenological undertakings can distort the data studied by historical-typologists. Yet, on the other hand, it seems important to recognize also that many historical-typologists are interested in clarifying the religiousness of others in order (ultimately) to clarify their own or, say, the religiousness of the western world—and that this sort of deeper aim need not necessarily distort alien traditions being studied. In fact, this aim is predicated on gaining as accurate a view as possible of alien traditions, for without such accuracy there can be no genuine clarification of one's own tradition. This aim is the other side of the coin of using comparison with traditions other than the one under scrutiny, for in using one's own tradition (or, e.g., those of the West) for comparative reference, the researcher gains a deeper understanding of not only his research object but also the comparative reference itself. And so, as Arthur observes in the conclusion to his selection in this volume, this sort of work can "be seen as purposeful in terms of exploring and defining our own religiousness, through a process of exploring the religiousness of others."

Method

The four integrally connected aims of the historical-typological phenomenology of religion significantly inform this voice's conception of an appropriate method of inquiry. That is, the four aims can be correlated with the distinctive steps or facets of this enterprise's phenomenological procedure. The aim of qualitative understanding of the forms of life of a religious tradition from that tradition's standpoint suggests immediately the propriety of empathetic understanding (imaginative experiencing and introspection), epoché (with respect to questions of truth, value, and theoretic-explanatory commitments), and evocative description (conveying a sense of how particular holistic worldviews experience and see life in the world). The aim of historical sensitivity and contextualization suggests the propriety of temporally structuring this qualitative understanding and evocative description so as to chart the chronological development of a particular tradition's ethos and worldview. The comparative aim, in turn, suggests the step of controlled elucidative comparison of a particular holistic worldview with other worlds of religious meaning, and the first aspect of the typological aim suggests that this controlled comparison relies on the use of constantly refined typological categories (ideal types) of religious phenomena. Finally, the second aspect of the typological aim suggests the step of elucidative interrogation of the standpoints of particular holistic traditions so that we may identify and clarify distinctly religious objectives and intentions that may constitute "universal" or "recurrent" features of all religious traditions.

These six facets of the historical-typological phenomenological method—qualitative understanding, epoché, evocative description, diachronic understanding, elucidative comparison, and elucidative interrogation—share some similarities with the method of the essentialists. By the same token, however, there are important differences as well. The similarities involve the use of tutored empathy, epoché, evocative description, and a concern with "universal" or "recurrent" features (or essences). The differences appear focused on matters of diachronic understanding and elucidative comparison of particular worldviews. The essentialist method appears more "static" and less interested in systematic comparison of data, while the historical-typological method appears to be more oriented to temporal change and the comparison of historical-empirical data. Let us now examine the similarities and differences by clarifying briefly each of these six methodological steps or facets.

The first step—empathetic understanding—is already familiar to us from our discussion of this notion in connection with the essential phenomenology of religion. Similar to the essentialists, the historical-typologists construe this step as involving both imaginative reexperiencing and systematic introspection of the contents thus imaginatively experienced. The difference from the essentialists' articulation of this step is associated with the intrinsic concern of the historical-typologists to understand a particular religious ethos and worldview. Thus, the historical-typologists focus their sympathetic reexperiencing and introspection on the data made available by other historical and social-scientific inquiry. Their empathetic inquiry into the meaning of this data is therefore controlled, shaped by, and in constant conversation with the work of other disciplines to a greater extent than that of the essentialists. In other words, the historical-typologists' use of empathetic understanding is self-consciously focused on the qualitative elucidation of empirical data, while that of the essentialists is more oriented toward the general philosophical elucidation of religious (versus nonreligious) consciousness.

This difference in the use of empathetic understanding is captured quite well in Kristensen's claim with regard to his study of prayer that:

> We want to know the spiritual factors which are active in all prayer, but faced with such extensive material, we must also have the courage, relying on a certain amount of intuition, to separate what is important from what is not. Then we must give our attention exclusively to the data which can reasonably well be approached and understood, and which therefore hold our promise of yielding positive results.

Kristensen's interest in empathetically understanding empirical data—involving both sympathetic reexperiencing as well as intuitive observation of religious contents—is representative of how historical-typologists conceive of this methodological step. Arthur's representation of this step is particularly vivid and illuminating, when he writes:

> ... phenomenology of religion so conceived provides a means of effectively "passing over" into the religious situation which one wants to investigate and "coming back" with a clearer understanding of it. It is a means of passing over to someone else's religious world so that we may try to see how things appear when viewed through that perspective. . . . Phenomenology of religion viewed as such seeks to offer to its sufficiently competent practitioner as non-secondhand an insight as it is possible to achieve into what animate the different vitalities and movements of meaning within any particular religious outlook. Its basic motivating idea is quite

straightforward: to try to apprehend someone else's religion *as it appears to them,* rather than focusing attention on how their religion appears to us from a non-phenomenological viewpoint.

The second methodological step—epoché or bracketing of evaluative and theoretic commitments—is also already reasonably familiar to us from our discussion of the essentialist method. To see the world accurately from the standpoint of a given tradition—in order to see as that tradition sees—it is clearly necessary to put aside any and all distorting "lenses" that might be associated with opinions about the truth or falsity or illusory quality of religion, about the supposed superiority of some religions over others, and about how various theories might explain religions in terms of psychological or sociological mechanisms. As Arthur puts it, "to achieve this [phenomenological] perspective it is necessary to maintain a deliberate open-mindedness, which postpones making any evaluative judgments, and to let oneself be moved, if only temporarily, by the same currents of significance as stir the believer [or tradition] under study." And, as he observes with reference to William Golding's *The Inheritors*—Arthur's case-example of the historical-typologist at work— "he [Golding] had, in other words, to sustain a disciplined empathy and open-mindedness throughout the book. He had to observe a holding back or bracketing out, familiar in the phenomenological vocabulary which disallowed the intrusion of analyses, explanations, value-judgments or clarifying comments from his own twentieth century point of view." Kristensen vigorously concurs when he objects to evolutionary evaluative theories of "higher" and "lower" types of prayer, saying "we must object to this kind of classification . . . evaluative comparison does not come with its [phenomenology of religion's] domain," and when he rejects Ludwig Feuerbach's classical projectionist theory of religion as applied to prayer:

Feuerbach tried to give a psychological answer to the question of how prayer originated and how it can be explained. His basic thesis is that man's desire, need, and hope are what have created the gods . . . God is a projection of the human mind; God is created in the image of man and not vice-versa; theology is anthropology. The gods are "wish beings" . . . prayer is an act by means of which man tries to fulfill his wish but the fulfillment of a wish, as long as there remains a wish is an illusion. Religion, therefore, which is the objectivizing of man's own essence, "is worthless illusion." . . . This is indeed a remarkable sample of a psychological explanation which is extraordinarily unpsychological and in conflict with the experience of all ages. . . .[26]

Kristensen's objections here are fully consonant with, and representative of, the phenomenological epoché employed by all historical-typologists in their study of religious traditions.

A third methodological step shared by both essentialists and historical-typologists is that of evocative description of the religious phenomena being studied. Again, this step is reasonably familiar to us, but it is nonetheless important to see how crucial historical-typologists regard this step for attaining their goal of qualitative understanding of particular religious traditions. Arthur indicates the close connection between qualitative understanding and evocative description when he writes that empathetic understanding "is an attempt to place us, so far as this is possible, in the other person's shoes, so that we might stand with them and walk with them, observing and feeling what occurs with a closeness which would be impossible for a 'external' descriptive study." And he further adumbrates this point with reference to Golding's *The Inheritors*: "in beginning his imagination from the inside and working out, in leading the reader around to discovering things for himself, rather than merely describing them, in building up a situation in which we can know imaginatively what it might be like to look through other eyes, to live in a different world of religious meaning, Golding does not rely on the fabrication of eroneous details." These features of "observing and feeling . . . with a closeness" and "discovering things for [one]self rather than merely describing them" are reminiscent of the performative factors of evocative description discussed in connection with the essentialists. For Arthur, evocative description is absolutely crucial to the attainment of truly qualitative understanding. This, for Arthur—and other historical-typologists as well—represents an important cognitive challenge and achievement of this enterprise, for through evocative description one is able to learn something about another religious tradition attainable in no other way: true understanding of the lived experience of participants from within that tradition. In short, evocative description performatively prompts existential understanding of the religious other that is otherwise impossible for the nonparticipant in that tradition. And historical-typologists further wager that such existential understanding may well be important to achieving further knowledge of a tradition under scrutiny—for example, by suggesting hypotheses to be explored by other disciplines, by suggesting insights into the "universals" of religion or about the spiritual nature of humankind, and so on.

Though Arthur is the most articulate of our authors in identifying and discussing this step of evocative description, we should also be aware that our other authors, while not discussing it, do in fact exemplify it in their work. Thus, for example, Kristensen actively seeks to evoke his reader's sympathetic appreciation and existential understanding of the prayerful activity of religious traditions rather far removed from our cultural world by quoting (e.g.) Algonquin, Incan, Christian, Babylonian, Hindu, and other prayer texts and then directing the reader's attention to the "spirit of these prayers." Eliade, for his part, goes to extraordinary lengths to pull his readers into the "existential meaning of 'living in one's own world'" and then to show how this existential meaning can be used to sympathize imaginatively with the "sacred space" of archaic religious traditions. In both cases, as well as others throughout the book, we can see (or rather experience) evocative description at work.

The fourth step of the historical-typological phenomenological method is diachronic understanding—temporally structured elucidation of a particular tradition's ethos and worldview and recording changes in that ethos and worldview. This is a step distinctive to the historical-typological voice and method, not shared in any self-conscious way by the essentialist voice and method. Of the authors included in this book, Kitagawa is one of the most articulate about this step. He begins his inquiry into types of pilgrimage in Japanese religions by noting the need to indicate universal structures, to highlight especially pertinent and illustrative events, to be senstive to change over time, and always to check typological structures against the historical materials. The result is that Kitagawa delineates the distinctive ethos of each of three types of pilgrimage—pilgrimage to sacred mountains, pilgrimage based on faith in divinities, and pilgrimage based on faith in charismatic persons—in a diachronic manner, tracing changes in the characteristic patterns of religious meaning associated with each type. In this manner he achieves diachronically qualitative understanding of each sort of pilgrimage in its internal developmental self-understanding over time. It seems clear that Kitagawa's effort hopes to produce what Smart refers to as a "moving" phenomenological picture of an element of a religious tradition as that tradition itself changes its own self-understanding of that element. Thus, unlike essential phenomenology of religion, the historical-typological enterprise is quite self-consciously non-static or dynamic in attempting to understand in a qualitative way the standpoint of particular religious traditions.

In its fifth step of controlled elucidative comparison, historical-typological phenomenology also seems distinctive from the essentialist voice, for although in this step the two voices share a concern with universal or recurrent structures or patterns, they do so for quite different reasons. One should recall that the essentialist voice is predominantly interested in identifying and characterizing the essential or defining traits of religious consciousness in general. By contrast, the historical-typological voice is predominantly interested in elucidating the internal perspective of a particular tradition by way of comparing it with other traditions, and for this purpose it employs typological categories as a way of assisting this comparison. Thus, for historical-typologists the notion of universal features (or "essences" as the essentialists would say) helps in the comparative elucidation of a particular tradition—and the universal features or patterns (or types) are used just so long as they genuinely assist in understanding a particular ethos. Should, however, a given universal feature turn out to be inapplicable or unhelpful, the historical-typologist will either refine the category or possibly drop it altogether as potentially distorting what may really be going on in a particular ethos or worldview. Thus, unlike the essentialists, the historical-typologists sit rather lightly on their typological categories or universal features, ever alert to the dangers of possible distortion of the particular phenomena in which they are particularly interested.

This attitude toward universal structures explains why both Kitagawa and Kristensen are prone to say things like "his conceptions and abstractions must be constantly re-examined in light of the integrity and the unique cluster of meanings of particular religious systems" (Kitagawa), "notwithstanding these universal features, which are shared by the pilgrimages of various traditions, each one tends to show a unique ethos of its own" (Kitagawa), "phenomenology makes use of comparison only to gain a deeper insight into the self-subsistent . . . meaning of each of the historical data" (Kristensen), "we can come to see the absolute character of particular religious data in an approximate way, but never more than approximately . . . the absolute character of the data offers resistance to the constitution of an 'ideal history' of prayer" (Kristensen). These are warnings to other historical-typologists—and to us as well—that, though universal features and recurrent types may often be useful to gaining comparative insight into the significance of a particular religious ethos, one must beware of imposing or forcing them where they do not fit.

What exactly does comparative elucidation involve? What does it look like? How is it done? These questions now beg for some clear answers. Perhaps the best way to answer them is to focus on a couple of clear exercises that highlight this methodological step. One such exercise is supplied by Kristensen's study of prayer. Kristensen is quite adept in using "comparison . . . to gain a deeper insight into the self-subsistent . . . meaning" of prayer. For example, he begins his study by comparing the Algonquin prayer to the Great Spirit to "cause that the water shall remain smooth," to the Christian prayer "give us bread for today," to the Incan prayer "to watch over them that they may live in health and peace," to the Zulu prayer to their ancestors "people of our house . . . you know what is good for us, give it to us," in order to display a basic attitude of "surrender to and trust in the leading of the Spirit, who created and governs man and cosmos." In another example he compares a Babylonian "magical prayer" to Shamash to "break the sorcerer's spell," to Luther's comment of religious assurance "God could do nothing else; the path was cut off for Him" in order to clarify the way in which a certain type of prayer exerts a certain compulsion on the gods. Now what is interesting about all this is the way in which, through identification of both similarities and differences among the prayers from different traditions, Kristensen is able to illuminate each prayer as well as reach some more general conclusions about the fundamental recurrent types of attitudes and actions represented in them all. Thus he is able to see the unique ethos associated with each prayer, use the ethos of one to clarify the ethos of another, and reach a tentative conclusion about some apparently universal features. This is the process of comparative elucidation at work, and it is quite evidently a rather powerful tool in the historical-typologist's method of inquiry.

Eliade's inquiry into "the world, the city, the house" represents another instance of elucidative comparison, this time focused on the study of "sacred space." Beginning with the way the historian Theodore Mommsen "lived in" the world of the Greeks and Romans as not simply history, but rather as a fundamental, though imaginative, orientation to the world, Eliade goes on to exploit this familiar comparative reference in order to illuminate "the cosmicized and . . . 'sacred' world" of archaic religious traditions, such as those of the Achilpas (an Australian tribe) and the Bororos of Brazil, who established their world by structuring their villages and territories around a central point representing a vertical axis open to the transcendent making possible their orientation in a now sacred world. Eliade continues by comparing the history of Rome's founding to those associated with the founding of cities in Iran, Southeast Asia, and China in order to illustrate the similarities of religious symbolism shared by these histories. The point is surely to compare such orientations to sacred space so as to clarify each as well as to suggest that a category of sacred space may well represent a universal structure of religious traditions. Again, we see the process of elucidative comparison at work as well as gain an appreciation for how it might deepen our understanding of particular traditions as well as possible universal structures of religion.

We need now to examine the sixth and final step of the historical-typological method—elucidative interrogation of the standpoints of particular religious traditions in order to identify distinctively religious objectives and intentions. This interrogation involves two aspects that may in some cases overlap or blend into one another. One aspect concerns distinguishing the distinctively religious objectives, intentions, and motiviations operative in a given tradition from other nonreligious motivations that may also be operative in that tradition's ambiant culture and may interact with the religious motivations. This sort of interrogation is aimed at clarifying the "mixed motives" (so to speak) that may lie behind some religious phenomena in a given tradition—it is clearly focused on gaining an understanding of the complexities that may be involved in a given tradition's ethos and worldview. The other aspect of this step involves futher clarification of distinctively religious motivations for the purpose of identifying and illuminating structures and phenomena apparently universal to all religious traditions. The first more modest aspect of elucidative interrogation is well represented by Kitagawa's work. The second more ambitious aspect is ably exemplified by Eliade's inquiry. Let us examine each of these examples briefly in order to clarify the function and logic of this final step of the historical-typological method.

In representing the first aspect of this step, Kitagawa quite straightforwardly points out that "in every religious tradition, the pilgrimage combines . . . diverse and often contradictory features, which are both spiritual and mundane." He further writes:

Usually, pilgrims are motivated by religious objectives, such as adoration of the deities or saints who are enshrined at various sacred places, gaining merit for one's salvation, paying penance for annullment of the sin, or praying for the repose of the spirits of the deceased, but these religious motives are often mixed with the desire to acquire healing, good forture, easy child-birth, prosperity, and other this-worldly benefits. Even the ascetic practices, which are usually imposed on the pilgrims, notably sexual abstinence and fasting or dietary restrictions, are interpreted as necessary investments for the expected rewards. Besides, the pilgrimage provides welcome relief from the routine of the dull everyday life of the people. Furthermore, seen from a broader perspective, the pilgrimage, which cements the solidarity of religious groups, also stimulates trade and commerce, dissemination of ideas, and intercultural exchange.

Thus, with respect to pilgrimage, Kitagawa notices that "spiritual," celebratory, worshipful motives are often intermixed with "mundane," instrumental, even materialistic motives. The first type of motive can only be achieved by distinctively religious activities, for these motives and activities are internally related—each needs the other and cannot be what it is without the other. The second type of motive, however, is only contingently and externally related to religious activity, since mundane ends can be achieved by many sorts of activities (e.g., medicine, commerce, and all the rest). Part of Kitagawa's task, therefore, is to distinguish between the distinctively religious motives and objectives intrinsically in-

volved in religious activities of pilgrimage, on the one hand, and the more
adventitious mundane motives and objectives only contingently related
to such activities, on the other. In this way, he seeks to interrogate the
phenomena in order to clarify their characteristic intrinsic religious traits.

In representing the second aspect of the step of elucidative interrogation, Eliade also evinces concern with the intrinsic religious objectives
and motives involved in "founding the world," but he goes far beyond
this concern to also try to identify what he regards as a universal structure of all religions—the notion of sacred space. Thus, as we noted earlier, he concludes his study with the bold claim that "what is relevant for
our theme is that we find everywhere the same fundamental conception
of the necessity to live in an intelligible and meaningful world, and we
find that this conception emerges ultimately from the experience of a sacred space . . . of houses, cities, and lands." And he further suggests that
this experience of sacred space is universal to "homo religiosus" (i.e., all
religious persons and communities). In effect, Eliade interrogates religious phenomena in order (finally) to identify and characterize what he
regards as a universal structure of all religions.

Issues

Thus far we have attempted to clarify the aims and method of the
historical-typological phenomenology of religion by focusing on the
work of some of its representative practitioners. We need now to go one
step farther to gain a more critical perspective on this voice, by identifying and discussing some of the typical problems and issues raised by this
voice. In this way we can become more aware of certain of its strengths
as well as its limitations. Our work is eased somewhat by the fact that
many of the same criticisms made of the essentialist voice are also levied
against the historical-typological enterprise. Interestingly, however, a
number of these criticisms can be more easily and decisively rebutted in
the historical-typological case. In addition to these shared criticisms,
there are also a few charges that appear to be more forcefully, if not
uniquely, raised against the phenomenological method of the historical-
typologists. We begin with a brief discussion of the criticisms that carry
over from the essentialist enterprise.

Five criticisms in particular appear to be shared by both the essentialist
and historical-typological voices. The first has been already identified—
namely, the concern over whether hidden normative agenda somehow
distort the descriptive and comparative results of the historical-typological
enterprise. A second problem is whether the phenomenological attitude
of the historical-typologists—in its apparent detached objectivity—is

able to do justice to religious phenomena of ultimate commitment associated with the "absolute" value-standpoints of particular religious traditions. A third problem is whether the phenomenological attitude of the historical-typologists is sufficiently "suspicious" of, and critical about, the factors involved in religious motivations, intentions, and activities. Yet a fourth problem concerns the seemingly "subjective" and therefore epistemically suspect status of empathetic understanding based on sympathetic reexperiencing. And a final problem—which may appear somewhat surprising, given our characterization of historical-typological method—concerns a perceived synchronic and anti-historical bias built into the method's use of typological categories and its concern with universal or recurrent structures of religion. Let us consider each of these criticisms with particular reference to the historical-typological voice.

The first criticism—the bias associated with normative agenda—clearly presents a genuine problem for those historical-typological researches that are governed by either theological or philosophical "missionary" (e.g., spiritual nature of man) aims. We have already admitted and discussed this problem. Such agenda can in fact constitute distorting "lenses" on historical data. But we need also to emphasize that the historical-typological method also builds in some checks against such biases—in the form of epoché or bracketing as well as comparative elucidation based on typological categories. Thus the danger of distortion is countervailed by the method itself, and so what is a possible risk is not an inevitable eventuality.

The second problem—deeper biasing effects of detached objectivity associated with the phenomenological attitude (or epoché)—has been effectively addressed in our earlier discussion of this criticism in connection with the essentialists. As we pointed out earlier, this criticism simply overlooks or discounts the fact that epoché is integrally bound up with and enhances the step of empathetic understanding based on sympathetic reenactment or reexperiencing. As Arthur very effectively puts it, "it is necessary to maintain a deliberate open-mindedness, which postpones making any value judgments, and to let oneself be moved . . . by the same currents of significance as stirred the believer under study." Thus, from his point of view, epoché and empathy are interactive and mutually reinforcing, resulting in "the idea of seeing another world meaning as it appears to its own inhabitants—whilst still maintaining the status of observer." That is, "detached objectivity" is not incompatible with empathetic understanding, as this second line of criticism appears to suggest or presuppose.

The third criticism—that the phenomenological attitude appears in-

sufficiently suspicious of hidden nonreligious motives and factors in-
fluencing religious forms of life—has also been addressed in our earlier
discussion of this problem. The point we made there is that phenomenologists, by focusing on consciously religious motives and intentions,
constitute religious "objects" of inquiry that may subsequently be investigated by other psycho-social disciplines interested in developing deeper
explanatory and theoretic accounts of religious phenomena. We might
furthermore add that historical-typologists—as represented by the work
of Kitagawa, for example—appear clearly cognizant of the fact that
mixed motives are at work in many religious phenomena. Such a perspective can hardly be charged with naiveté if it then proceeds to try
to separate out what appear to the be intrinsically religious motives
and intentions constituting the distinctively religious dimensions of such
phenomena.

The fourth problem—concerning the epistemic status of empathetic
understanding—has also been addressed in our earlier discussion. There
we made the point—with reference to the work of Westphal and
Smart—that the step of sympathetic reexperiencing is uncontroversially
at work in other disciplines and that therefore the phenomenological
method does not suffer from any epistemic difficulty peculiar to it. Furthermore, we suggested that in all these disciplines the process of empathetic understanding clearly yields incontrovertibly significant and inter-
subjectively verifiable results, shifting the burden of proof (so to speak)
back on the critics of this methodological procedure. Adding to our earlier discussion, Arthur tries to locate one of the important factors lying
behind the critics' position: "the problem is, of course, how an approach
which claims to be non-factual, personal and holistic can possibly offer
us any insight into religion at all. For, on first hearing at least, such terms
sound anything but reassuring about the provision of any legitimate
means of knowing." And his answer to this problem involves exploiting
a discussion by contemporary philosopher Renford Bambrough on how
writing and reading stories and novels can in fact assist our comprehension of facts precisely through the process of sympathetic reexperiencing:

Renford Bambrough has drawn attention to occasions when "we can achieve and
convey knowledge and understanding by seeing and showing a pattern of relationships in between a set of items in which each separate item is already available
for inspection." Imaginative re-experiencing is, or seeks to be, such an occasion,
when an advancement in learning takes place without our acquiring any increase
in itemizable bits of information which were not available to us before. . . . As
Bambrough went on to show, in reading a story we may learn something which
is quite "disproportionate to the number of new facts we learn" or to whether we
learn any new facts at all. Indeed, many works of literature can be said to teach

us about things we might already claim to know about. . . . Imaginative re-experiencing does not advocate an *abandonment* of information in favor of some kind of factually unfounded excercise in speculation. Rather, it sees being well informed as a pre-requisite for its imaginative endeavor. The information is seen as the raw material for that endeavor, it is not however, accepted as the final product which is sought. . . . There would seem to be no immediate reason, then, for rejecting a methodology which is non-factual, personal and holistic . . . simply on the grounds that it could not provide any legitimate means of knowing. It might not be easy to specify precisely what we *do* learn from such an approach, since the nature of the knowledge it offers resists any process of itemization, but it seems clear that it can teach us some things—perhaps a great deal—even in those areas where we may feel fully informed already . . .

One of Arthur's points here is that imaginative reexperiencing of another's worldview can lead us to see significant and meaningful patterns and relationships among facts and, further, that identifying and elucidating these patterns and relationships constitutes a cognitive achievement enhancing our knowledge of a particular religious tradition. There is, we submit, nothing murky or mysterious about either this achievement or the process leading up to it.

The fifth problem of anti-historical bias may at first blush appear to be a very improbable line of criticism against an enterprise explicitly concerned with features of historical context and development. Though, as we conceded earlier, this criticism may have some bite with respect to some research done within the essentialist voice, it is less obviously applicable to the historical-typological enterprise. Nevertheless, the charge is often made, and we must consider carefully its rationale and merit. The criticism focuses most directly on the steps of comparative elucidation and interrogation, which employ as well as forge typological categories for the purposes of gaining a deeper understanding into the nature of particular religious traditions as well as religions in general. The claim is that typological categories (e.g., prayer, sacred space, pilgrimage, sacred persons, sacred communities) are static, unduly reifying, and, when applied to complex and ever-changing historical data, ultimately skew that data. For example (and this is only hypothetical), it might be charged that applying Kristensen's category of "magical prayer" (ritually exerting compulsion on the gods) to Christian materials might result in a radical misunderstanding of the phenomenon of petitionary prayer in that tradition (which some argue is more expressive of surrender to God's will whatever His will might be). If this were done, then distortion of Christian petitionary prayer would result. Or, for another example (again, hypothetical), some might argue that in proposing the category of sacred space as a religious universal, researchers might be lead to overlook or discount aspects of those traditions (e.g., Theravada Buddhism) that deny a transcendent referent and thus the sensibility of a spatial orientation to a god or gods. Again, the result might be a significant distortion in understanding a religious tradition from its own internal standpoint.

While there may be real dangers associated with the insensitive use of such typological categories, it does appear that this line of criticism overlooks significant checks against such dangers built into the historical-typological method. We have, for example, pointed out that practitioners of this method are ever alert to refining and adjusting (or even rejecting) their typological categories when they are dealing with subtle and nuanced data that either stretch or do not fit the categories. For historical-typologists focused on the qualitative understanding of particular religious traditions, typological categories are heuristic devices or guides to uncovering nonobvious features of the data under scrutiny—assisted by comparison to the data of other traditions that might fall within those categories. Heuristic devices are used only so long as they assist the primary investigation, and are modified or dropped if they are found to be not doing their job. The point is that historical-typologists work dialectically back and forth between their comparative types and the particular data, constantly revising their understanding of each—types and data—until they reach a satisfactory and defensible (to a community of scholars) understanding of a particular tradition.

While possibly conceding the presence of such a dialectical process, the critics might press their point more forcefully against that mode of elucidative interrogation interested in proposing religious universals. So-called universals, they might charge, once in place and accepted as universals, might be henceforth used unthinkingly and uncritically when coming up against new data. Moreover, a so-called universal once accepted by a community of scholars is less likely to be called into question than an heuristic device, and therefore might be employed in a prejudicial fashion. There is no denying a legitimate danger here, but, by the same token, being aware of this danger constitutes both a challenge and the possibility of avoiding the danger in the first place—by treating even so-called universals as heuristic to the understanding of religious dimensions of human existence.

Now that we have completed our review of the criticisms brought against both the essentialists and the historical-typological voices—and seeing the nuanced responses of the latter—we need to consider whether there are any additional problems that might be relatively distinctive to the historical-typological enterprise. There are at least two such problems—one is concerned with cultural bias ("if I were a horse" fallacy), the other with a difficulty we will call "diachronic bias." The "if I were a

horse" fallacy charges that the historical-typological method is ineluctably infected with cultural bias because the investigator employing sympathetic reenactment inevitably imports his or her own cultural baggage
into the imaginative empathetic process, for the investigator's imaginative
experience and thought is shaped at the deepest possible level by the language and conceptuality of that person's cultural tradition.[27] There is
considerable truth to this sort of contention—researchers are shaped by
their cultural traditions—but the charge of inevitable bias overlooks the
power and prospects of checks within the historical-typological method.
Epoché clearly helps to nullify the effects of "cultural baggage," and the
process of comparison based on constantly reexamined typological categories also assists in freeing the investigator's research from distorting
cultural biases. Furthermore, trans-cultural and cross-traditional understanding is obviously possible as shown by activities ranging from
language-translation to inter-cultural dialogue. So again we encounter a
risk, but one that can be counteracted by an appropriately sensitive and
controlled method.

The problem of diachronic bias is perhaps most perceptively discussed
by the contemporary phenomenologist/philosopher/historian of religions,
Ninian Smart.[28] In his discussion of how historical-typologists attempt to
construct a dynamic moving picture of a tradition's self-understanding
(diachronically qualitative understanding), he points out that the researcher is faced with the problem of how to identify which temporal
community's self-understanding—within a given religious tradition—is
to be taken as normative or definitive for the tradition. For example,
within the Christian tradition, which historical community's conception
of God is normative for the entire tradition (if any), so that we may speak
of a Christian tradition that subsumes (e.g.) Catholic and Protestant, medieval and modern, church and sect, and even fringe religious groups
such as Unitarian universalists? Questions such as these point up the
problem of whether the researcher's choice of (e.g.) a conception of God
as normative for the entire tradition might not build in a diachronic bias
toward an historically and socially particular conception of God that
might distort the researcher's understanding of other historically and
socially located communities within the tradition. There seems to be a
real problem here, and Smart's suggested solution is that the historical-
typologist must try to identify the typical conceptions of God of these
various historical communities of worship and then within these typical
conceptions discern the "regulative ideal" toward which they all tend,
while simultaneously being self-consciously sensitive to the finer differences among their particular conceptions. That is, Smart proposes that

the phenomenological researcher must construct an "ideal type" for conceptions of God within the tradition, while simultaneously recognizing that various instantiations of this ideal type have differences. This, suggests Smart, will help to correct for diachronic bias: being self-consciously alert to both the similarities within the different conceptions (the ideal type or regulative ideal) and the differences within the similarities (the finer grain of particular conceptions). This solution to the problem appears both possible and plausible. Awareness of this problem and a way of checking it permit us to be more critically alert to an issue seemingly endemic to the historical-typological voice.

As with the essentialist voice, reviewing these problems or concerns about the historical-typological voice assists us in seeing some of the weaknesses and strengths of its method. Though, again, we have tended to rebut these concerns, we should remain aware that continuing perceptions of them have no small role in helping to generate or at least strengthen the resolve of other methodological voices both within and outside the field of phenomenology of religion. Thus, for example, the criticisms of static typology, insufficient suspicion, diachronic bias, and so on have helped to support the development of other nonphenomenological methods in the history of religions, while the issues of detached objectivity as well as inescapable cultural bias have helped to support the emergence of the existential-hermeneutical phenomenology of religion. Nevertheless, none of these various methodological voices—whether within or outside the field of phenomenology of religion—would deny that the historical-typological voice has had and continues to have an important role in the academic study of religion.

Third Voice: Existential-Hermeneutical Phenomenology of Religion

The third voice in the phenomenology of religion is what we call, following Paul Ricoeur and his interpreters, the existential-hermeneutical phenomenology of religion.[29] "Existential" and "hermeneutical" here have rather precise meanings, and their linkage is intended to signal a distinctive turn in some recent research in phenomenology of religion. "Existential" refers to this voice's preoccupation with structures and problems of human existence in the world, including such broad themes as freedom, intersubjectivity, temporality, corporeality, finitude, and death as well as particular human experiences such as anxiety, hope, despair, guilt, caring. "Hermeneutical" refers to this voice's perception that all human experience is mediated by language (or, more broadly symbolic systems). The linkage of the two—"existential" and "hermeneutical"—indicates this voice's further perception that all structures and problems of human existence and experience require an approach explicitly focused on exploring them through interpretation of their linguistic or symbolic expression. Thus, at the very outset of our discussion of this voice, we can see that it is oriented to both a particular subject-matter and a distinctive methodological approach. Before we move on to discuss this voice's aims and method, it may be useful to first identify in a more general way some of the basic traits of existential-hermeneutical phenomenology. For this part of our discussion, we draw freely on Ricoeur's justly famous *Encyclopedie Française* article on existential phenomenology as well as the discussions of other existential phenomenologists such as Gabriel Marcel and Maurice Merleau-Ponty.[30] As we do this, we will try self-consciously to connect certain points of our discussion to some of the issues and problems we identified in our examination of the two previous voices. In this way, we should gain a strong foundation for our subsequent examination of the distinctive aims, method, and problems of the existential-hermeneutical phenomenology of religion.

Orientation to Existential Phenomenology

The most important observation that Ricoeur makes about existential phenomenology in general is that it is an "oriented" enterprise.[31] By this he means that it quite explicitly and self-consciously serves normative aims associated with the philosophy of human existence. Existential phenomenologists use the phenomenological method to explore the great problems of human existence (mentioned above), and they do this in such a way as to privilege one or another normative aim—for example, to counteract human alienation from the natural and/or social world, to recover the metaphysical dimensions of human existence, to rediscover humankind's bond with a transcendent sacred, and so on. Furthermore, in pursuing one or another of these aims, different investigators tend also to emphasize different forms of human experiences as being the "key" or central access to advancing a deeper understanding of the human condition—one might focus on experiences of radical freedom to make choices and create values (Sartre), another might focus on experiences of anxiety and dread (Heidegger), yet another might focus on experiences of hope and liberation (Marcel).[32] And, in turn, these aims and pursuits tend to produce distinctively different "styles" of existential phenomenology.[33] Ricoeur's point is that existential phenomenology in all of its variations is a radically oriented field in which the phenomenological method is clearly subordinated to dominant, organizing, and normative existential aims, insights, and hunches about what is most important in the human condition.

This aggressive openness on the part of existential phenomenologists about their normative orientations contrasts quite strongly with the stances of essentialists and historical-typological phenomenologists of religion, who, while often possessing hidden normative aims and agenda, appear to be trying to pursue within their phenomenology more descriptive aims associated with either explicating the essential traits of religious consciousness in general or understanding the ethos and worldview of particular religious traditions. Phenomenologists within the latter two voices do not self-consciously intend to be normatively existential within their phenomenological investigations—in fact, they try constantly to "check" or bracket out these aims because of their constant worry about distorting or biasing the data. This is a very different attitude from that of existential phenomenologists, who openly embrace and aggressively pursue normative existential aims. What factors might account for such a radical difference in attitude?

Answering this question takes us to the heart of what existential phenomenology is all about in terms of its shared insights into the nature of human consciousness and existence in the world. Though in his article Ricoeur discusses only four of these shared insights or themes, there appear in fact to be six such dominant themes. They are: (1) "consciousness is bound to a pre-given world," (2) "we are incarnated," (3) "we are temporal or historical," (4) "we are essentially related to others in an intersubjective world," (5) "we are linguistic beings through and through," and (6) "we are free." Individually and collectively these six organizing insights or themes explicate in a deeper way why and how existential phenomenology is an oriented field of inquiry, for they identify distinctive modes of human existential orientation in the world that, according to existential phenomenologists, all phenomenological inquiry must take into account as it works out its programs of research. These insights constitute "givens" (or "pre-givens") that, from their perspective, all phenomenological programs must acknowledge on pain of fundamental shortsightedness (or even incoherence) in their aims and method. Let us now briefly discuss these insights, with a constant eye on how they might modify, add to, or correct features of our other two voices in phenomenology of religion.

The first organizing insight—the link between consciousness and a pre-given world—is absolutely crucial, for it "founds" in a sense all the other insights. The claim is that upon becoming reflectively aware of itself all consciousness finds a world already there, "pre-given." In Ricoeur's words, "the 'world' . . . is pre-given in the sense that every present activity [of a conscious being] surges into a world already there."[34] Merleau-Ponty puts this point well when he writes in his *Phenomenology of Perception*, "the world is there beyond any possible analysis of mine," or, again, the world is given in our experience as "the background from which all acts stand out" and as "the field for all my thoughts and all my explicit perceptions."[35] Now, how, one might ask, do these phenomenologists gain this insight, and what precisely is its significance? Merleau-Ponty provides the clue to answering this question when he suggests that we are so thoroughly embedded in the world that the only way to become aware of this fact is to suspend (bracket) this involvement, "put it out of play" in the manner of phenomenological epoché. And, he further suggests, when reflection is thereby enabled to stand back from its involvement it can "watch the forms of transcendence fly up like sparks from a fire; it slackens the intentional threads which attach us to the world and thus brings them to our notice." But then, he points out, by learning of "the unmotivated upsurge of the world" in us, in our being, we can see as well that complete reduction or epoché is for us—as beings in the world—not possible.[36] And so through epoché we see that epoché itself refers us to an existential structure underlying our experience—the fact that we are essentially beings in the world. In a sense, phenomenological reduction or epoché self-destructs—it finds that it is not attainable in a complete way, because our consciousness is tied inextricably to a pre-given world. As Ricoeur observes, "this shift in accent marks the passage to existential phenomenology."[37]

The significance of this insight is no doubt beginning to emerge in the reader's mind: phenomenological reduction (epoché)—one of the linchpins of the phenomenological method—is radically bounded by the existential fact that our consciousness is linked to a pre-given world. And seeing this gives rise to the question, are there any other existential facts (or structures) that bound our understanding of life in the world? Further, are there perhaps such structures that concern some sort of significant link between humankind and the sacred? Being able to ask such questions as these indicates just how fundamental the first insight of existential phenomenology is, for with the establishment of a link between consciousness and a pre-given world comes also an approach to human existence replete with rich possibilities and opportunities for investigating the nature of our being in the world, for understanding ourselves at what is perhaps the deepest possible level. Is this insight shared by our other two voices in the phenomenology of religion? If not, what are the possible implications of this for our critical understanding and appraisal of these two voices?

What seems reasonably clear is that the notion of a "bound" epoché is quite different from the essentialists' understanding of the step of epoché or bracketing. Their conception of this step appears to presuppose the idea of a detached objective observer who, through sympathy assisted by bracketing, focuses on religious consciousness as the Other to be understood and examined. Within the essentialist method, the phenomenological observer does not share a pre-given world with the other precisely because the observer does not acknowledge a pre-given world at all. But, in not acknowledging such a world bounding all consciousness, the question is raised as to whether the phenomenological observer might not be alienated in an important way from the standpoint of the religious consciousness he or she is investigating. If this line of reasoning is cogent, then the problem is re-raised of the possible biasing effect of the phenomenological attitude's radical detachment. Perhaps some essential features of religious consciousness will slip by the detached investigator unnoticed, unacknowledged, or uninvestigated. Similarly, with respect to the historical-typologist's phenomenological attitude, which, though supplemented by steps of diachronic understanding and comparative reference, is nonetheless shaped by the ideal of a detached objective observer—it too runs the risk of being alienated from the particular ethos and worldview it is attempting to investigate and thus may miss certain of its significant features. This possible bias in both the essentialist and historical-typological voices needs, of course, to be investigated further, and we will do this in connection with our discussion of the other insights of existential phenomenology.

The second insight of existential phenomenology—captured in Marcel's claim that "we are incarnated"—is related to the first but takes the latter a step farther in the direction of concreteness.[38] The claim here is that our consciousness is tied to a pre-given world in the specific form of being incarnate or embodied: I am my body, or more accurately, I am embodied, and there is no escaping this. Both Marcel and Merleau-Ponty contend that the feature of corporeality represents a fundamental and inescapable datum of our consciousness, implying that we are essentially "situated" and "oriented" in the world in a particular way. To put it roughly, "where my body is" shapes what and how I perceive; "how my body is" shapes the quality of my perception; "what happens to my body" also happens to my consciousness; and so on. Our bodies are not merely objects in the world to which we are contingently or accidentally attached or related; rather they are part of how we are as conscious beings, orienting us in particular ways as spatial conscious beings. According to existential phenomenologists, this insight has significant implications for phenomenological inquiry into the nature of human consciousness and existence in the world.

One important implication is that phenomenological inquiry needs to be alert to the corporeal and, more broadly, spatially oriented features of conscious experience. This much seems obvious. Another less obvious implication pointed out quite effectively by Marcel is that our incarnateness so situates us in the world that it prevents us from being able to attain a radically detached objective and comprehensive view of ourselves.[39] Precisely because we "see" the world from only an oriented perspective, we find it difficult (indeed impossible) to gain a complete and neutral perspective on the world, including, of course, ourselves, our very own being. Indeed, this difficulty is especially stark in the case of ourselves (our being) because we are never simply objects to ourselves, able to investigate ourselves in a totally detached manner in the way of scientific inquiry into natural objects and events. Rather we are opaque to ourselves, and our being is a mystery to us in many respects. The further implication of this difficulty in being able to attain a detached, standpointless perspective is that the supposed cognitive ideal of "the anonymous epistemological subject" (to use Ricoeur's phrase) in phenomenology, who uses himself or herself as a neutral and impartial sounding board for understanding human experience and consciousness, is called into question.[40] That is, not only is the epistemological subject (the inquirer) bound to the world but he or she is also oriented in the world in a particular way—corporeally and spatially. Thus, the subject is no longer so "anonymous." Now how does the existential phenomenological perspective and its implications bear on our other two voices in phenomenology of religion?

One such bearing should be obvious. Since the essentialist method apparently presupposes the standpoint of the anonymous epistemological subject (the image of the detached, neutral, and objective observer), it fails to recognize and take account of the inquirer's corporeal orientation in the world. We in fact saw this vividly illustrated, for example, in the way that Earle so casually separated the (transcendental) ego or consciousness from the body in his investigation into the essence of mystical consciousness. And we need to ask whether this sort of separation of mind from body and dismissal from the latter's importance might not have the possible consequence of "blinding" the phenomenological inquirer to seeing or appreciating "embodied" aspects of (e.g.) mystical

experience—for example, the significance of physical discipline in medi-
tational practices, the significance of kinesthetic elements in the experiences of mystical union or mystical love, and so on. Such distortional
effects seem quite possible, and it may be no simple oversight that many
Western essentialists (e.g., Otto, Scheler, Earle) fail to discuss or even
explicitly acknowledge the corporeal elements in mystical or, more
broadly, religious consciousness.

   Clearly, a similar sort of problem could also affect the work of historical-
typologists who also appear to presuppose the ideal of an anonymous
epistemological subject. However, we must be cautious here, for it is
equally important to recognize that by virtue of their focus on particular
religious traditions and their methodological step of comparative elucidation, historical-typologists gain a "check" of sorts against any whole-
sale blindness to corporeality and orientation in the world. If, for example, a particular tradition emphasizes physical disciplines of some sort
or perhaps the notion of some sort of sacred space, then it would be
difficult for a self-consciously historical and comparative method to overlook, ignore, or dismiss these features of the tradition. Possible evidence
for the efficacy of such a check may be seen in Eliade's work, which
clearly recognizes the fact and significance of spatial orientation in the
"worlds" of various (if not all) religious traditions. Indeed, Eliade is quite
well known for his studies of Yoga practices in Eastern religious traditions, and these practices involve important elements of physical discipline (phenomena of embodied consciousness) of which Eliade is fully
cognizant.[41] So we must conclude that historical-typologists are not
nearly as prone as the essentialists to underestimate the significance
of corporeality and spatial orientation in the world. This may be due in
part to direct influence of existential phenomenology on some historical-
typological research—Eliade, for example, is quite conversant with and
frequently mentions influential existential phenomenologists in some of
his methodological discussions. Nonetheless, it cannot be said that all
historical-typological phenomenology of religion is so influenced and has
shed the ideal of the anonymous epistemological subject—therefore, the
risk of distortion remains with this voice.

   The next three insights of existential phenomenology—temporality
(or historicity), intersubjectivity, and linguisticality—are also related to
the first theme of pre-given world, extending its range into additional
modalities of our being oriented in the world. "Temporality" refers, of
course, to the way we are oriented in the world in terms of time (past,
present, and future) in addition to space: in the present we project ourselves from our past into the future. Our presents are shaped and con-

and "the reality of God as understood in a specific, historical tradition," on the other; in Westphal's case, the implications of the experience of guilt for appreciation of the way that the sacred can heal "the wounded self-consciousness"; and so the list continues. And it is further apparent that diverse inquiries within this voice view various experiences as constituting the key access for advancing human existential self-understanding; again, for example, experience of critical situations and times revealing the "precariousness of our existence" and calling for "momentous decisions" (Smith); confessions of experiences of evil as well as experiences of grace, hope, and liberation (Ricoeur); experiences of guilt, morbid self-awareness, and defensive denial of moral responsibility (Westphal).

Besides being oriented to the specific subject-matter of religiously significant existential structures and experiences, the existential-hermeneutical voice in the phenomenology of religion (like existential phenomenology in general) also possesses a reasonably distinctive methodological orientation as well. In the case of existential phenomenology, we saw that its methodology, while incorporating features of epoché and sympathetic re-experiencing, conceives of itself as radically "bounded" by the "pre-given" existential traits of human consciousness of being in the world. This conception is no less true of the existential-hermeneutical voice in phenomenology of religion. And so we find, for example, Smith delineating his methodology in the following way:

The phenomenological approach to any philosophical problem means an approach through the analysis of primary experience and the reflective grasp of what we actually encounter. This view, though positive, implies the negation of other views. First, it means that experience is not to be understood either as a way of transforming reality into mere phenomena devoid of power and otherness, or of reducing reality to the data of sense; second, it means that experience is not to be identified with an exclusively private or "mental" content confined to an individual mind; third, it means that ingredient in experience is a real world of things, events, and selves transcending the encounter had by any one individual or any finite collection of individuals. The general assumption behind these negations is that experience is neither a substitute for reality nor a veil that falls between us and what there is, but rather a *reliable medium of disclosure* through which the real world is made manifest and comes to be aprehended by us.

What seems clear from this passage is that Smith conceives of the phenomenological method as radically oriented or bounded (e.g.) by a pre-given world disclosing itself in experience that is fundamentally intersubjective in nature ("not exclusively private or 'mental' content confined to an individual mind"). And so he goes on to argue that "instead of beginning with special experiences . . . recorded and interpreted in biblical . . . literature [as he argues, Otto tended to do] . . . it would be more in accord with a phenomenological approach to start from a broader base and consider recurrent situations that are to be found universally in experience" [i.e., experiences of crucial times and decisions and special places]. Thus does Smith see his methodology also "bounded" and "oriented" to existential structures of temporality, freedom, and corporeality. Later in his study, Smith signals the way in which his methodology is additionally bounded and oriented to the existential trait of linguisticality when he acknowledges that:

it is, however, an error to identify the experience of the holy, as it is open to any human being, with the apprehension of a definite being as such . . . there are too many possibilities for interpretation . . . just because there is such a plurality of religious traditions and cultural forms, we are not justified in identifying the experience of the holy, taken as a phenomenon of universal scope, with the intuition of God as understood from the standpoint of any one religious tradition. . . . The way is left open for *interpreting* the power present in crucial events and places encountered in living experience, in terms of the doctrine of God to be found in that tradition.

Here Smith acknowledges that his method is constrained by the existential structure of human linguisticality in the sense that diverse cultural traditions (including, of course, language) shape human understanding and interpretation of "the power present in . . . crucial events and places." And so we see his method as fully both embracing and oriented by the insights of existential phenomenology.

Ricoeur's method is similarly so oriented, though he accords a special primacy to the existential insight of linguisticality at the very outset of his inquiry:

I propose, first, to consider this term [guilt], not in its psychological, psychiatric or psychoanalytic usage, but in the *texts* where its meaning has been constituted and fixed. These texts are of penitential literature wherein the believing communities have expressed their avowal of evil; the language of these texts is a specific language which can be designated, in a very general way, as "confession of sins." . . . My point of departure is in a *phenomenology of confession* or avowal.

Ricoeur's focus on primary religious language as an expressive access to religious experience of evil is, of course, striking in its clear methodological acknowledgment of the existential structure of linguisticality. No less striking, however, is his orientation to existential structures of intersubjectivity (texts and language of "believing communities," "experience of sin rooted in the life of the community"), freedom ("in a first state of reflection, I say: to affirm freedom is to take upon oneself the origin of evil"), temporality (in the avowal of evil, "I declare myself, after the fact, as being he who could have done otherwise . . . this movement from in front of to behind the responsibility is essential. It constitutes the identity of the moral subject through past, present, and future"), a pre-given world ("freedom has already chosen in an evil way. This evil is already there. It is in this sense that it is radical, that it is anterior. . . . Evil is this prior captivity"), and even elements of corporeality and spatial orientation ("the return to the origin is a return to that place where freedom discovers itself"). Thus we can see that Ricoeur, like Smith, is radically oriented by the insights of existential phenomenology.

Both the aims and method, then, of this third voice in phenomenology of religion are significantly shaped by the dominant themes of existential phenomenology. This is not to say, however, that this voice simply reduces to philosophical explanation of human existence as pursued by existential phenomenology in general, for this voice does exhibit rather distinctive aims and methodological concerns not held by all existential phenomenologists. We need now to clarify these distinctive aims and method.

Aims

As a general organizational principle, we might begin by noting that investigators working within this voice appear to pursue two distinctive types of aims: one is descriptive-interpretive, the other is ontological-explorative. The first descriptive-interpretive aim is focused on gaining access to, describing, and analyzing the believing soul's (and community's) existential orientation to the sacred—in terms of its (or their) distinctive experiential expression and understanding of the basic existential structures of human being in the world (pre-given world, corporeality-spatiality, temporality, intersubjectivity, linguisticality, and freedom). The dominating concern of this aim is to describe and interpret the believing soul's and community's own self-understanding of their experience in the world within the framework provided by the six basic existential structures—how these structures are experienced and interpreted by the believing soul and community. The second ontological-explorative aim then takes the findings achieved within the first aim and interrogates them with an eye to seeing what they might reveal, suggest, or imply about human existence or the human condition in a more general way—Are there basic religious dimensions of human existence in the world? Is there a sacred or transcendent realm, and, if so, how is it conceived and experienced? Is humankind naturally religious (*homo-religiosus*)? and so on. Often this ontological-explorative aim and inquiry are conducted in explicit dialogue with the findings and insights of other humanistic disciplines (e.g., other schools of philosophical inquiry, other disciplines of religious studies, the disciplines of psychology, sociology, and social anthropology, the disciplines of literary criticism, even the disciplines of theology as well as inter-religious dialogue). This aim is a "wager" made by such inquirers that the self-understanding, expression, and experience of believing souls and communities have something important to teach us about ourselves, whether or not we are religious.

Method

In addition to expousing distinctive aims, existential-hermeneutical phenomenologists of religion also share a reasonably unified method of inquiry which, for convenience, we divide into five steps: (1) "bounded" epoché, (2) sympathetic re-experiencing, (3) evocative description, (4) interpretive interrogation, and (5) ontological exploration. "Bounded" epoché is our construal of the temporary bracketing or suspension of judgment practiced by our existential-hermeneutical phenomenologists with respect to all matters of truth, value, and commitment *except* those inescapable pre-given existential structures of all conscious experience. With respect to the latter, we understand the inquirer to acknowledge that such basic existential structures as corporeality, temporality, inter-subjectivity, and the like "bound" or orient all conscious experience, though we also understand him to suspend temporarily his own specific interpretations of these structures in the interest of trying to understand and appreciate how the subjects of his inquiry experience and interpret these structures. In this way, the inquirer is able to use these structures as "probes" into how the believing soul and community are affected by and understand these structures, without imposing his own specific experience and understanding of these structures on the self-understanding of his subjects. On this construal, epoché is still operative in the method of this voice, but it is understood to be oriented or bounded by the basic organizing insights of existential phenomenology about our being in the world.

Though our authors do not speak explicitly of "bounded" epoché in the way that we have, they do say or imply things about epoché that suggest this construal; more important, perhaps, they appear to conduct their inquiries according to this understanding of "bounded" epoché. In his introduction to *God, Guilt, and Death*, for example, Westphal explicitly argues for the importance of the methodological step "in which evaluation (determination of truth and value) is temporarily suspended in order that description and thereby understanding may progress."[42] At first glance, this formulation seems no different from the other voices' understanding of epoché, but in the face of an impending charge of pre-supposing an ideal of detached objectivity, Westphal later qualifies his understanding of the method of existential phenomenology in the following manner: "To establish that the stance of detachment and disengagement which defines the descriptive attitude is not motivated by the desire to be rigorously scientific, but rather by a passion for self-understanding that is itself neither detached nor engaged."[43] Now this qualification could be taken to refer only to the subsequent step of ontological exploration or it could be taken to refer to the method through and through. If the first interpretation were followed, then we suggest Westphal runs the risk of introducing a fundamental incoherence in his understanding of the existential-hermeneutical method, especially since existential phenomenology appears to reject the stance of the anonymous epistemological inquirer. The second interpretation, then, appears preferable, and we have what is, in effect, a formulation of "bounded" epoché.

Ricoeur too, for another example, appears to be committed to a notion of bounded epoché when he speaks of sympathetic reexperiencing as a form of provisionally adopting "the motivations and intentions of the believing soul" in "a second naiveté," "a mode of as if," ultimately linked to an oriented field of investigation "situated" in a philosophical and cultural tradition shaped by a "Greek memory, from which rises the question: what is being?"[44] Ricoeur refers to this orientation—which, of course, shapes existential phenomenology—as a "principal methodological bondage"—and it is difficult to credit that this could not affect the step of epoché itself. And, in fact, Ricoeur himself is compelled to conclude his introduction to *The Symbolism of Evil* with the observation that "anyone who wished to escape the contingency of historical encounters and stand apart from the game in the name of a non-situated 'objectivity' would at most know everything, but would understand nothing. In truth, he would seek nothing, not being motivated by concern about any question."[45] So Ricoeur, like Westphal, rejects the supposed ideal of the anonymous epistemological inquirer, and this cannot but affect his use and construal of epoché—as oriented by the insights of existential phenomenology.

The second step of the method of existential-hermeneutical phenomenology of religion—sympathetic re-experiencing—has already been introduced in connection with Ricoeur's remarks about the first step. Though we are by now sufficiently familiar with the notion of sympathetic re-experiencing not to have to discuss it in any great detail,

we do need to be aware of a very distinctive "turn" in the existential-
hermeneutical understanding of the step. This "turn" is very precisely
captured in Ricoeur's representation of this step:

> My point of departure is in a *phenomenology of confession* or avowal. Here I
> understand by phenomenology a description of meanings implied in experience
> in general . . . a phenomenology of confession is therefore a description of mean-
> ings and of signified intentions, present in a certain activity of language: the lan-
> guage of confession. Our task, in the framework of such a phenomenology is to
> re-enact in ourselves the confession of evil, in order to uncover its aims. By sym-
> pathy and through imagination, the philosopher adopts the motivations and in-
> tentions of the confessing consciousness; he does not "feel," he "experiences" in
> a neutral manner, in the manner of an "as if," that which has been lived in the
> confessing consciousness. But with which expression shall we start? Not with
> expressions of confessions that are the most developed, the most rationalized, for
> example, the concept or quasi-concept of "original sin" . . . we should not be
> embarrased by the fact that behind these rationalized expressions, behind these
> speculations, we encounter myths, that is, traditional narratives which tell of
> events which happened at the origin of time . . . precisely because they have lost
> their explanatory pretention, they reveal an exploratory signification; they mani-
> fest a symbolic function, that is, a way of expressing indirectly the bond between
> man and what he considers sacred . . . in its turn, myth refers us to a level of
> expressions, more fundamental that any narration and any speculation. . . .
> Therefore it is to this experience and to its language that we must have recourse;
> or rather, to this experience *in* its language.

The "turn," of course, comes in Ricoeur's emphasis on the way that the
religious experience of evil is embodied within the performative language
of confession of sins. In his view, there is no other access to these religious
experiences of evil—or, indeed, religious experiences in general—than
through the way these experiences are expressed in language. Thus does
he see the phenomenological step of sympathy quite explicitly "bounded"
by the existential structure of linguisticality. The inquirer sympathetically
reexperiences the consciousness and attitudes of the believing soul and
community by sympathetically re-avowing their confessions of evil and
through this re-avowal reenacting their motivations, intentions, and emotions as expressed in this discourse. It is important, according to Ricoeur,
to focus on performative—not speculative—religious discourse, for it is
in the performative use of language that one comes the closest to the
primary intentions and experiences of the believing soul and community:
this is the spontaneous and most revealing language of evil, unadulter-
ated (so to speak) by subsequent rationalization, systematic reflection,
and possible false consciousness. And, he further notes, this language of
confession is symbolic, encoding layers and dimensions of meaning and
signification that need to be reenacted and reexperienced to be recovered.

It seems reasonably obvious that in order to be recovered, this performative language must be carefully interpreted in addition to being reenacted, but before we move on to consider that methodological step, we need first to consider the intermediary step of evocative description.

Ricoeur, of course, is not alone among the existential-hermeneutical phenomenologists of religion in his focus on an appreciation of the sympathetic reenactment of the performative language of the believing soul and community. Westphal, for another example, makes much of the model of acting as an analogue for understanding the step of sympathetic reexperiencing. And he focuses attention on this analogous model precisely because, as he says, "when a great actress plays Lady Macbeth, she interprets the latter's experience by re-enacting it . . . [she] (re)*feels* the motivations and intentions of Lady Macbeth and (re)*enacts* her deeds and her consequent torment."[46] Westphal's point might be better expressed by saying that the actress sympathetically refeels the motivations, intentions, as well as torment of Lady Macbeth *in* reenacting her words and deeds. Performative reenactment accesses, so to speak, the intentions and experience of the character. And, according to existential phenomenologists, this way of performatively accessing a subject's consciousness as expressed in language is no less true for the consumer than for the inquirer himself—and this, of course, introduces the step, reasonably familiar to us, of evocative description.

The rationale for this third step of evocative description is really no different than in the case of the other voices in phenomenology of religion—to permit and encourage the reader to reenact and reexperience individually the fundamental religious intentions, motivations, emotions of the believing soul and community. We can, of course, express this aim in a distinctively pointed way: the existential-hermeneutical inquirers aim to have their readers reenact for themselves the existential stance of the believer, in order that they, together with their inquiring guides, might fully and directly appreciate the insights and investigations of existential-hermeneutical inquiry into religion. To accomplish this aim, the existential-hermeneuticists consistently employ performative language to permit and prompt this existential engagement on the part of their readers. Thus, for example, Smith, Ricoeur, and Westphal consistently invite their readers to reenact with them the performative language of believers, to consider points in their own lives where they have encountered and been aware of key existential phenomena such as guilt, hope, and even redemption, to reconsider the deep meaning embodied in existentially moving literary and even mythic texts. They apparently wager that these invitational comparisons can be successful precisely because they and their readers share basic existential structures—as points of orientation and access—to the stance of the believing soul and community.

The fourth step of the existential-hermeneutical method—interpretive interrogation—brings us to the heart of this voice. Building upon the preceeding three steps, inquirers within this voice launch careful, nuanced, and extraordinarily provocative probes into the levels of meaning embodied in the performative, symbolically structured, and experientially expressive language of the believing soul and community. Since this step is so important and distinctive to this voice, it will behoove us to spend some time on explicating its nature and implications.

The step of interpretive interrogation is nicely imaged in another of Westphal's models for existential-hermeneutical inquiry: the "good listening" that we tend to associate with the role of a professional counsellor or psychotherapist, who listens to the discourse of his or her client with patience, sensitivity, and nonjudgmental openness. Westphal describes the good listener as follows:

If I am a good listener, I don't interrupt the other nor plan my own next speech while pretending to be listening. I try to hear what is said, but I listen just as hard for what is not said and for what is said between the lines. I am not in a hurry, for there is no pre-appointed destination for the conversation. There's no need to get there, for we are already here; and in this present I am able to be fully present to the other who speaks. The speaker is not an object to be categorized or manipulated, but a subject whose life situation is enough like my own that I can understand it in spite of the differences between us. If I am a good listener, what we have in common will seem more important than what we have in conflict. This does not mean that I never say anything, but I am more likely to ask questions than to issue manifestos or make accusations. . . . They will be the kind of questions the prosecuting attorney asks on cross examination, but they will not be asked in a prosecuting manner. They will rather be asked as a confessor or therapist asks them. For the purpose is not to win the case but to free understanding from self-deception. Though the goal is to "permit the believing soul to speak," it does not follow that the believing soul is automatically taken at face value.[47]

Important in this image, of course, are those "virtues" that appear to be involved in the steps of existentially oriented and bounded epoché and sympathy—respect for the other, full presence to the other, recognition of commonality, patience. But equally important is the method of asking probing questions in a nonprosecutorial, nonjudgmental manner in order to get the other to reveal his or her basic intentions, motivations, and understanding of the world. This method corresponds to the step of interpretive interrogation—the gentle, insightful, but nonetheless critical probing that permits (indeed encourages) the believing soul to reveal himself or herself in a successively deepening way. Though this image of good listening and gentle but critical probing helps us to understand the step of interpretive interrogation in its broad outlines, it needs to be taken farther if we are to gain an adequate comprehension of its features, and for this deeper and more systematic view we turn to Ricoeur's discussion of this step.

Ricoeur's representation of this step is predicated on his understanding of the believing soul and community's language as both performative and symbolic. We have already discussed the way in which this language is performative and therefore expressive of underlying (or better, embedded) motivations, intentions, and experiences, but now we need to focus on the symbolic aspect. Suggests Ricoeur, this language is symbolic in the sense that it "designates a thing in an indirect way, by designating another thing which it directly indicates." For example, the confessional expression of evil as a stain or impurity uses "the quasi-material representation of [literal] stain" as "symbolic of something else"—"a clear-obscure of a quasi-physical infection and of a quasi-moral indignity." Since this is so, continues Ricoeur, "the work of repetition as applied to the expression of evil is, in essence, the explicitation, the development of different levels of direct and indirect signification which are intermingled in the same symbol." Ricoeur's point is surely that in order to understand the symbolic language, we must probe it in such a way as to interpret its various levels of meaning and significance. And as much of this language is found embedded in complex dramatic narratives about the origins of evil, the task of interpretation turns out to be an extensive and demanding one, focused as it is on ever-deepening realms of meaning. Thus, the existential-hermeneuticist finds himself or herself contending with both the primary performative-symbolic language of awareness of evil (or, more broadly, religious experience) and the secondary symbolic-dramatic language of narrative myths. Furthermore, if he or she is to be fully alert to the reaches of this symbolic language, he or she must also be aware of their cosmic (ontological), oneiric (psychic), and poetic (imaginative) uses and dimensions of meaning.[48]

Throughout this interpretive interrogative inquiry into the symbolic language of the believing soul and community, the inquirer is guided by the basic insights provided by existential phenomenology—corporeality, temporality, intersubjectivity, freedom, and the rest—using these to probe the contours and complexities of the existential stance and self-understanding being expressed by the religious consciousness. It is important to be aware of this guiding function provided by the basic existential structures, for they function to keep the inquirer's investigation grounded in existential reality as well as offer an orientation to his or her interrogative probings. Ricoeur in particular is quite self-conscious about this guiding function of existential structures and, in fact, takes it a step farther by suggesting that his inquiry into religious experiences of evil is both bound and guided by distinctively Western sources (i.e., myths of evil) that permit him to see and appreciate various sorts of relation (of depth, lateral relations, retroactive and anticipative relations) internal to his sources that develop over time.[49] So his inquiry is additionally guided by what he calls our common "cultural memory" (itself expressive of the existential structures of temporality and intersubjectivity). Where, we might ask at this point, is this step of interpretive interrogation headed? What is its endpoint or goal? This brings us to the final step of the existential-hermeneutical method—ontological exploration.

We began our discussion of the existential-hermeneutical voice by observing that it is radically oriented toward one or another normative aim associated with clarifying and probing the basic religious dimensions of human existence in the world. This sort of aim is reflected in this voice's final methodological step of ontological exploration. Needless to say, the way that this step is taken will vary according to the existential concerns and interests of a given existential-hermeneuticist as well as the findings yielded by his or her use of the preceding four steps. Thus, for example, the Christian philosopher Gabriel Marcel is preoccupied with exploring the nature and implications of hope and liberation for a deeper understanding of the human condition; Ricoeur, while clearly interested in the theme of hope, suspects that the phenomena and myths of evil will yield a deeper understanding of humankind's "strained" or "broken" bond with the sacred; Smith appears preoccupied with the ontological implications of "crisis times" in human life and the way that these seem to disclose the holy in a mediated way to all humankind, and so on. Despite these differences, what all of these investigators appear to share in their ontological investigations—in addition to an interest in the structures of human existence—is a basic "wager" or "bet" that their various existential-hermeneutical inquiries reveal some sort of fundamental religious orientation within human existence in the world. They furthermore share the same methodological insight that their previous existential-hermeneutical researches may be more deeply interpreted to disclose or reveal this fundamental religious orientation if their "wager" is taken up, followed, or enacted. This implies still further that they think their various wagers can be somehow validated.

Smith, for example, follows this pattern of ontological exploration. He begins by suggesting that "certain recurrent situations [crucial times, special spaces] that are to be found universally in experience" will, if properly understood, reveal or disclose something significant about the religious dimension of human existence in the world. He then carefully describes (in a modestly evocative way) the precise existential character of these turning points and special spaces—in terms, for example, of their temporal or spatial uniqueness, capacity to evoke synoptic perspectives on life as a whole, self-revelation, significant decision—concluding that they "bring us to a realization of the problematic character of our existence, of our dependence upon a power not ourselves, and of the need to find an object of supreme devotion." Though he admits that "the most they can do is arrest us and impel us to consider the question and the possibility of a form of Holy Life upon which our existence depends," implying that "there is no necessary . . . transition" from these experiences to "the reality of God as understood in a specific, historical tradition," he nonetheless probes deeper that "the ways left open for *interpreting* the power present in the crucial events and places . . . in terms of the doctrine of God" because these experiences do ground "a mediating concept which we may call the general concept of God." The mediating concept thematized in the experiences of crucial times and events "finds its basis in philosophic reflection in the world and ourselves . . . [it] embraces the idea of a supremely worshipful reality which gives being and controls the final destiny of all finite realities." And, in turn, this general, experientially derived concept "mediates between the pervasive experience of the holy and the specific idea of God existing within an historical religious community." The adequacy of this concept—conceived as a religious existential structure—proves its worth (is validated) by its power to connect general human experience, on the one hand, and specific religious traditions, on the other, in an intelligible manner. Thus does Smith move from initial wager to existential-hermeneutical inquiry to deeper ontological exploration concluding with a validation of his initial wager. Whatever else we might think of the analysis—and it does seem to be theistically "loaded"—the pattern of analysis and argument seems clear enough.

Ricoeur, to take another example, also follows this general pattern of ontological exploration in his study of the symbolism of evil. He begins with the wager that, as he puts its, "I shall have a better understanding of man and of the bond between the being of man and the being of all beings if I follow the *indication* of symbolic thought."[50] He then goes on to conduct an existential-hermeneutical phenomenological "reading," so to speak, of the experiences of evil through the primary performative-symbolic language of confession and the secondary dramatic narrations or myths of evil found in the religious consciousness and traditions of the west. His study, however, does not end there, for he subsequently moves into a phase of ontological exploration of these myths of evil based on a specific wager that these will assist him in understanding our existential situation. That is, he interprets, in an ontologically explorative way, the symbols and myths of evil to "speak of the situation of the being of man in the being of the world . . . the task, then, is, starting from the symbols, to elaborate existential concepts" [pertaining to human evil].[51] He sees, for example, the whole series of primary symbols—defilement, sin, and guilt—as converging in the paradoxical but existentially operative notion of the "servile will" (bound will, unfree freedom) which raises questions of how and why we are in this state of unfreedom that are, in turn, answered in diverse ways by four principal types of myths of the origin of evil. He further interprets these myths of evil—primordial chaos, tragedy, exiled soul, and Adamic fall—in a dynamic or dialectical manner, resulting in a new reading of the origin of evil as ascribable to both misuse of human freedom *and* objective factors outside of human control (symbolized by seduction, infection, etc.). In effect, Ricoeur's exploration warrants the utility of some sort of concept of original sin—a paradoxical theological concept combining human responsibility for evil with an objective side to evil that precedes human freedom. And he concludes his study by arguing that his initial wager is "verified by its power to raise up, to illuminate, to give order to that region of human experience, that region of confession" known as moral evil.[52] Again, whatever we might think of this analysis—and it too seems theistically "loaded"—it too clearly follows the general pattern of ontological exploration elaborated above: from wager to existential-hermeneutical inquiry to yet deeper ontological interpretation to validation of the initial wager.

There is one additional feature shared by the steps of both ontological exploration and interpretive interrogation that requires brief comment. In the process of both steps, existential-hermeneutical inquirers display a clear tendency to engage in dialogue with other disciplines interested in the same phenomenon. We might call this feature "hermeneutical conversation across disciplines." There appear to be a number of rationales accounting for this feature. One involves the insight that other disciplines—such as psychology, sociology, social anthropology, other philosophical schools of inquiry, history of religions, and so on—are themselves concerned to investigate the basic existential structures of human being in the world. Thus, existential-hermeneuticists are naturally interested in learning the results of similarly focused inquiries, in order to benefit their own work and contribute to the work of others. A second rationale involves the fact that some existential-hermeneutical inquiry—

for example, interpretation and exploration of mythic texts—crucially depends on the scholarship provided by other disciplines—in the case of myths, for example, history of religions, classics, literary criticism provide the mythic texts that the existential-hermeneuticists wish to investigate. Yet a third rationale involves the perception that existential-hermeneutical phenomenology of religion itself may "constitute" data to be investigated by other disciplines, and therefore in the interest of supplying such data in the most useful form, existential-hermeneuticists have to learn, through conversation, how these disciplines currently conceive and constitute the data from their disciplinary points of view in comparison and contrast with existential-hermeneutical phenomenology of religion. Without belaboring the obvious, we simply note that Ricoeur's inquiry into the myths of evil, for example, appears to rely in crucial ways on other disciplines concerned with mythic texts. By contrast, Westphal's inquiry appears to engage in hermeneutical conversation with other disciplines (e.g., psychoanalysis, sociology of deviance) in order to enrich his own work as well as to correct these disciplines' understanding of guilt. Paul Pruyser's inquiry into the phenomena of hope seems clearly focused not so much on making an original statement about hope as rather correcting and enriching psychological perspectives on these phenomena.

Issues

Thus far we have been attempting to clarify the aims and method of existential-hermeneutical phenomenology of religion by focusing on the work of some of its representative practitioners. We need now to go a step farther to gain a more critical perspective on this voice—by identifying and discussing certain of its possible problems. In that way, as with the other two voices, we can become more aware of this voice's strengths and limitations. As seems evident from our earlier discussion of existential phenomenology in general and the way that it compares with the other two voices in phenomenology of religion—as well as from our detailed discussion of the existential-hermeneutical method—this third voice appears to undercut or mitigate a number of the problems associated with the other voices.

For example, the notion of "bounded" epoché—in its rejection of the anonymous epistemological subject—appears to undercut in a decisive way the criticism of the biasing effects of detached objectivity associated with the other two voices. In its presumption of existential structures shared with the believing soul and community, "bounded" epoché avoids "alienation" from the religious Other that it is investigating. Moreover, the step of interpretive interrogation—in hermeneutical conversation with the methods, researches, and results of other disciplines—appears to mitigate the criticism of insufficient suspicion (or simple naiveté) associated with the essentialist voice. The existential-hermeneuticist is well aware of the so-called schools of suspicion and is well positioned to argue with them about the shortcomings of reductive approaches to religious phenomena (see, e.g., Westphal's effective critique of Nietzsche's and Freud's handling of guilt in his contribution to this volume). Furthermore, the fact that this voice's method is oriented by the basic insights of existential phenomenology appears to "ground" its use of sympathetic reenactment so as to decisively undercut charges of epistemic murkiness associated with this procedure. In effect, this procedure is made possible by those existential structures shared by both the inquirer and the believing soul and community. And, this voice's evident acknowledgment of and concern with the existential structure of temporality appear to counter the criticism of anti-historical bias associated principally with the essentialist voice. Indeed, many existential-hermeneuticists go to great lengths both in discussing the temporal and historical aspects of religious phenomena and in making use of research provided by the history of religions. Finally, even the criticism of possible cultural bias has been seemingly anticipated and addressed by this voice—for its representatives often openly acknowledge their "methodological bondage" to Western cultural traditions and thus appear somewhat restrained in making more "universal" claims (consider, for example, the work of Ricoeur in this regard).

By this point in our discussion, we suspect that the reader is well able to appreciate the force of this brief recitation of how the existential-hermeneutical voice is able to escape many of the criticisms targeted against the other two voices. Nevertheless, he or she is also likely to feel some unease about the dominant characteristics of this voice—namely, its obvious and self-conscious service to normative aims advancing the cause, so to speak, of religious dimensions of human existence. Do not these characteristics, one might ask, run significant risks about gaining an impartial view of human existence in the world? Might not inquirers within this voice—methodologically oriented and bound as they are—be prevented from seeing and appreciating other perspectives on the issues and problems that interest them? Is it not disingenuous to think that open acknowledgment of methodological orientation and normative aim somehow diffuses criticisms of cultural and religious bias?

There is both something right and something wrong with the apparent rhetorical force of such questions as these. What is right is this: often existential-hermeneutical inquiries are, in fact, partial, perspectival, and (if one wishes to use the term) biased. They are explicitly partial to Western cultural and religious experience; they are focused on existential structures discerned and formulated by Western scholarship; they are biased by their normative aims (some of which may be theological and Christian). What seems wrong is this: the questions appear to assume that totally impartial views of existential phenomena are both possible and desirable, and, further, that "partiality" prevents the attainment of knowledge and truth. Both of these assumptions are questionable, if not downright false. If the existential phenomenologists are right about pre-given existential structures, then all views are partial, perspectival, and biased when dealing with matters of human existence. This is inescapable and may as well be admitted. Acknowledging such partiality, however, does not prevent our attainment of increasingly more adequate views if we both admit this partiality and attempt to work within its constraints—for example, by opening our research to intersubjective assessment by others (as existential-hermeneuticists do), by engaging in critical conversations across disciplines (as existential-hermeneuticists do), by being open to new or hitherto unexplained phenomena (as existential-hermeneuticists are). In this way, it is possible to attain knowledge about existential matters so far as any such knowledge can be attained—relative to constraints of context.[53] Of course, what seems knowledge today may be overturned tomorrow, but that does not mean that we are unable to acquire over time increasingly more adequate and defensible views, again, if we will admit our partiality and work within its constraints.

We can see this dialectically corrective process—leading to a more adequate view of religious existence and experience—at work in the contribution of Carolyn Bynum in this volume. Bynum's aim is to correct the phenomenology of religion's focus on the religious experience of males (*homo religiosus*), by introducing the needed perspectival corrective of women's religious experience. This she does most effectively by laying out a series of case-examples of religious symbols, asking about each, "How do such symbols refer to and make use of gender?" "Whose meaning are we analyzing?" "Do female[s] . . . see God as mother and mean by 'mother' what their male counterparts mean?" Though she is enormously appreciative of Ricoeur's existential-hermeneutical understanding of religious symbolism—and in fact adopts that understanding for her own work—she nevertheless argues that "the phenomenological emphasis of Ricoeur on the process by which the symbol is appropriated may need to be expanded by the phenomenological emphasis of French feminism on genderedness until we have a more varied and rich notion of the experiences of symbol users." Her point is well taken, and we suggest that it has the potential of providing a corrective to Ricoeur's work and the existential-hermeneutical voice, more broadly. Thus Bynum squares off the French feminist phenomenology (a partial view) against Ricoeur's existential-hermeneutical inquiry (another partial view) to come up with a gender-complex notion of religious symbolism (a more adequate view). Her effort provides a clear example of how partial views can be used to achieve a no doubt still partial but more adequate view of religious experience and its significance.

As with the other two voices in the phenomenology of religion, reviewing these problems or concerns about the existential-hermeneutical voice assists us in seeing some of its strengths and weaknesses. Though once again, we have tended to rebut these concerns, we need to be aware that continuing perceptions of them have an important role in helping to generate or strengthen the resolve of other methodological voices both inside and outside the field of phenomenology of religion. In particular, continuing concern about this third voice's strong normative orientation helps to support the enterprise of historical-typological phenomenology of religion as well as other methods in the history of religions. And, similarly, continuing worries about "insufficient suspicion" as well as the legitimacy of "sympathetic reenactment" help to increase the attention given to more "suspicious" and "formal" methods in the study of religion (e.g., deconstruction). Nonetheless, none would deny that existential-hermeneutical phenomenology of religion has been and continues to be a very "live option" in the academic study of religion.

This completes our review of the three principal voices defining the field of the phenomenology of religion. As we have seen, there are three distinct voices but with overlaps sufficient to speak of one unified field of inquiry. The reader of this anthology is now equipped to understand in an informed way the selections that follow. Though each selection stands on its own and makes a distinctive contribution to the phenomenological study of religion (as indicated by the headnote preceding each selection), the reader is encouraged to return periodically to this general introduction and use it for tracing out in particular selections those typical aims, methodological steps, and issues associated with their respective voices. In this manner, the reader can gain maximal advantage for appreciating critically the power and prospect of each voice's contribution to the rich melody of the phenomenology of religion.

NOTES

1. These developments are illuminatingly discussed by John Wilson in his introduction to Paul Ramsey and John Wilson (eds.), *The Study of Religion in Colleges and Universities* (Princeton: Princeton University Press, 1970), pp. 3–21. See also Thomas L. Benson, "Religious Studies as an Academic Disci-

pline" (sub-entry of the three-part article "Study of Religion"), *Encyclopedia of Religion*, Mircea Eliade, Editor in Chief (New York: Macmillan, 1987).

2. Rudolph Otto, *The Idea of the Holy*, 2nd ed., translated by John W. Harvey (New York & London: Oxford University Press, 1950).

3. Gerardus van der Leeuw, *Religion in Essence and Manifestation*, 2 vols., translated by J. E. Turner with additions by Hans H. Penner (Gloucester, Mass.: Peter Smith, 1967).

4. The third voice is well represented by the work of Gabriel Marcel and Paul Ricoeur among others. See, for example, Gabriel Marcel, *Creative Fidelity*, translated by Robert Rosthal (New York: Farrar, Straus & Giroux, 1964), and Paul Ricoeur, *The Symbolism of Evil*, translated by Emerson Buchanan (New York: Harper & Row, 1967).

5. P. D. Chantepie de la Saussaye, *Manual of the Science of Religion*, translated by Beatrice S. Colyer-Fergusson (London & New York: Longmans, 1891).

6. Husserl was a prolific author. Especially useful are the following of his writings: *The Paris Lectures*, 2nd ed., translated by Peter Koestenbaum (The Hague: Martinus Nijhoff, 1975); *The Idea of Phenomenology*, translated by William P. Alston and George Naknikian (The Hague: Martinus Nijhoff, 1970); *Cartesian Meditations*, translated by Dorion Cairns (The Hague: Martinus Nijhoff, 1973); *Ideas*, translated by W. R. Boyce Gibson (New York: Collier Books, 1962); *Phenomenology and the Crisis of Philosophy*, translated by Quentin Lauer (New York: Harper & Row, 1965). All the translators provide helpful commentary; also helpful in this regard is Herbert Spiegelberg, *The Phenomenological Movement*, 2 vols., 2nd ed. (The Hague: Martinus Nijhoff, 1971), esp. chs. III and XIV. Spiegelberg provides masterful interpretations of many of the thinkers associated with philosophical phenomenology.

7. Robert Solomon (ed.), *Phenomenology and Existentialism* (New York: Harper & Row, 1972), pp. 6–7.

8. Max Scheler, "Phenomenology and the Theory of Cognition," in *Max Scheler: Selected Philosophical Essays*, translated by David R. Lachterman (Evanston: Northwestern University Press, 1973), pp. 136–201; quotation from p. 152.

9. Dilthey was another prolific author. Especially useful are the following selections translated from his writings: *Pattern and Meaning in History*, edited by H. P. Rickman (New York: Harper & Row, 1962), and H. P. Rickman (ed.), *W. Dilthey: Selected Writings* (Cambridge: Cambridge University Press, 1976). Helpful interpretations of Dilthey's philosophy include: Rudolf A. Makkreel, *Dilthey: Philosopher of Human Studies* (Princeton: Princeton University Press, 1975); Michael Ermarth, *Wilhelm Dilthey: The Critique of Historical Reason* (Chicago: University of Chicago Press, 1978); H. P. Rickman, *Wilhelm Dilthey: Pioneer of Human Studies* (Berkeley: University of California Press, 1979).

10. Max Scheler, *On the Eternal in Man*, translated by Bernard Noble (New York: Harper & Row, 1960), pp. 18–19, 159–161.

11. This phrase is used by Otto in the selection from his *The Idea of the Holy* included below in this anthology. Except where indicated, all quotations in the remainder of this editorial introduction are to be found in the selections of the authors quoted; since these quotations can be readily found, we will dispense with footnoting them.

12. Ninian Smart introduces and discusses this idea of evocative description

in both his *The Science of Religion and the Sociology of Knowledge* (Princeton: Princeton University Press, 1973), pp. 21–22, and his *The Phenomenon of Religion* (London: Macmillan Press, 1973), pp. 32–34.

13. The complete text of Husserl's March 5, 1919, letter to Otto can be found (in German) in Hans-Walter Schütte, *Religion und Christentum in der Theologie Rudolf Ottos* (Berlin: De Gruyter, 1969), pp. 139–142. The letter contains several important statements. To begin with, Husserl observes that "your book [*The Idea of the Holy*] has affected me as scarcely another book has for many years," and he considers it to be "a first beginning for a phenomenology of religion." It "will hold a firm place in the history of the philosophy of religion, particularly the phenomenology of religion. It is a beginning, in the sense that it focuses on beginnings, on origins, and thus in the best sense of the word is 'original'." It is important to note here that while Husserl believed there was more work to be done "before a theory of religious consciousness as a philosophical theory can be presented," the use of the word "beginning" is not a negative or slighting evaluation on Husserl's part. As we mentioned above, Husserl always called himself a "perpetual beginner." Thus his evaluation is not that Otto's work is merely a preliminary step that must be superseded but rather a solid first step, a foundation for further phenomenological exploration of religious experience and consciousness. The letter concludes with Husserl recalling their personal acquaintance at Göttingen: "From our Göttingen years you know how highly I have always esteemed you and with what pleasure I sought intellectual contact with you."

14. Wilhelm Wundt (1832–1920), a founder of experimental psychology. For a brief discussion of Wundt's "folk psychology of religion," see David M. Wulff, *Psychology of Religion: Classic and Contemporary Views* (New York: John Wiley, 1991), pp. 14–15.

15. Van der Leeuw provides the classical discussion of this problem in *Religion in Essence and Manifestation*, vol. 2, pp. 683–684.

16. In addition to Dupré (discussed below), Westphal has a penetrating discussion of this problem which he characterizes as "Nietzsche's objection" to "the transparency of consciousness to itself." See Merold Westphal, *God, Guilt, and Death* (Bloomington: Indiana University Press, 1984), pp. 16–20.

17. Chris Arthur, in his contribution to this volume, mentions this sort of rebuttal and also finds it somewhat question-begging.

18. Westphal, *God, Guilt, and Death*, pp. 10–12.

19. Smart, *Phenomenon of Religion*, pp. 69–76.

20. Evidence for this acknowledgment on Scheler's part can be seen throughout his lengthy study "Problems in Religion" found in *On the Eternal in Man*, pp. 105–356.

21. Smart, *Phenomenon of Religion*, pp. 38–39.

22. Husserl's avoidance of this problem is perceptively noted by David Stewart and Algis Mickunas in their useful study, *Exploring Phenomenology*, 2nd Edition (Athens: Ohio University Press, 1990), pp. 65–66.

23. See Marcel, *Creative Fidelity*, p. 20, where he writes: "To be incarnated is to appear to oneself as body, as this particular body, without being identified with it nor distinguished from it—identification and distinction being correlative operations which are significant only in the realm of objects. What clearly emerges from the foregoing reflections is the fact that there is no distinct haven to which I can repair either outside of or within my body. Disincarnation is

not practically possible and is precluded by my very structure." This notion of our being incarnated will be discussed further in connection with existential-hermeneutical phenomenology of religion.

24. Although he does not himself coin this precise label, Smart does empha-size the interaction and interdependence of what he calls "historical phenome-nology" and "typological phenomenology" of religion; see his *Phenomenon of Religion*, chs. 1–2. Smart is following in the footsteps of van der Leeuw whose work reflected an explicit commitment to typological presentations as well as the incorporation of larger numbers of, and more diverse materials from, the history of religions. Lying in the background of the work of both van der Leeuw and Smart is the influence of Dilthey's philosophy of human existence.

25. Smart, *Phenomenon of Religion*, pp. 38–39.

26. Ludwig Feuerbach (1804–1872). See his classic *The Essence of Christi-anity*, translated by G. Eliot (New York: Harper and Row, 1957).

27. This fallacy is discussed by both Arthur (in his selection below) and Smart (in his *Phenomenon of Religion*, p. 70). Both are responding to E. E. Evans-Pritchard's classic discussion of this fallacy in his *Theories of Primitive Religion* (Oxford: Oxford University Press, 1965), ch. II.

28. Smart, *Phenomenon of Religion*, ch. 2; see also his *Science of Religion*, ch. 3.

29. Although he does not himself coin this precise label, Ricoeur does empha-size the interaction of hermeneutics and existential phenomenology in the study of religious meaning. See, for example, his *Symbolism of Evil* and the articles collected in his *The Conflict of Interpretations*, edited by Don Idhe (Evanston: Northwestern University Press, 1974).

30. Ricoeur's article is available in English translation as ch. 8 ("Existential Phenomenology") of his *Husserl: An Analysis of his Phenomenology*, translated by Edward G. Ballard and Lester E. Embree (Evanston: Northwestern University Press, 1967). This article forms the basis for the illuminating discussion of exis-tential phenomenology in Stewart and Mickunas, *Exploring Phenomenology*, ch. 4. Particularly useful and accessible works by Marcel and Merleau-Ponty in-clude the former's *Creative Fidelity*, chs. I, III, VII, and the latter's *Phenome-nology of Perception*, translated by Colin Smith (London: Routledge and Kegan Paul, 1962).

31. Ricoeur, *Husserl*, p. 212.

32. See, for example, Jean-Paul Sartre, *Being and Nothingness*, special abridged edition, translated by Hazel E. Barnes (New York: Citadel Press, 1956), Martin Heidegger, *Being and Time*, translated by John Macquarrie and Edward Robinson (New York: Harper and Row, 1962), and Gabriel Marcel, *The Mystery of Being*, 2 vols., translated by G. S. Fraser (Chicago: Regnery, 1960).

33. Ricoeur, *Husserl*, p. 208.

34. Ricoeur, *Husserl*, p. 205.

35. Merleau-Ponty, *Phenomenology of Perception*, pp. x–xi.

36. Merleau-Ponty, *Phenomenology of Perception*, pp. xii–xiv.

37. Ricoeur, *Husserl*, p. 204.

38. Marcel, *Creative Fidelity*, pp. 12–23. Merleau-Ponty's discussion of cor-poreality can be found in *Phenomenology of Perception*, part one.

39. Marcel, *Creative Fidelity*, p. 69.

40. Ricoeur, *Husserl*, p. 208.

41. Mircea Eliade, *Yoga: Immortality and Freedom*, translated by Willard R. Trask (London: Routledge and Kegan Paul, 1958).

42. Westphal, *God, Guilt, and Death*, p. 5.

43. Westphal, *God, Guilt, and Death*, p. 22.

44. Ricoeur, *Symbolism of Evil*, pp. 19–20.

45. Ricoeur, *Symbolism of Evil*, p. 24.

46. Westphal, *God, Guilt, and Death*, p. 11.

47. Westphal, *God, Guilt, and Death*, p. 12.

48. Ricoeur discusses these dimensions of symbolic meaning in *Symbolism of Evil*, pp. 10–14; see also his *Freud and Philosophy*, translated by Denis Savage (New Haven: Yale University Press, 1970), pp. 13–16.

49. Ricoeur, *Symbolism of Evil*, pp. 20–23.

50. Ricoeur, *Symbolism of Evil*, p. 355. For an illuminating critical discussion of Ricoeur's hermeneutics of evil, see Don Idhe, *Hermeneutical Phenomenology: The Philosophy of Paul Ricoeur* (Evanston: Northwestern University Press, 1971), ch. 5.

51. Ricoeur, *Symbolism of Evil*, p. 356.

52. Ricoeur, *Symbolism of Evil*, p. 357.

53. Merleau-Ponty provides a version of this dialectical, rational, and corrective process in *Phenomenology of Perception*, pp. xvii–xxi.

❖

Religious Experience: Numinous, Mystical, and Feminist

(Essential Phenomenology of Religion)

❖ RUDOLF OTTO ❖

Rudolf Otto (1869–1937) was professor at the University of Marburg and his publications include numerous articles as well as *The Idea of the Holy, Religious Essays*, and *Mysticism: East and West*. Before he took the position at Marburg, Otto served for many years, together with Edmund Husserl, on the faculty at the University of Göttingen. Later, after they had both left Göttingen, Husserl recalled the pleasure of Otto's friendship and praised Otto's book on the holy, predicting that it "will hold a firm place in the history of the true philosophy of religion, particularly the phenomenology of religion. It is a beginning, in the sense that it focuses on beginnings, on origins, and thus in the best sense of the word is 'original.'" Husserl was not one to give out compliments lightly. Moreover, Husserl's evaluation was not slighting, for he always called himself "a perpetual beginner." Thus he did not mean that Otto's work was merely a preliminary sketch that needed to be superseded. Rather, he judged it to be a solid first step, a foundation for further phenomenological explorations of religious experience and consciousness. Much as Husserl anticipated, Rudolf Otto's analysis of the holy has become a landmark in the history of the phenomenology of religion. His insistence on a nonreductive analysis of religious experience was timely. Beyond that, his evocative analysis of the numinous, that dimension of religious consciousness which was neither the knowing of rationalism nor the doing of moralism, provoked enormous interest. Finally, his phenomenological descriptions of creature-feeling, of mysterium (including the aspects of the wholly other and of fascination), and of tremendum (including the elements of awefulness, overpoweringness, and energy) continue to influence students of religion even today.

On Numinous Experience as *Mysterium Tremendum et Fascinans*

In the probing and analysis of such states of the soul as that of solemn worship, it will be well if regard be paid to what is unique in them rather than to what they have in common with other similar states. To be rapt in worship is one thing; to be morally uplifted by the contemplation of a good deed is another; and it is not to their common features, but to those elements of emotional content peculiar to the first that we would have attention directed as precisely as possible. . . . .

"Mysterium Tremendum"

The Analysis of "Tremendum"

. . . [T]he nature of the numinous can only be suggested by means of the special way in which it is reflected in the mind in terms of feeling. "Its nature is such that it grips or stirs the human mind with this and that determinate affective state." We have now to attempt to give a further indication of these determinate states. We must once again endeavour, by adducing feelings akin to them for the purpose of analogy or contrast, and by the use of metaphor and symbolic expressions, to make the states of mind we are investigating ring out, as it were, of themselves.

Let us consider the deepest and most fundamental element in all strong and sincerely felt religious emotion. Faith unto salvation, trust, love—all these are there. But over and above these is an element which may also on occasion, quite apart from them, profoundly affect us and occupy the mind with a wellnigh bewildering strength. Let us follow it up with every effort of sympathy and imaginative intuition wherever it is to be found, in the lives of those around us, in sudden, strong ebullitions of personal piety and the frames of mind such ebullitions evince, in the fixed and ordered solemnities of rites and liturgies, and again in the atmosphere that clings to old religious monuments and buildings, to temples and to churches. If we do so we shall find we are dealing with something for which there is only one appropriate expression, "mysterium tremendum." The feeling of it may at times come sweeping like a gentle tide, pervading the mind with a tranquil mood of deepest worship. It may pass over into a more set and lasting attitude of the soul, continuing, as it were, thrillingly vibrant and resonant, until at last it dies away and the soul resumes its "profane," non-religious mood of everyday experience. It may burst in sudden eruption up from the depths of the soul with spasms and convulsions, or lead to the strangest excitements, to intoxicated frenzy, to transport, and to ecstasy. It has its wild and demonic forms and can sink to an almost grisly horror and shuddering. It has its crude, barbaric antecedents and early manifestations, and again it may be developed into something beautiful and pure and glorious. It may become the hushed, trembling, and speechless humility of the creature in the presence of—whom or what? In the presence of that which is a mystery inexpressible and above all creatures.

1. The Element of Awefulness

. . . Before going on to consider the elements which unfold as the "tremendum" develops, let us give a little further consideration to the first crude, primitive forms in which this "numinous dread" or awe shows itself. It is the mark which really characterizes the so-called "religion of primitive man," and there it appears as "daemonic dread." This crudely naive and primordial emotional disturbance, and the fantastic images to which it gives rise, are later overborne and ousted by more highly developed forms of the numinous emotion, with all its mysteriously impelling power. But even when this has long attained its higher and purer mode of expression it is possible for the primitive types of excitation that were formerly a part of it to break out in the soul in all their original naiveté and so to be experienced afresh. That this is so is shown by the potent attraction again and again exercised by the element of horror and "shudder" in ghost stories, even among persons of high all-round education. It is a remarkable fact that the physical reaction to which this unique "dread" of the uncanny gives rise is also unique, and is not found in the case of any "natural" fear or terror. We say:

"my blood ran icy cold," and "my flesh crept." The "cold blood" feeling
may be a symptom of ordinary, natural fear, but there is something non-
natural or supernatural about the symptom of "creeping flesh." And any
one who is capable of more precise introspection must recognize that the
distinction between such a "dread" and natural fear is not simply one of
degree and intensity. The awe or "dread" may indeed be so overwhelm-
ingly great that it seems to penetrate to the very marrow, making the
man's hair bristle and his limbs quake. But it may also steal upon him
almost unobserved as the gentlest of agitations, a mere fleeting shadow
passing across his mood. It has therefore nothing to do with intensity,
and no natural fear passes over into it merely by being intensified. I may
be beyond all measure afraid and terrified without there being even a
trace of the feeling of uncanniness in my emotion. . . .

Though the numinous emotion in its completest development shows a
world of difference from the mere "daemonic dread," yet not even at the
highest level does it belie its pedigree or kindred. Even when the worship
of "daemons" has long since reached the higher level of worship of
"gods," these gods still retain as numina something of the "ghost" in the
impress they make on the feelings of the worshipper, viz. the peculiar
quality of the "uncanny" and "aweful," which survives with the quality
of exaltedness and sublimity or is symbolized by means of it. And this
element, softened though it is, does not disappear even on the highest
level of all, where the worship of God is at its purest. Its disappearance
would be indeed an essential loss. The "shudder" reappears in a form
ennobled beyond measure where the soul, held speechless, trembles inwardly to the farthest fibre of its being. It invades the mind mightily in
Christian worship with the words: "Holy, holy, holy"; The "shudder" has
here lost its crazy and bewildering note, but not the ineffable something
that holds the mind. It has become a mystical awe, and sets free as its
accompaniment, reflected in self-consciousness, that "creature-feeling"
that has already been described as the feeling of personal nothingness and
submergence before the awe-inspiring object directly experienced.

The referring of this feeling numinous tremor to its object in the numen brings into relief a property of the latter which plays an important
part in our Holy Scriptures, and which has been the occasion of many
difficulties, both to commentators and to theologians, from its puzzling
and baffling nature. This is the ὀργή ("orge"), the Wrath of Yahweh,
which recurs in the New Testament as ὀργή Θεοῦ, and which is clearly
analogous to the idea occurring in many religions of a mysterious *ira
deorum*. To pass through the Indian Pantheon of gods is to find deities
who seem to be made up altogether out of such an ὀργή; and even the

higher Indian gods of grace and pardon have frequently, beside their merciful, their "wrath" form. But as regards the "wrath of Yahweh," the strange features about it have for long been a matter for constant remark. In the first place, it is patent from many passages of the Old Testament that this "wrath" has no concern whatever with moral qualities. There is something very baffling in the way in which it "is kindled" and manifested. It is, as has been well said, "like a hidden force of nature," like stored-up electricity, discharging itself upon anyone who comes too near. It is "incalculable" and "arbitrary." Anyone who is accustomed to think of deity only by its rational attributes must see in this "wrath" mere caprice and wilful passion. But such a view would have been emphatically rejected by the religious men of the Old Covenant, for to them the Wrath of God, so far from being a diminution of His Godhead, appears as a natural expression of it, an element of "holiness" itself, and a quite indispensable one. And in this they are entirely right. This ὀργή is nothing but the *tremendum* itself, apprehended and expressed by the aid of a naive analogy from the domain of natural experience, in this case from the ordinary passional life of men. But naive as it may be, the analogy is most disconcertingly apt and striking; so much so that it will always retain its value and for us no less than for the men of old be an inevitable way of expressing one element in the religious emotion. It cannot be doubted that, despite the protest of Schleiermacher and Ritschl, Christianity also has something to teach of the "wrath of God."

It will be again at once apparent that in the use of this word we are not concerned with a genuine intellectual "concept," but only with a sort of illustrative substitute for a concept. "Wrath" here is the "ideogram" of a unique emotional moment in religious experience, a moment whose singularly *daunting* and awe-inspiring character must be gravely disturbing to those persons who will recognize nothing in the divine nature but goodness, gentleness, love, and a sort of confidential intimacy, in a word, only those aspects of God which turn towards the world of men. . . .

2. *The Element of "Overpoweringness" ("majestas")*

We have been attempting to unfold the implications of that aspect of the *mysterium tremendum* indicated by the adjective, and the result so far may be summarized in two words, constituting, as before, what may be called an "ideogram," rather than a concept proper, viz "absolute unapproachability."

It will be felt at once that there is yet a further element which must be added, that, namely, of "might," "power," "absolute overpoweringness." We will take to represent this the term *majestas*, majesty—the more readily because anyone with a feeling for language must detect a last faint trace of the numinous still clinging to the word. The *tremendum* may then be rendered more adequately *tremenda majestas*, or "aweful majesty." This second element of majesty may continue to be vividly preserved, where the first, that of unapproachability, recedes and dies away, as may be seen, for example, in mysticism. It is especially in relation to this element of majesty or absolute overpoweringness that the creature-consciousness, of which we have already spoken, comes upon the scene, as a sort of shadow or subjective reflection of it. Thus, in contrast to "the overpowering" of which we are conscious as an object over against the self, there is the feeling of one's own submergence, of being but "dust and ashes" and nothingness. And this forms the numinous raw material for the feeling of religious humility. . . .

3. The Element of "Energy" or Urgency

There is, finally, a third element comprised in those of *tremendum* and *majestas*, awefulness and majesty, and this I venture to call the "urgency" or "energy" of the numinous object. It is particularly vividly perceptible in the ὀργή or wrath; and it everywhere clothes itself in symbolical expressions—vitality, passion, emotional temper, will, force, movement, excitement, activity, impetus. These features are typical and recur again and again from the daemonic level up to the Idea of the "living" God. We have here the factor that has everywhere more than any other prompted the fiercest opposition to the "philosophic" God of mere rational speculation, who can be put into a definition. And for their part the philosophers have condemned these expressions of the energy of the numen, whenever they are brought on to the scene, as sheer anthropomorphism. Insofar as their opponents have for the most part themselves failed to recognize that the terms they have borrowed from the sphere of human conative and affective life have merely value as analogies, the philosophers are right to condemn them. But they are wrong, in so far as, this error notwithstanding, these terms stood for a genuine aspect of the divine nature—its non-rational aspect—a due consciousness of which served to protect religion itself from being "rationalized" away.

For wherever men have been contending for the "living" or for voluntarism, there, we may be sure, have been non-rationalists fighting rationalists and rationalism. It was so with Luther in his controversy with Erasmus; and Luther's *omnipotentia Dei* in his *De Servo Arbitrio* is nothing but the union of "majesty"—in the sense of absolute supremacy—with this "energy," in the sense of a force that knows not stint nor stay, which is urgent, active, compelling, and alive. In mysticism, too, this element of "energy" is a very living and vigorous factor, at any rate in the "voluntaristic" mysticism, the mysticism of love, where it is very forcibly seen in that "consuming fire" of love whose burning strength the mystic can hardly bear, but begs that the heat that has scorched him may be mitigated, lest he be himself destroyed by it. And in this urgency and pressure the mystic's "love" claims a perceptible kinship with the ὀργη̃ itself, the scorching and consuming wrath of God; it is the same "energy," only differently directed. "Love," says one of the mystics, "is nothing else than quenched wrath." . . .

The Analysis of "Mysterium"

We gave to the object to which the numinous consciousness is directed the name *mysterium tremendum*, and we then set ourselves first to determine the meaning of the adjective *tremendum*—which we found to be itself only justified by analogy—because it is more easily analysed than the substantive idea mysterium. We have now to turn to this, and try, as best we may, by hint and suggestion, to get to a clearer apprehension of what it implies.

4. The "Wholly Other"

. . . Taken, indeed, in its purely natural sense, *mysterium* would first mean merely a secret or a mystery in the sense of that which is alien to us, uncomprehended and unexplained; and so far *mysterium* is itself merely an ideogram, an analogical notion taken from the natural sphere, illustrating, but incapable of exhaustively rendering, our real meaning. Taken in the religious sense, that which is "mysterious" is—to give it perhaps the most striking expression—the "wholly other" (Θατερον, *anyad, alienum*), that which is quite beyond the sphere of the usual, the intelligible, and the familiar, which therefore falls quite outside the limits of the "canny," and is contrasted with it, filling the mind with blank wonder and astonishment. . . .

It might be objected that the mysterious is something which is and remains absolutely and invariably beyond our understanding, whereas that which merely eludes our understanding for a time but is perfectly intelligible in principle should be called, not a "mystery," but merely a "problem." But this is by no means an adequate account of the matter. The truly "mysterious" object is beyond our apprehension and comprehension, not only because our knowledge has certain irremovable limits, but because in it we come upon something inherently "wholly other," whose kind and character are incommensurable with our own, and before which we therefore recoil in a wonder that strikes us chill and numb.

This may be made still clearer by a consideration of that degraded offshoot and travesty of the genuine "numinous" dread or awe, the fear of ghosts. Let us try to analyse this experience. We have already specified the peculiar feeling-element of "dread" aroused by the ghost as that of "grue," grisly horror. Now this "grue" obviously contributes something to the attraction which ghost-stories exercise, in so far, namely, as the relaxation of tension ensuing upon our release from it relieves the mind in a pleasant and agreeable way. So far, however, it is not really the ghost itself that gives us pleasure, but the fact that we are rid of it. But obviously this is quite insufficient to explain the ensnaring attraction of the ghost-story. The ghost's real attraction rather consists in this, that of itself and in an uncommon degree it entices the imagination, awakening strong interest and curiosity; it is the weird thing itself that allures the fancy. But it does this, not because it is "something long and white" (as someone once defined a ghost), nor yet through any of the positive and conceptual attributes which fancies about ghosts have invented, but because it is a thing that "doesn't really exist at all," the "wholly other," something which has no place in our scheme of reality but belongs to an absolutely different one, and which at the same time arouses an irrepressible interest in the mind.

But that which is perceptibly true in the fear of ghosts, which is, after all, only a caricature of the genuine thing, is in a far stronger sense true of the "daemonic" experience itself, of which the fear of ghosts is a mere off-shoot. And while, following this main line of development, this element in the numinous consciousness, the feeling of the "wholly other," is heightened and clarified, its higher modes of manifestation come into being, which set the numinous object in contrast not only to everything wonted and familiar (i.e. in the end, to nature in general), thereby turning it into the "supernatural," but finally to the world itself, and thereby exalt it to the "supramundane," that which is above the whole world-order.

In mysticism we have in the "beyond" (ἐπέκεινα) again the strongest stressing and over-stressing of those non-rational elements which are already inherent in all religion. Mysticism continues to its extreme point this contrasting of the numinous object (the numen), as the "wholly other," with ordinary experience. Not content with contrasting it with all that is of nature or this world, mysticism concludes by contrasting it with Being itself and all that "is," and finally actually calls it "that which is nothing." By this "nothing" is meant not only that of which nothing can be predicated, but that which is absolutely and intrinsically other than and opposite of everything that is and can be thought. But while exaggerating to the point of paradox this *negation* and contrast—the only means open to conceptual thought to apprehend the *mysterium*—mysticism at the same time retains the *positive quality* of the "wholly other" as a very living factor in its overbrimming religious emotion. . . .

5. *The Element of Fascination*

The qualitative content of the numinous experience, to which "the mysterious" stand as *form* is in one of its aspects the element of daunting "awefulness" and "majesty," which has already been dealt with in detail; but it is clear that it has at the same time another aspect, in which it shows itself as something uniquely attractive and *fascinating*.

These two qualities, the daunting and the fascinating, now combine in a strange harmony of contrasts, and the resultant dual character of the numinous consciousness, to which the entire religious development bears witness, at any rate from the level of the "daemonic dread" onwards, is at once the strangest and most noteworthy phenomenon in the whole history of religion. The daemonic-divine object may appear to the mind an object of horror and dread, but at the same time it is no less something that allures with a potent charm, and the creature, who trembles before it, utterly cowed and cast down, has always at the same time the impulse to turn to it, nay even to make it somehow his own. The "mystery" is for him not merely something to be wondered at but something that entrances him; and beside that in it which bewilders and confounds, he feels a something that captivates and transports him with a strange ravishment, rising often enough to the pitch of dizzy intoxication; it is the Dionysiac-element in the numen.

❖ MAX SCHELER ❖

Max Scheler (1874–1928) studied with Wilhelm Dilthey and Rudolf Eucken at the Universities of Berlin and Jena. He first met Edmund Husserl in 1901 and assisted Husserl for several years in editing the *Yearbook for Philosophy and Phenomenological Research*. Scheler's wide-ranging philosophical interests are represented in his many publications, including *The Nature of Sympathy, On the Eternal in Man*, and *Man's Place in Nature*. In the following selection Scheler provides a phenomenological analysis of the natural religious act and finds two essential attributes of the divine disclosed in such an act: it is an absolute being and it is holy. Further investigation of the absolute quality of the divine reveals a consciousness of nothingness, an experience of creatureliness on the part of the believer, while the confrontation with the category of the holy indicates its irreducibility to any other modalities. Well versed in the phenomenological tradition and clearly building on the work of Rudolf Otto, Max Scheler in this selection makes a distinctive and independent investment in the rich tradition of the essential phenomenology of religion.

Basic Character of the Divine

Just as in all fields of knowledge the being and the object are given to man earlier than knowledge of the being, and earlier still than the *manner* of acquiring such knowledge, so the objects of the essence called "divine"—God or the gods—also belong directly to the *primal datum* of the human consciousness. In and through all other things which are given to him as existent and possessing such and such qualities, man has learned by dint of natural religious acts to see, sense or imagine that an entity is being disclosed ("revealed") to him which possesses at least two essential attributes: *it "is" in absolute being, and it is holy.* However many additional attributes this holy and absolute being may receive from religions both primitive and developed, it invariably possesses *these.* Always it is given to man as an "absolute entity," that is, as one which is unconditionally superior to all others (including the *ego* so thinking) in capacity for sheer "being," and one on which man is therefore utterly dependent in his whole existence. Yet the "absolute entity" is not inferred, constructed or excogitated from an initial sense of awareness of utter dependence: such a feeling could always be ascribed to weakness in the subject—his inadequate reserves of will-power or the underdevelopment (by himself or society) of his latent capabilities. No; what happens is that the positive attribute of *supremacy* in a being X (implying the dynamic predicates of might, power and the like) becomes perspicuous to intuition "in" some one contingent entity. Furthermore, it is not himself alone whom the individual subject sees to be dependent on this absolute being— this entity founded in and "resting on" itself—but also, even without inductive scrutiny of their being and qualities, all other entities there are; indeed it is as a *part* of contingent being in general that he feels himself dependent.

This unconditional self-inclusion in the sphere of relative being—to the last jot of selfhood—is the foremost characteristic in the religious conception of this first attribute of divinity. On this point there is no reservation on the ground of distinctions between soul and body, spirit and flesh, I and thou, etc. No; utter dependence affects the human being as an undivided whole, as a simple fragment of this "world"—"world" being the heading under which man subsumes the totality of relative being. In the *religious* conception of this primacy content of the divine essence there is no question either of an "inference" or of any theoretical, philosophical perception such as underlies the "proof from contingency." If for no other reason, this is so because only the relative entity, whichever it may be, that exercises the *primary* indicative function of pointing the way to the absolute being could be the starting-point of such an inference, and this entity does not acquire any special religious significance until there is a reflexive retrospection to the fact that it *has* shown the way to the absolute, *i.e.* the divine. But here too, as everywhere, "to stand revealed" means to have been the reverse of extrapolated, inferred, abstracted. It means that when the absolute being of an object qualified as "divine" becomes, of and *out of* itself, "trans-parent" and "trans-lucent" (in the active senses) within an empirical object from the relative sphere, it is only the operation of the shining and looking through which lifts the latter object into prominence and singles it out from among all other objects of relative existence. Just as, when a man or woman looks out of a window, that window becomes from the very fact conspicuous beyond the others in its row, so the finite object becomes "special" and "holy" from the fact that it is symbolizing the absolute being.

If the metaphysical idea of the *ens a se* coincides in this way with the primary *religious* definition of the divine, it nonetheless remains true that the religious and metaphysical paths to knowledge are altogether different. The correlative religious act *accepts* a thing in *process* of revelation and self-presentation within another thing: the act of metaphysical cognition *goes to meet it* spontaneously in logical operations. The relation inherent in a thing's "process of revelation" (the objective *standing for something, one object's* pointing on to another or, in the case of higher forms of revelation, a self-annunciation, self-communication, self-expression)—belongs to the class of symbolic and intuitive relations. In this there is no more question of abstracted relational *concepts* than of inferential or interpretative, meaning-seizing operations of the intellect. Again, the symbolic relation of self-presentation certainly does not originate in an item contained by the human mind—as happens when the meaning of a word presents itself on its utterance—but in the very *object* of the relative entity "in" which the possessor of absolute being presents or "discloses himself." Hence we are dealing with an *objective* relation, not one objectively logical (such as identity or similarity), not one objectively causal, but a symbolic and, in the event, *intuitive* relation. The mind discovers it only in the religious act. Hence another vast distinction: the metaphysical thought-process leading to the *ens a se* can be applied quite indiscriminately to *any* contingent, relative existent, whereas in the religious conception of this basic definition of the divine, the divine invariably reveals itself in specific, *isolated* or strictly limited *concrete things* and *happenings*, including *also* such psychic experiences as may arise. All further substantive definition of the "gods" or "God" beyond the general essential category of the divine is always determined subsequently in various ways from the essential material of these things and happenings.

Even the world's *"dependence"* on the absolute being thus disclosed is given only in the religious act. It is not a logically objective or objectively causal dependence, corresponding to the relations of reason and consequence or cause and effect. It rests rather on the intuitively evident activity of the "effecting process," which enters into all observable causal connections as an irreducible phenomenal factor. This activity is distinguished by the fact that God equated with the *ens a se* appears as the *utterly* active, strong and almighty, and everything else as the utterly passive and enacted—appears enacted in that the active presents itself, in turn, *dynamically* and *symbolically*. In the purely objective causal connection of two events or things (in the case of direct interaction) the cause does not in any way present itself *in* the effect; one cannot tell from the effect alone what thing is its cause; inductive practical knowledge must precede the connection of C and E, if one wishes to conclude C from E, and C is to be more than "some cause unknown." It is otherwise in the religious act, which conceives the finite and contingent entity as the *"creature"* of the mighty or (in monotheism) almighty deity. Here the creatureliness of the creature bears the original stamp of a *phenomenal characteristic*: thus it points to a symbolic connection with the creator and "mirrors" him in its own defective and inadequate way. It is true that in this way the relations of reason and consequence, cause and effect, enter into the content of the religious act. But here these relations are *sensed*, not excogitated, and are always also *symbolic*. For that reason there can *here* be no question of metaphysical inferences.

In varying ways—some illustrating the purity and sublimity of religion, some the different attributes of God—"God expresses himself" in the events of nature. All nature is indeed the field of his expression, just as a human face is available to express joy or grief in smiles or tears. Or God proclaims and manifests himself in nature as mighty and active. Everywhere there lies in or beside the intuitive causal connection one other symbolic relation which is not present in simple objective causality. That a certain acid will turn litmus-paper blue or red is not something we can deduce from the acid alone, however exactly we know its constituents. Still less, conversely, can we deduce from a blueness the actual cause of blueness. We may not come to any conclusion in the matter until we have made many inductions on the hypothesis of regularity. The substance of the effect is not contained in the substance of the cause. If, as here, where we are dealing not with a multiplicity of gods and worlds but with the concrete causal relationship between *one world* and *one God*, there is (from the fact of uniqueness) a complete absence of regularity, we cannot make any statement about the nature of the world-cause from the *mere* objective causality subsisting between God and the world. However, we have quite a different situation when we come, for example, to the relationship of a work of art to the mind of the artist and the individual nature of that mind. Certainly the artist is *likewise* the cause of his work. But beyond that fact, the work also contains *phenomenally* something of the artist's individual spirit and essence: it mirrors him, his spirit lives in it—is present to us in his work. Here the substance of the effect is itself a pointer to the nature of its author, even though we have no previous knowledge of him. Thus the work is "a Rembrandt," "a Grünewald" and so on. Yet take but one step down from art to craft, and the same is no longer true. The craftsman has merely clothed a traditional form with material (*e.g.* the form of a table with wood). Nevertheless, we conclude as to the cause of the table in the way in which we conclude as to the cause of a natural event. For before we know the craftsman we see from the table *itself* that it is the "work of man" or that reason and industry had their parts in its production. A presence of God in the creature, *analogous to the presence of the artist in the work of art*, is visible and sensible in the religious act.

To these two basic definitions of the divine, the *ens a se* and the mightiest or almighty active principle, there exactly correspond two empirically known *reactions* to the *divine apprehended in self-revelation* in the religious act—the sense of the partial *nothingness* and impotence of all *relative* being, and the sense of the *creatureliness* of all relative being and of one's own being as part or member thereof.

These two experiences cannot take shape *unless* both basic definitions of the divine have already been apprehended in the religious act, or can only enter the mind to the extent that these definitions are apprehended and present within it. In no sense therefore are they the first experiences from which one either can or should infer God. For it is only when *God* is confronted as the *ens a se* that there ensues an extremely characteristic "conversion" of whatever existential phenomenon is the immediate object of experience—a transformation whereby that which *before* the religious act was perceived as positively existing now appears relatively non-existent, a relative nonentity. Anybody who experiences a *transition* from a state outside to one inside the active religious sphere may observe the nature of this *conversion of perspective* in his own person. It is not in the presence of the purely conceptual idea of the *ens a se*, but in the presence of the *ens a se* naturally revealing itself via the religious act in an object of some kind, that *all* other existing entities acquire with varying intensity their character of *nothingness*. "I nothing—Thou all" is always the most primitive expression of the religious consciousness in the *first* stage of its evolution. The second experience, of *createdness* and *creatureliness*, can enter only when we reflect on the positive entity which every thing still *is* and we as men still are—regardless of that partial nonentity and nothingness which we first apprehended in the presence of God. In that reflection both things are made plain, both the nothingness experienced in submission to God and the positive selfhood grasped in the self-assertion of the positive entity we "still" bear within us. "I am not utterly nothing, but a creature of God" is the sense of the second experience.

Here, too, we are concerned with a *sense of enactment*, not a conclusion from effect to cause. As such it precedes the experience of creatureliness proper, which postulates the analogy with personal human volitional activity, in other words the idea of the divine as personal and intelligent. For to *create* is something other than to be the mere cause, and implies the intelligent personality of the cause in question. So it is in the first place on theistic religious grounds that the sense of enactment becomes that of three things: (1.) it is intrinsic in the contingent existence of an object in *any* given sphere of being that the existence must have an effective cause; (2.) *resistance* of an object to the exercise of volition; (3.) the only model on which we apprehend the mode of *possible* realization of a purely qualitative essence is that of the manner in which we apprehend the original realization of a merely imagined thing when, in and through volition, we enact a project of the will—irrespective of the intermediary processes of a psychophysical organism and mechanism.

Unlike the above-described prime causality, all kinds of *lateral* causality between contingent existents affect not the realness or realization of such existents but only their *arrangement in time and space*; they are therefore subordinate to the idea of the initial causation of *any* given existent by an *ens a se*.

But, however much the religious act in which we apprehend our own and the world's createdness conforms to these metaphysical perceptions and accords with them in results, the logical operations which give rise to the perceptions are wholly *absent* from the natural religious act which teaches us our created status as a work of God. One may therefore have the sense of that status *without* thought or conclusion, and one may think and conclude yet not have it. Suppose, moreover, one were to formulate the following conclusion: the cause of human reason, and the cause of the existence of forms of being which correspond to its thought-forms, must likewise be rational—indeed, by virtue of the formally absolute and infinite character bestowed on all divine attributes by the nature of the *ens a se*, it must be "absolutely and infinitely rational." Such a conclusion would be utterly different from the *experience* of infinite reason as it pours its light into finite reason and shines forth out of created things. This sense of the godly attribute shining into the light of finite reason is expressed in the thought of Saint Augustine that in so far as we truly understand all things, that is, as they are in themselves, we understand them *"in lumine Dei"*—though perhaps we may not see God thereby.

In the idea of the divine there is a direct, necessary and real connection for the religious consciousness between the *ens a se*, the all-pervading active force and the *value*-modality known as *holiness*, with all its attendant wealth of value-qualities.

Metaphysics may try by various means of deduction and proof to represent this connection as logically necessary. Thus, for example, the attempt has been made, taking the idea of the *ens a se* as an ideal limit, to arrange every kind of entity in a sequence of such a nature that the things within it would be ordered according to the degree in which they owed their being to themselves or derived it *ab alio*. In this sense the concept of the *degree* of being is meaningful and justified. Thus there can be no doubt that as an autonomous rational being man is an *ens* which is self-dependent to a higher degree than the living creature devoid of reason; but this latter in turn, as an *auto*motive phenomenon, is at a higher degree than the inanimate body which *as* inanimate must clearly be determined in its movements by bodies *other* than itself. Believing that these degrees of ontological perfection might also be regarded as the measure of *an entity's perfection of value*, the metaphysician now proceeded with an appearance of strict *analytical* logic from the ontological to the value-definitions of the divine. And so without more ado the *ens a se* was to be the *ens perfectissimum* because its being is the most complete; hence, it becomes the *summum bonum*, hence again, the absolutely holy. It is possible to go yet farther. Since freedom and intelligence (= ability to be

cause rather than effect) represent the highest degree of ontological perfection, as pre-eminently enjoyed by the human spirit among all *entia ab
alio*, it seems inherent in the concept of *ens a se* = *ens perfectissimum* that
if it is real at all it should also be absolutely spiritual, intelligent, free and
rational.

Whatever justice may lie in these deductions' claim to logic, this much
is certain: the *religious* consciousness does not arrive by this route at the
idea of a holy God. For the *religious* consciousness it is a composite
axiom about the nature of things that what is absolutely valuable must
also exist—that is, what has value only *through* and *in* itself (not that
the absolute entity is necessarily also valuable in itself). In this connection, by the way, it is immaterial what the people (or other repository of
religious awareness) actually consider to be of absolute value. For that
reason love of God, in a special sense, and fear of God for that matter,
precedes, in the evolution of a given individual religious consciousness,
even the religious act in which the existence of the "godly" thing is posited; here "love of God" is understood not as love of a deity whose existence is already assumed, but as the qualitative character of the act of
loving when addressed to "something" within the *value-modality* of holiness. And again it is for the religious consciousness a composite axiom
about the nature of things that whatever has "absolute" value derived
exclusively from itself belongs to the value-*category* of the holy, which
category cannot be resolved into any other group of values, whether logical cognitive values, or axiological, moral, aesthetic values, etc.

Within the multiplicity of positive religions the value-category "holy"
may appear very elastic in its separate *qualities* and their *combination*.
As a *category* it is an absolutely stable quantum which has not "evolved"
from anything else. All that the history of human value-preferences can
show is that many kinds and qualities of value, which in earlier stages of
development had "right of entry" into the category of holiness, possessed
religious "sanction," have gradually lost that right and become extra religious, profane values.

As a further proposition it is also axiomatic that the holy (*i.e.* whatever is of holy worth at a given time) is to be preferred before all other
values, and has therefore the intrinsic right to demand the free *sacrifice*
of every good belonging to another value-category. This is the *basic
liaison-principle* linking religion and morality. "Sacrifice to holiness" is
not only the very morality of religion, but also the religion of morality.

A most estimable writer on the philosophy of religion, Rudolf Otto,
has recently expounded the qualities of holiness with remarkable depth
and subtlety. In his book *Das Heilige* [*The Holy*] he distinguishes a num-

ber of elements in that part of the holy which may be considered an "irrational" supplement to those attributes of the divine which he groups together as "rational." To these elements Otto gives special Latin names in order to distinguish them clearly from similar but *extra*-religious values. Thus he adduces the *mysterium tremendum*, the element of *maiestas*, the elements of the *energeticum, mysteriosum, fascinosum* (this last being that of attraction and enticement, which counteracts the deterrent *tremendum*), the element affording protection or atonement, etc. Little as I can accept the religious epistemology which Otto develops in the later sections of his book, I the more gladly salute in its purely *descriptive* section the first serious endeavour to analyse the chief qualities of the value-modality "holy"—the objective characteristic of all and every religion—by the dialectical method of phenomenology. In the true spirit of the phenomenological method Otto rightly says of his own procedure: "This (the category of holiness) is perfectly *sui generis* and irreducible to any other; and therefore, like every absolutely primary and elementary datum, while it admits of being discussed, it cannot be strictly defined. There is only one way to help another to an understanding of it. He must be guided and led on by consideration and discussion of the matter through the ways of his own mind, until he reach the point at which 'the numinous' in him perforce begins to stir, to start into life and into consciousness. We can co-operate in this process by bringing before his notice all that can be found in other regions of the mind, already known and familiar, to resemble, or again to afford some special contrast to, the particular experience we wish to elucidate. Then we must add: 'This X of ours is not precisely this experience, but akin to this one and the opposite of that other. Cannot you now realize for yourself what it is?' In other words our X cannot, strictly speaking, be taught, it can only be evoked, awakened in the mind; as everything that comes 'of the spirit' must be awakened."

This on the whole negative method of successively peeling away the correlates and contraries that are felt to offer progressive indications to the "phenomenon *demonstrandum*," with the consequent laying bare of the phenomenon and its presence to the inspecting mind, is the way which leads to the *phenomenological scrutiny of the essence*. The indefinability of the X under investigation (*per genus et differentia specifica*) is a sure sign that in this X we have a genuine elementary essence which underlies ultimate concepts but is itself "inconceivable." For "to conceive" means to reduce the object of a concept in terms of other concepts. It is not surprising that the rationalistic philosopher decries this method as generally fruitless. Unaware of its character as a mind-awakening and

guiding procedure (into which indirect thinking in judgments and inferences enters only as a means of leading the mind to the threshold of
discovery), he sees only those judgments and inferences and overlooks
the sense and nerve of the whole procedure. He then agrees with the
finding of Wilhelm Wundt that phenomenology is a wholly profitless affair, since it consists in negative judgments and always ends in a tautology
(such as that the holy is simply—the holy). Where this priceless verdict is
unutterably mistaken is in this: Wundt takes the negative judgments—
which in this method are no more than dialectic invitations to redirect
the mind's attention closer to the all-important object—to imply theoretical rational definitions of some thing, and even the so-called tautology
he regards as a theoretical rational definition instead of merely the concluding invitation to look here and now upon the supreconceptual datum
which can only be beheld, to gaze directly upon its pure self-given state,
now that the husks of approximation have been stripped away. Nobody
in his senses could believe, however, that as a theoretical rational definition the "tautology" would be anything but absurd.

Many who make use of this method (in our present field or any other)
are surprisingly unaware that as a method it is basically none other than
that of "negative theology." For the method of "negative theology" itself
arose purely from the deep conviction that the *divine* and holy form as
such a prime elementary quality which can only be demonstrated by a
slow process of elimination and analogy, a quality which must satisfy all
concepts of the divine—positive and negative—but itself remains inconceivable. There is no doubt that as an approach and method phenomenology was first employed, in the time of Plotinus, in exactly this theological context. "Negative theology" has also been a frequent victim of
the misunderstanding that it employed negations to define the divine
theoretically and not on the contrary to prevent its being prematurely
defined in rational terms *before* its essence had been grasped. But to understand the meaning of negative theology one need only be clear about
one constantly recurring fact concerning all religious discourse. This is
the enormous disproportion subsisting, in rational linguistic expression
describing religious experience of divinity, between what is truly and
positively vouchsafed to mental vision and its often, indeed mostly, negative definitions. Otto himself gives an example which is very much to the
point—indeed conclusive: " 'Eye hath not seen, nor ear heard, neither
have entered into the heart of man, the things which God hath prepared
for them that love him.' Who does not feel the exalted sound of these
words and the 'Dionysiac' element of transport and fervour in them? It is
instructive that in such phrases as these, in which consciousness would

fain put its highest consummation into words, 'all images fall away' and the mind turns from them to grasp expressions that are purely negative. And *it is still more instructive that in reading and hearing such words their merely negative character simply is not noticed*; that we can let whole chains of such negations enrapture, even intoxicate us, and that . . . deeply impressive hymns—have been composed, in which there is really nothing positive at all! All this teaches us the independence of the positive content of this experience from the implications of its overt conceptual expression, and how it can be firmly grasped, thoroughly understood, and profoundly appreciated, purely in, with, and from the feeling itself."

Now if negative theology is rationalistically misunderstood, the reader or hearer is left with only the negative propositions in place of the positive datum which these propositions single out for us from the chaos of the finite, non-divine or merely analogically similar and seek to place before the mind's eye. And this is also true: if negative theology, which by nature is mystical technique rather than theory, is accepted, even by its champion, as *rational* theory, it must necessarily lead to religious nihilism—even to atheism. For an object whose every definition is negative is—even apart from formal categorical exactitude—nothing. So the result of such misunderstanding is that the most positive, most high repository of being and value is supplanted by its exact opposite—nothing.

But if negative theology, or rather its method, is understood properly in accordance with the business in hand, the proposition that it is the *basis of all positive theology* (and not *vice versa*) is as certainly true as that the eidetic phenomenology of any object-group is the ultimate basis of the positive science concerned with that group. All *positive* conceptual definitions of God are therefore by nature (*i.e.* as conceptual) no more than quasi-definitions or *analogical* definitions. Measuring the varying *nearness* of these analogical definitions to the intentional object is a task demanding more than simply an investigation of their obvious rational interconnection—though that they *should* so interlock is a requirement whose observance undoubtedly helps the progress of religious cognition. But the *final decision* as to the possibility or extent of *cognitive* value in any such analogy (or, for that matter, in any positive conceptual definition) lies with the religious consciousness, to be settled according to its own autonomous principles and in the light of the quality of divinity *self-"given"* to it (by negative theology, demonstrably *self*-given if at all)—together with a normative notion of the divine's internal consistency.

❖ WILLIAM EARLE ❖

William Earle (1919–) is professor of philosophy at Northwestern University. He is the author of *Objectivity, Christianity and Existentialism* (with James Edie and John H. Wild), *The Autobiographical Consciousness, Mystical Reason* as well as other works. His selection phenomenologically describes mystical experience and focuses on the experience of the identity of the believer with Absolute Reality as the essential characteristic of mysticism.

Earle's findings are intriguing for they raise the question of mysticism's relation to other states of religious consciousness. Following Earle, one could seek phenomenologically to distinguish mysticism from the experience of divine or demonic possession as found, for example, in charismatic Christianity, Tibetan Buddhism, or the religion of the Dinka in Africa. One could also contrast the phenomenologically derived description of the mystical identity of the individual and Absolute Reality with the phenomenological analysis of the shamanic experience provided by Ivar Paulson with its emphasis on the experience of the ecstatic trance state and the flight of the free soul. Beyond these considerations, Earle also argues for the connection between mystical and common experience and thus raises again the challenge of phenomenologically identifying the attributes and nature of the religious experience as well as specifying the realms of disjunction and continuity between the religious and non-religious spheres of experience.

❖

Phenomenology of Mysticism

I suppose it is safe to say there are mystics in every culture, time and place. Evelyn Underhill's *Mysticism* displays before us an enormous panorama of mystical experience drawn from ancient Greece, Israel, Persia, India, as well as the modern Christian world. And if one impression is that mysticism is infinitely various, another is that remarkably enough through that variety, the same thing is being expressed. I shall try, in a moment, to say what I imagine that "same thing" to be. But beforehand, and more or less in self-defense, I should also like to say that any effort such as the present which seeks to disengage and examine the essence of mysticism is doomed to a certain sterility and abstractness. The genuine mystics themselves, far from being inarticulate, can hardly stop talking, and revel in startling images drawn from virtually every domain of life. Light which is darkness, or darkness light, suns which shine at midnight, stones looking at you, spheres whose center is everywhere and circumference nowhere, Absolute Reality as an object of erotic love, the world in a grain of sand, a fixed explosion, eternity in an hour, etc., an exuberance in which at first sight almost anything at all can be said now that reason is thrown to the winds. If indeed, reality itself is a *coincidence of opposites*, as Nicalos of Cusa says, then have we not left poor logic far behind? And yet, on second glance, all this luxuriant irrationality begins to take on its own logic, its own reason, and perhaps through it all one can begin to perceive a common essence. But since it is a common essence, it must abstain from the glorious particular imagery of the mystics themselves, and one can well ask why bother.

And the answer, and therewith the justification for this present effort, is that mystics are not simply playing with words for the sake of poetic effects, nor simply trying to outrage common logic by an act of effrontery. They are all, clearly, trying to say or I should say, are saying *what reality is*. And since there are other disciplines and interests of mind which also concern themselves with this question, in fact it would be difficult to name one interest of mind which was not concerned with reality, the claims of the mystic must be adjudicated in their abstract essence. It is therefore an obligation of philosophy at least, to examine those claims, even when what remains may look more like a skeleton than the living experience itself.

And so, for the rest of this essay, I shall try to restate abstractly what I imagine the essence of the mystic experience to be, examine it phenomenologically, and arrive at some conclusions. I shall state those conclusions at once; the essential claims of the mystics are not merely absolutely sound, and can be known to be so, but are of extraordinary importance, and finally, far from being a matter of swoons, ecstasies, visions and hallucinations, hysterical stigmata, or unintelligible mutterings, there is such a direct connection between mysticism and common experience, that common experience on any terms would not be possible at all unless the philosophical claims of the mystic were granted. The effect here desired is a reconciliation between common experience and those extraordinary trances, such that while not many of us are mystics in the hyperbolic sense of that term, everyone is so in varying degrees of explicitness and expression. No doubt this will offend both sides; the mystics will find their unique experiences degraded by being related to common experience, and the man who most detests mystic experience will be invited to look again; maybe he too is a mystic without knowing it, even against his will.

To come immediately to the point, I take the very essence of mysticism to be *the experience of the identity of the soul and God.* It is the validity of the claim embodied in that experience which will be under examination. However, I would like to make a slight retranslation: *the experience of the identity of myself with Absolute Reality.* The reason for the retranslation is largely rhetorical; the first phrasing raises to the philosophical mind almost insuperable difficulties: the soul? God? what are they? do they exist? And since every key term in that formulation has behind it some two thousand years of very heated dispute, it might be useful to rephrase it in the most neutral terms possible. After all, the term, Absolute Reality, has never had much currency and no doubt never will, hence it is ideal for our purposes; we can within limits define it as we will. And the "myself" also puts the matter in terms less theologically colored than "soul." In the long run it hardly makes much difference, but then to approach the question neutrally, it seems best to use neutral language. Also, while not everybody's God is the same as Absolute Reality, nor everyone's idea of soul the same as an I myself, I shall not try to talk about all those other possible meanings, but only about what I have phrased above, as the experienced identity of an I myself with Absolute Reality.

Our method of examination will be phenomenological, a standpoint elaborated if not discovered by Edmund Husserl. The ins and outs of that method are a matter of infinite technical discussion; I shall use of it only this: the attempt to reflect radically upon experience as that experience presents itself to the experiencer. It will be then mind reflecting upon itself, without presupposition, in an effort to discern explicitly what the structure and content of that experience is. This reflection from first to last will try to confine itself to experience as it offers itself without presupposing from the start what reality "must" be, what the ego experiencing "must" be, notions drawn from sources external to that experience itself. In a word, that phenomenological reflection does not begin with any logical, biological, physical or philosophical presuppositions. All of that must be put in brackets; the effort will be to reflect upon experience itself, to see once again what it is rather than to attempt a critique from supposed truths drawn from elsewhere. Phenomenology thus understood is nothing but an attempt to make clear to oneself the phenomenon of any experience whatsoever just as it offers itself to the mind reflecting. If this self-examination seems condemned from the outset to remaining *within* experience, hence being incapable of answering the question whether the mystic experience is an experience *of* something independent of experience, that is Absolute Reality, I hope to show in a moment that this fear is groundless. That will be one burden of the discussion.

And now a phenomenological clarification of our principal terms, the I, or Ego, then Absolute Reality, finally their identity. When Meister Eckhardt said: I am God, and was immediately condemned by the church as a heretic and blasphemer, precisely what on earth did he mean? And why was the Church offended? The offense of the Church is obvious; Meister Eckhardt was a man with two legs, visible and audible in his parish, who ate, slept, and certainly would die. How could any such creature claim identity with the invisible, inaudible and eternal God? Could confusion go further? And in a nutshell, such represents, in one way or another, the perpetual battle between the mystic, thought to be a madman, and the objective, empirical world of science, thought to be the repository of all truth. Or then maybe there is a *profound misunderstanding*, which phenomenology can help remove.

First the I, our version of "soul"; the I or Ego, is to be taken phenomenologically, that is, as it appears to itself. Since it is the Ego or I which experiences its identity with Absolute Reality, we must explore at some length precisely what this ego is as it grasps itself in reflection. It is certainly not Meister Eckhardt, the forked animal, who says he is identical with reality, but his very soul, that is his self. And it is not his self or personality as it might be encountered by others, or which has a name, or which is anything whatsoever other than that which grasps itself reflexively as a self, a self for itself. The ego or self then is taken here as a self, conscious of itself as a self. But yet another quagmire must be avoided. This reflexive self-awareness must at all costs be distinguished from a derived and related phenomenon, namely, that of "thinking about" myself, forming a picture of myself, or forming some sort of objective concept of myself. My *primordial* awareness of myself can not be the awareness of some sort of *object*, later to be identified with "myself." In fact, any such thing when taken as basic, is nothing short of schizophrenia, a division within the self, rather than its identity. How indeed would I ever know that such an objective thing, the concept of myself, was really I myself? My selfhood would thereby become an hypothesis; that the I I was thinking *about* or conceptualizing, was indeed one and the same as the I which was thinking that concept, or posing such an object before it. All of which is pure absurdity, and not in the least what we are at present discussing: the reflexive self-grasp or immediate consciousness of each ego of itself as itself. The net result of these considerations is simply the self as self-*awareness*, and not either a self as a material thing nor a self condemned to *look at* itself in concepts or images, as if it were an ontological stranger to itself. The self, so taken, is to put it weakly, most remarkable; for while nothing could be more familiar or more immediately known, it is precisely that self which declares itself to be identical to God or Absolute Reality. It will claim to be the divine element in man.

All of which puts at great length what Descartes, not exactly known for mysticism, says briefly: I think, therefore I am. Or more precisely, everytime I reflect on my thinking, even if that thinking is wrong or full of doubt, at least I can know immediately and with certainty, that I, the *ego cogito*, or thinking ego, am. And, of course, the thinking upon which I reflect, is any sort of awareness whatsoever, not merely abstract reasoning. In a word, the ego or I which anyone can make explicit to himself by reflection, is given in that act of reflection the immediate certainty that it is. But then, what is it? For Descartes who in this respect anticipates the phenomenological stand-point, as given to itself it is simply and purely a "thinker," that is, a unity or "substance" as he puts it, whose whole nature is exhausted in thinking or awareness.

And with that move, we need no longer consider anything but it; or rather in repeating Descartes's reflection, each now need consider nothing but himself as a thinking self. My own body, other persons, and the physical world of nature are not ingredient in the very essence of that thinking self. The I as it is for itself, is only *accidentally* related to its body, to the physical world, to other persons. It may turn its thinking attention to them, but it is not they, or even like them. It is this which we are discussing. Now in anticipation, if each self must say: I am I, that expression expressing the very essence of being a self, and feels in itself something ontologically remarkable, something that can consider the world but is not itself a part of that world, perhaps it will not appear outrageous that Moses' God also gave as his proper name, *I am that I am*. "Tell them that The Same sent me. . . ." The secret connection between the self and Absolute Reality was known implicitly from the beginning. Much of course has happened in the history of thought in between, whether improvement or confusion must be left to the judgment of each; but at least the mystics are always around to remind us of what we've lost.

Phenomenologically speaking, what could be more obvious than that the very language of religion and metaphysics, the sense of their terms, the meaning of such terms as eternity, God, Absolute, Reality, Identity, and the rest would be impossible for us, unless there were *in* each self *resources* out of which those terms could draw their sense? The question then at this point is not whether such things exist, but simply their signification. To whatever degree these words and their like *speak at all*, to that degree, the self which understands them has already implicitly implied the proof of their truth and reality. Something or other, the self, must be so constituted that language of this transcendental order is at least significant. If it is so constituted, then indeed some existent thing, the self so understanding this language, must be itself transcendentally constituted, hence confirm what the language alluded to. Otherwise the language would collapse into what in the strictest sense of that term is *babbling*, or sounds without the least signification. Only like knows like, unlikes can only stare uncomprehendingly at one another. But all this by way of anticipation.

To return to more mundane matters, the ego which perceives, remembers, desires, anticipates, and entertains transcendental meanings if only by way of wondering about them, must have a most remarkable structure. Or as Edmund Husserl put it, "the transcendental ego is the wonder of all wonders." Further, this wonder of all wonders is nothing remote from each self at all; it is that self, as it shows itself to itself.

A few examples might suffice to indicate the extraordinary character of the ego. I see this room. Or, to put it more accurately, I *seem* to see it; I don't wish to quarrel here whether there really is such a room, or whether I really am seeing it. For our purposes, it is enough to focus our attention on the whole affair as a phenomenon. At least the phenomenon is certain, if nothing else is; and the phenomenon is enough. But precisely what is this banal event? I am immediately aware of a three-dimensional room, full of people. But the banal event of seeing a spatial object is itself an event of the most extraordinary sort. My object, spread out in three dimensions, all comes together into my *perception* of it, a perceiving which in and of itself, is not spread out in three dimensions. That is, by my *perception* of it, it is assimilated or reduced to an act of perception, which in no way whatsoever resembles its object. Neither I, the perceiving self, nor my act of perception, is a three-dimensional object. Indeed if either I or my act of perception were themselves three-dimensional, we would be faced with a pure absurdity: there would be within this room, two rooms of equal size, the room I look at, and then I and my perception of it, now become another room occupying this very room. No, there is only one room! The ego and its perception of it, is not a second room at all; and if it were, it could not perceive this room, but only be another funny spatial object lying within the originally perceived room. In any event, what could be clearer than the fact that the *I perceive* is a nonspatial act, *related* to a spatial object, but not in and of itself spatial?

And so, as we explore the extraordinary character of the I, the first thing perhaps to note, is that it is not in the least spatial, hence certainly not physical at all. As I hope is apparent, we are trying to make plausible our final conclusion, that the thinking ego is indeed a *transcendental* something or other, and therefore a fit candidate for its own mystic claim that it is indeed identical with Absolute Reality or God. Our method however is not by fits and trances, with all due credit given to them, but by a somewhat patient exploration of mundane phenomena which anyone can verify.

But then, no doubt, the ego is in *time*? The word, time, of course, means many things and perhaps no one is very clear about what it means. But for our present purposes, let us take it as naming the very *flux and flow of the world*. I do not mean the obvious fact that some things are moving while others remain at rest. I mean that even for things clearly at rest for us, each moment of their rest is different from the next moment and from the previous moment, although the thing itself sits there with recognizably the same face. But the real time I wish to talk about is that Heraclitean flux which pervades the world like some ever-blowing wind. Again, the banal truth, is that everyone is *aware* of this flux of time.

Everyone knows at heart, even if we choose not to think of it, that the entire experienced world is some sort of ontological bonfire forever consuming and forever renewing itself, within the now. But then the odd feature of it all is that the I *knows* it immediately; what sort of thing then is the I which is aware of the fire? Is it too caught up in it, a participant in the fire, or is it something above the flames? Yet is it not immediately clear upon reflection, that nothing *wholly and exclusively* temporal could possibly be aware of time? Being itself wholly different at each moment, how could it *apprehend* this difference? How can anything wholly in flux be aware *that* it is in flux? To take another example, how is it possible to *understand* a simple sentence or a simple melody? A sentence is not understood until the last word has sounded, nor a melody until its last note, unless either is so banal as to permit us to anticipate it. But then when the last word or note has sounded, the *whole* sentence and the *whole* melody is somehow present; that is, the words and notes at the beginning are *retained* at the end. And so what is no longer literally sounding in our ears, must still be *present* in retention, or no sentence, no melody could appear to our mind. If then the ego itself did not preside nontemporally over these movements, in order to gather together at the end all that preceded, neither linguistic nor musical sense would be possible. That which can so preside over the flux, retain what was *as past*, but still *retain* it, obviously can not be exclusively a temporal event itself. It is *related* to time but not itself temporal. The comprehension of the flux, then, cannot be itself exclusively an item in it. If the I think, the ego, then is neither a spatial volume, nor an instant in the flux, it is *transcendental* to both and begins to disclose something of what Husserl called, the wonder of wonders. And yet, it is indeed ourselves, and not a hypothetical entity; it is closest to us, being *identical* with ourselves.

A final example drawn now from logic, an area especially despised by mystics who usually know little about it. And yet their instincts are right, for logic, as I hope to show, reveals a poor comprehension of itself, and the limitations of its own valid operations. For it too is only possible under the nonlogical conditions explicit in mysticism. The I think thinks many things; we have been considering the most ordinary acts of perception; but then what about more abstract assertions of propositions?

Logic operates under its own master law, the law of noncontradiction. Two genuinely contradictory propositions cannot both be true. Or, if transferred to the realm of facts, nothing can have contradictory properties. Bishop Butler put it: *each thing is what it is and not another thing.* Now this grand idea is also held to be the very condition of meaningful discourse. Both to say something and deny it at the same time and in the same respect is, for Aristotle, sheer babbling, and a philosopher is under no obligation to enter into discourse with babblers. They are the same as vegetables.

But is it all that easy? A phenomenological reflection upon the operation of reason asserting anything at all equally shows that to assert anything is at the same time to deny its contradiction. But then, for the contradiction *to be denied* simply says that reason can indeed *entertain* contradictories if only to stoutly deny them. And so the mind is, after all, perfectly able to envisage contradictories, and *must* do so if it is to reject them. There must therefore be at least one thing which can envisage the contradictory, namely, mind; and, in the very act of entertaining the hated contradiction, it is itself contradictorily qualified. Further, it would be foolish indeed to assert that the transcendental ego in its reasoning capacity is in fact *never* contradictorily qualified; that would amount to nothing but the boast that in fact we never contradicted ourselves, and happy indeed is the man who could honestly say that! The state of perfect coherence might be something some desire, but they could hardly *desire* it if they automatically or necessarily had it. And so, the logical ego, in its effort to avoid the contradictory is *perfectly aware* of the contradictory, and in fact dwells in the contradictory far more than it has nerve enough to admit.

Rational *assertions* of course are not made by reason which can literally *do* nothing at all, but by the *will*; it is the will out of its freedom, which asserts what it asserts in the *light* of reason. The rejection of the contradictory is an act of will, affirming or denying. And as every student of Descartes knows, for that philosopher, the will is *absolutely free*; this absolute freedom in the very heart of the will was adopted by Jean-Paul Sartre as constitutive of the very essence of consciousness itself. But no matter, looking now at the will, it is clear, I think, that in our transcendental will, we have the absolute freedom to affirm or deny anything whatsoever, and indeed to will anything whatsoever, whether we can *do* what we will or not being beside the point. Anyone can always say either yes or no, and also both, at the same time and in the same respect.

Now the contradictory itself has very peculiar properties. Anything whatsoever combined with its contradictory, exhausts the universe of discourse; anything whatsoever will fall into one camp or the other. The contradictory therefore has precisely the same structure as Being itself; together, contradictories constitute a universe. Clearly there can *be* nothing which is not an instance of Being. Absolute Being then is not identical with any of its instances. And so, through our common-sensical path, we have met again that which has exactly the same formula as God or

Absolute Reality. For Cusanus, God is the coincidence of opposites, or the ocean in which all that *is* and all that now *is not*, are engulfed. This ocean, or Absolute Reality philosophically speaking, or God, religiously speaking, is Being, but then since Being isn't any particular thing at all, it is also nothing; measured against its own specifications or "creations," it is the same as Nothingness.

Perhaps this is sufficient to assign logic to its proper place; its applicability is strictly to the finite and determinate world of particular things; it is false when applied without restriction to Being or Absolute Reality. And if for formal logic, it is a horror to have contradictory premises, since absolutely *every* proposition follows from a contradiction, hence one cannot validly arrive at *any* specific proposition rather than its opposite, for the metaphysical or mystic consciousness it is, on the contrary, a delight to arrive at an absolute principle from which everything indeed does follow. This would assure us of its infinite fertility, exactly what is needed for an ultimate principle which is understood to be generative of everything.

If we have uncovered this principle in the very heart of the transcendental ego, it follows without much argument that no such thing can be called "finite." We have seen how it is nonspatial, nontemporal, and now indeed that it is no finite entity at all, but rather a transcendental, absolute and free unitary act of exactly the *same structure* as Absolute Reality itself. *I am God*, said Meister Eckhardt. This must be understood not merely as an exultant and extravagant *feeling* or metaphysical *euphoria*, but as a literal truth, a truth moreover which is the keystone to every rational system of metaphysics, particularly those prominent in the seventeenth century.

The argument so far has tried to make evident that the I which is aware of a variety of mundane or finite phenomena space, the flux of time, and the logical distinctness of each thing taken by itself, cannot itself be characterized by those categories, but must be transcendental to them in order to be aware of them. Earlier, however, the argument was that the ego must be transcendental if it is to have even an inkling of the sense of transcendental terms; only like knows like. Now it seems that only unlike knows unlike. But the resolution of this difficulty comes again through a phenomenological reflection upon exactly what it is we do "know" of these mundane phenomena. Again, to stare at something or be immediately acquainted with it is not knowing it in any preeminent sense.

Knowing space and time can only be recovering in these phenomena what the transcendental ego already had out of its own resources, ideas usually called "innate ideas," the recovery of them in the phenomenal field being akin to Platonic recollection. Hence Descartes proceeded to consider of extension only that aspect of it which is reducible to number, and invented analytic geometry to do the task; what was left out was the extendedness of extension, that part belonging to space as it affected the imagination of the body. And so with flux, movement, time. The inherent flux in the flux or the temporality of time, is not accessible to reason; only its number and formula are. The mind can only be aware that there is flux by encountering it, and what it then encounters is unintelligible, except insofar as it illustrates a formula. Number, on the other hand, as well as the other innate ideas and categories, such as substance, actuality, eternity, and the rest, never exhaustibly listed or listable, all derive their primary meanings from the self's own self-reflection, and are therefore innate, and not acquired.

And for mystics again and again, it is never the world in its flux, oppositions, distinctions or sensory character which is intelligible; the world is primarily and fundamentally unintelligible, and God alone is capable of being known. He alone is intelligible because of the peculiar affinity of the transcendental ego with him. What is known of the world is only what it reflects of that Absolute. This amounts to a change of view upon the world so that it may be experienced as proceeding from a transcendental reality and therefore being absolutely insufficient in and of itself to be.

The whole issue comes to a focus in the famous or infamous "ontological argument." There are many forms of it, from Anselm through Descartes, Spinoza, and Leibniz; but let us summarize them all in the following form. I can conceive of an absolutely perfect Being; since existence is a perfection, such a Being must necessarily exist as I conceive it. That is, it is not a mere hypothesis that God exists, or suggestion that needs additional support. It can be known with certitude that Absolute Reality is, since the denial is itself contradictory. The essence of God necessarily implies his existence.

Now all this would be not merely suspicious or invalid, but patently false if God or Absolute Reality were some sort of entity, thing, or specific event. And it would be equally absurd if the "existence" of it were of the same sort as the existence of any such finite entity, thing or event. Needless to say, although it would be hard to say exactly how much ink has been spilled on the question, neither is Absolute Reality nor its mode of being remotely like the existence of things. If Absolute Reality were like a thing, a large thing, an important thing, or even an indefinitely large and indefinitely lasting thing or event, it could of course not be absolute;

and if its mode of being were like things or events, then it would like them be dependent or contingent upon *other* things and events, hence not be necessary and eternal *in and of itself.* All of which is captured in traditional phrases such as God is that *in which* all things live, move and have their being; philosophically speaking, Absolute Reality is not by definition dependent upon anything independent of itself; that is what *absolute* means. Nor is it a summation of things, as though those things were independent parts which need only be added arithmetically to achieve the status of an absolute whole; as every rational metaphysics has demonstrated, these "things" which look independent in themselves, are and can be nothing but limitations of something absolute whose nature is to be independent. Theologically, God is not the sum of his creatures, but rather their origin and creator. Analogously, space itself is not a sum- mation of spatial things, since each one of them presupposes space itself; nor is time a summation of events, each one of which is already temporal. The priority works the other way around; space and time are prior to their particularizations. Analogously, Absolute Reality is absolutely prior to any finite thing whatsoever, things which for their part are nothing but finitizations or limitations of what is ontologically prior to them, the Absolute.

If then we think a reality which is absolute, and here the important term is "think" for obviously no such thing according to its own proper intention is imaginable or experienceable through the senses, we think that which the ontological argument is about. Such a reality must be the ground of not merely all that is now, in all its infinite detail and extent, throughout all its types and forms, but also all that was and all that will be. Further, since what *could have been* also has its distinctive reality, the domain of possibility is necessarily included along with temporal *exis- tence. Impossibility* also is a form of reality, since there are many things which are true of impossibility, among which is the fact that it is impos- sible. The list is of course in principle infinite, and no purpose would be served by extending the inventory of what is to be included; the answer at the other end is simple: everything.

But if, up to this point, we have been trying to isolate the idea of Absolute Reality, by distinguishing it from other ideas, perhaps there is one aspect of it which has escaped our notice. We have perhaps been implicitly directing our attention to an infinite or absolute Object, within which every experienceable and nonexperienceable thing is as a delimi- tation of it. And now it is essential to remove the last barrier: *no Object could possibly be absolute.* Absolute Reality *can* not be considered as an object exclusively. By thinking of an absolute object, of which the natural

❖

Samadhi

In studying Zen we start with practice. Now, it is true that Zen is concerned with the problem of the nature of mind, so it necessarily includes an element of philosophical speculation. However, while the philosopher relies mainly on speculation and reasoning, in Zen we are never separated from our personal practice, which we carry out with our body and mind. Edmund Husserl, the founder of phenomenology, may seem to come close to Zen in his ideas when he advocates a technique called "phenomenological reduction." He says that he ignores "the ego as a person arranged on objective time," and arrives at the "pure phenomenon." However, like other philosophers, he does not seem to go beyond a purely mental exercise. In Zen training we also seek to extinguish the self-centered, individual ego, but we do not try to do this merely by thinking about it. It is with our own body and mind that we actually experience what we call "pure existence."

The basic kind of Zen practice is called *zazen* (sitting Zen), and in zazen we attain *samadhi*. In this state the activity of consciousness is stopped and we cease to be aware of time, space, and causation. The mode of existence which thus makes its appearance may at first sight seem to be nothing more than mere being, or existence. However, if you really attain this state you will find it to be a remarkable thing. At the extremity of having denied all and having nothing left to deny, we reach a state in which absolute silence and stillness reign, bathed in a pure, serene light. Buddhists of former times called this state annihilation, or Nirvana. But it is not a vacuum or mere nothingness. It is utterly different, too, from the unconscious state of the patient under anesthesia upon the operating table. There is a definite wakefulness in it. It is a condition of existence that recalls the impressive silence and stillness that we experience in the heart of the mountains.

In ordinary daily life our consciousness works ceaselessly to protect

and maintain our interests. It has acquired the habit of utilitarian thinking, looking upon the things in the world as so many tools—in Heidegger's phrase, it treats them "in the context of equipment." It looks at
objects in the light of how they can be made use of. We call this attitude
the habitual way of consciousness. This way of looking at things is the
origin of man's distorted view of the world. And he comes to look upon
himself, too, in the context of equipment, and fails to see into his own
true nature. This way of treating oneself and the world leads to a mechanical way of thinking, which is the cause of so much of the suffering
of modern man, and which can, under some conditions, lead to the development of mental illnesses. Zen aims at overthrowing this distorted
view of the world, and zazen is the means of doing it.

On coming out of samadhi it can happen that one becomes fully aware
of one's being in its pure form; that is, one experiences pure existence.
This experience of the pure existence of one's being, associated with the
recovery of pure consciousness in samadhi, leads us to the recognition of
pure existence in the external world too. Discussion of these topics inevitably leads us into epistemological tangles, but let us proceed for the
moment, granting that such recognition of pure existence is possible. To
look at oneself and the objects of the external world in the context of
pure existence is *kensho* or realization. And this has been achieved, since
Buddha himself did so, by men and women of every generation, who bear
witness to its feasibility. . . .

Samadhi

Rinzai Zenji's four categories are as follows:
1. Man is deprived; circumstances are not deprived.
2. Circumstances are deprived; man is not deprived.
3. Both man and circumstances are deprived.
4. Neither man nor circumstances are deprived.
What do these statements mean?

The First Category

"Man is deprived; circumstances are not deprived" denotes a situation
in which one's mind is absorbed in outward circumstances. A famous
surgeon was once performing an operation that required great concentra-
tion. While he was working there was a sudden earthquake. The shocks
were so severe that most of the attendants involuntarily ran out of the
room for safety. But the surgeon was so absorbed in the operation that

he did not feel the shocks at all. After the operation was over he was told of the earthquake, and this was the first he knew of it. He had been completely absorbed in his work, in a kind of samadhi.

We experience this kind of samadhi when we are watching a football game, reading, writing, thinking, fishing, looking at pictures, talking about the weather, or even stretching out a hand to open the door—in the moment of sitting down or stepping forward. In fact, we are at every moment absorbed in that moment's action or thought. There are various degrees of absorption, various periods of duration, and differences between voluntary and involuntary attention: the differences, for example, between our watching a football game (involuntary attention) and the surgeon performing his operation (voluntary attention). But we are almost always experiencing a minor or major condition of momentary samadhi, so to speak. When we are in this sort of samadhi we are quite forgetful of ourselves. We are not self-conscious about our behavior, emotions, or thought. The inner man is forgotten and outer circumstances occupy our whole attention. To put it another way: inward concern is absent; outward concern dominates.

It should be remembered that consciousness works in two different ways, one directed outward, the other inward. When consciousness is concerned with outward matters, inward attention is forgotten, and vice versa. There are two kinds and several phases of samadhi. We have already drawn a distinction between absolute and positive samadhi; Rinzai Zenji's four categories provide the basis for a further characterization of the different phases.

Now, it is important to recognize the difference between true samadhi with self-mastery and the false kind of samadhi without it. In the first, even when the inner man is forgotten, he is not forsaken. The firmly established man is getting along well within, ready to make his appearance at any time. False samadhi lacks this self-mastery from the outset. There can be fighting samadhi, stealing samadhi, hating samadhi, but all without the guidance of self-mastery. These are not true samadhi as it is understood in Zen.

An animal or bird enjoys samadhi every moment. When it grazes in a meadow it is in a grazing samadhi. When it flies up at the sound of a gun, it is in a flying samadhi. Mellowed by the evening sun, standing quietly for a long time motionless in the meadow, it is in what we might call a "mellowing samadhi"—a beautiful picture and a condition to be envied even by a human being. But the animal has no self-consciousness; though much to be admired, the animal's samadhi is after all an animal samadhi, a lower state than that which man is capable of. The mellow condition attained by some under the influence of drugs like LSD, though greatly attractive to weaker characters, can be compared to that of animal samadhi. It is a retrogression to the primitive life. Not losing self-mastery but at the same time being involved in external conditions is the real meaning of "Man is deprived; circumstances are not deprived." In this state the inner man is simply inactive.

The Second Category

The second category, "Circumstances are deprived; man is not deprived," denotes inward attention. When we work on Mu or practice shikantaza, we concentrate inwardly and there develops a samadhi in which a certain self-ruling spiritual power dominates the mind. This spiritual power is the ultimate thing that we can reach in the innermost part of our existence. We do not introspect it, because subjectivity does not reflect itself, just as the eye does not see itself, but we are this ultimate thing itself. It contains in itself all sources of emotion and reasoning power, and it is a fact we directly realize in ourselves.

Rinzai Zenji calls this ultimate thing "man." When this "man" rules within us in profound samadhi, circumstances are forgotten. No outward concern appears. This state of mind is "Circumstances are deprived; man is not deprived." It is an inward samadhi and it is what I have called absolute samadhi, because it forms the foundation of all zazen practice. It contrasts with the outwardly directed samadhi described in the first category, which I call positive samadhi. Positive samadhi is a samadhi in the world of conscious activity. Absolute samadhi is a samadhi that transcends consciousness. When we simply use the term samadhi by itself we generally refer to this absolute samadhi.

The Third Category

The third category is "Both man and circumstances are deprived." A discussion of this category must be preceded by an explanation of self-consciousness. I have said that consciousness functions in two ways, outwardly and inwardly. There is another important action exercised by consciousness: one that reflects upon its own thought. This kind of reflection must be distinguished from general introspection, which deals with character or behavior. When we think, "It is fine today," we are noting the weather, but we are not noting that we are thinking about the weather. The thought about the weather may last only a fraction of a second, and unless our next action of consciousness reflects upon it and recognizes it, our thought about the weather is allowed to pass away unnoticed. Self-consciousness appears when you notice your thought, which immediately precedes your noticing it, and you then recognize the thought as your own.

If we do not perform this noticing action we do not become aware of our thinking, and we will never know that we have been conscious at all. We may call this action of noticing our own thoughts "the reflecting action of consciousness," to distinguish it from general introspection. I take some trouble to identify this reflecting action of consciousness because, as will be seen, it plays an important role in dealing with topics in zazen.

Now, when one is in absolute samadhi in its most profound phase, no reflecting action of consciousness appears. This is Rinzai's third category, "Both man and circumstances are deprived." In a more shallow phase of samadhi, a reflecting action of consciousness occasionally breaks in and makes us aware of our samadhi. Such reflection comes and goes momentarily, and each time momentarily interrupts the samadhi to a slight degree. The deeper samadhi becomes, the less frequent becomes the appearance of the reflecting action of consciousness. Ultimately the time comes when no reflection appears at all. One comes to notice nothing, feel nothing, hear nothing see nothing. This state of mind is called "nothing." But it is not vacant emptiness. Rather is it the purest condition of our existence. It is not reflected, and nothing is directly known of it. This nothingness is "Both man and circumstances are deprived," the condition Hakuin Zenji called "the Great Death." The experience of this Great Death is no doubt not common in the ordinary practice of zazen among most Zen students. Nevertheless, if you want to attain genuine enlightenment and emancipation, you must go completely through this condition, because enlightenment can be achieved only after once shaking off our old habitual way of consciousness.

Jishu-zammai

What is the difference between sleep and samadhi? Samadhi never loses its wakefulness. "Jishu-zammai" is the expression that describes the quality of samadhi. *Ji* means "self," *shu* means "mastery," and *zammai* is "samadhi," so the term denotes the samadhi of self-mastery. Jishu-zammai never loses its independence and freedom. It is spiritual power, and it contains within itself all sources of emotion and intellect. When you come out of absolute samadhi, you find yourself full of peace and serenity, equipped with strong mental power and dignity. You are intellectually alert and clear, emotionally pure and sensitive. You have the exalted condition of a great artist. You can appreciate music, art, and the beauties of nature with greatly increased understanding and delight.

Therefore, it may be, the sound of a stone striking a bamboo trunk, or the sight of blossoms, makes a vivid impression on your mind, as is related in so many descriptions of kensho. This impression is so overwhelming that "the whole universe comes tumbling down."

Kensho is nothing more nor less than your recognition of your own purified mind as it is emancipated from the delusive way of consciousness. It is rather seldom that one notices the inner man, because the reflecting action of consciousness is not at work in the most exalted moments of existence. But when your mind is projected to the outside world in the form of, say, the sound of a stone striking bamboo, or the sight of blossoms, and the sound or the sight strikes the door of your mind, you are then greatly moved by this impression, and the experience of kensho occurs. You seem to see and hear beautiful things, but the truth is that you yourself have become beautiful and exalted. Kensho is the recognition of your own purified mind in a roundabout way.

The Fourth Category

This category, "Neither man nor circumstances are deprived," is the condition attained in the Zen student's maturity. He goes out into the actual world of routine and lets his mind work with no hindrance, never losing the "man" he has established in his absolute samadhi. If we accept that there is an object in Zen practice, then it is this freedom of mind in actual living.

To put it another way: when you are mature in practicing absolute samadhi, returning to ordinary daily life you spontaneously combine in yourself the first and third categories. You are active in positive samadhi and at the same time you are firmly rooted in jishu-zammai—the self-mastery of absolute samadhi. This is "Neither man nor circumstances are deprived," the highest condition of Zen maturity. True positive samadhi achieved through Zen practice ultimately resolves itself into this fourth category.

A man may practice zazen and make certain progress in absolute samadhi and be successful in establishing the "man" within himself. Then a new problem will arise, that of how he can exercise this man in his actual life in the busy world. When sitting on the cushion doing zazen he can attain samadhi and experience the man, and can realize that the man is really his absolute self. But when he comes out into his daily routine and eats, talks, and is active in his business, he often finds he has lost the inner man. He wonders how he can manage to maintain the man in himself in his daily life.

To take another example, the Zen student may be told first to work on Mu. At first he does not know what to do with this Mu. But in the course of practice he comes to know Mu in the pure condition of his existence that appears in his samadhi, and he realizes that Mu is his own true self. But when returning to actual life he finds that even in walking his Mu is disturbed, and he is unable to maintain the condition he enjoyed in his samadhi. When he moves his spoon to his mouth, or stretches his hand to something on the table, his mind is not in the same condition as in the samadhi that he experiences at sesshin time, at the monastery or elsewhere. He would sweep, broom in hand, earnestly trying to maintain the Mu, but alas! things around him intrude into his mind or attract his eyes, and he finds he is distracted. Circumstances are rampant; man has no place to settle down in his mind. Where has the man gone who was described as "not deprived" in the second category?

The student may now change his attitude and, returning to the state of the first category, try to be absorbed in outward circumstances. But he finds this, too, very difficult. While sweeping, he cannot become sweeping itself. In other words, he is unable to forget all other things besides sweeping, as the surgeon was absorbed in his operation. Of course, when he sees a football game he becomes absorbed in it. But this is a case of passive, involuntary attention, in which anyone can be excited and shout, forgetting all other things, including the inner man. There can be absorption in fighting, absorption in dissipation, absorption in amorous passion, all with the inner man forsaken. The victim is at the mercy of outer circumstances. This is false or superficial samadhi. The samadhi of the first category is not this sort of thing. The missing ingredient is inner control, jishu-zammai. Although the man is not on the stage, in genuine samadhi he is wakeful inside.

In short, the student who is puzzled how to retain the inner man in his daily life—who wonders how he can embody Mu in himself in his actual life—is striving for the condition in which both the inner man and the outward concerns—man and circumstances—are not deprived but are freely in action. In the first category man was inactive; in the fourth category man has returned to the front line. One who has attained maturity in Zen can behave freely and does not violate the sacred law: both man and circumstances are in vigorous activity and there is no hindrance. Only maturity in Zen will secure this condition—the ultimate aim of Zen practice.

❖ CAROL P. CHRIST ❖

Carol P. Christ is a contemporary feminist writer whose works include *Laughter of Aphrodite* and *Womanspirit Rising*. She describes the piece from which this selection is taken as "a phenomenological description of *a* common pattern in women's spiritual quest." As she analyzes this quest, she notes that it takes the form of a recurring spiral rather than a linear process and that it includes four distinct components—nothingness, awakening, insight, and new naming. She indicates, moreover, the contexts and qualities that make these female experiences different from those of men. Her phenomenological analysis of the content and implications of difference marks both an addition to contemporary feminist literature and a testimony to the need for further phenomenological exploration of women's religious consciousness.

❖

Nothingness, Awakening, Insight, New Naming

Women's Spiritual Quest takes a distinctive form in the fiction and poetry of women writers. It begins in an *experience of nothingness*. Women experience emptiness in their own lives—in self-hatred, in self-negation, and in being a victim; in relationships with men; and in the values that have shaped their lives. Experiencing nothingness, women reject conventional solutions and question the meaning of their lives, thus opening themselves to the revelation of deeper sources of power and value. The experience of nothingness often precedes an awakening, similar to a conversion experience, in which the powers of being are revealed. A woman's awakening to great powers grounds her in a new sense of self and a new orientation in the world. Through awakening to new powers, women overcome self-negation and self-hatred and refuse to be victims.

Awakening often occurs through *mystical identification*, which women's traditional attunement to the body and mothering processes have prepared them for. Women's mystical experiences often occur in nature or in community with other women. Awakening is followed by a new naming of self and reality that articulates the new orientation to self and world achieved through experiencing the powers of being. Women's *new naming* of self and world often reflects wholeness, a movement toward overcoming the dualisms of self and world, body and soul, nature and spirit, rational and emotional, which have plagued Western consciousness. Women's new naming of self and world suggests directions for social change and looks forward to the realization of spiritual insight in social reality—the integration of spiritual and social quests.

Though a woman's spiritual quest may proceed linearly from the experience of nothingness, through awakening, to mystical insight, and new naming, this order is not necessary. Sometimes awakening precedes awareness of the experience of nothingness, and mystical insight can intensify a woman's experience of the nothingness of conventional reality.

It should not be assumed that a woman can ever be through with the experience of nothingness. As long as she lives—and especially in a male-centered society—the experience of nothingness will reappear. The moments of women's quest are part of a process in which experiences of nothingness, awakenings, insights, and namings form a spiral of ever-deepening but never final understanding.

The *experience of nothingness* in women's spiritual quest has analogies to the dark night described in classical mystical texts. In *The Experience of Nothingness* Michael Novak pointed out the contemporary relevance of the mystical perception of the world. For him the mystic's notion of the "dark night of the soul" provided a useful paradigm for understanding the spirit of social unrest and protest that inspired the American civil rights, antiwar, and counterculture movements of the 1960s. The experience of the dark night of the soul is well expressed in the mystic's epigram, "*if you desire to possess everything, desire to have nothing.*" For the mystic, the dark night of the soul is a period of purgation in which all ties with the conventional world are broken in anticipation of revelation and union with a higher source of being and value. The "dark night" is a metaphor for the sense of emptiness felt by those who have broken their ties with conventional sources of value, but have not yet discovered their grounding in new sources. Novak felt that the experience of nothingness did not have to be feared if it could be seen as a stage in a journey toward greater insight. He argued that the experience of nothingness is not paralyzing—it is liberating. In its dark light, nothing is beyond questioning, sacred, immobile. Nonetheless, he believed that the "experience of nothingness may be absorbed in full sanity; that a clear and troubling recognition of our fragility, our mortality, and our ignorance need not subvert our relation to the world in which we find ourselves." He felt that familiarity with the experience of nothingness was a good antidote to political naiveté and shallow idealism.

Though Michael Novak did not consider the sense of emptiness women feel as they realize their position in a world where women's experience is not valued, his notions provide a powerful paradigm for naming women's experience. Mary Daly recognized this first in her review of *The Experience of Nothingness* and later in her book *Beyond God the Father*, where the experience of nothingness is a central category in her analysis of women's quest. Every human being is vulnerable to the experience of nothingness if each is willing to recognize what Novak calls "the formlessness, the aimlessness, and the disunity implicit in [one's] own insignificance, [one's] mortality, [one's] ultimate dissolution." And while women share in the general human experience of finitude, women's experience of nothingness is more far reaching than men's. Women's experiences of nothingness begin at birth and continue throughout their lives. At a very young age a girl realizes that being female means understanding that her brothers have a right to demand more of their mother's attention, that her father will not play ball with her. Being female means that even if she gets A's, her career will not be as important as that of a boy who gets B's. Being female means that *she* is not important, except in her relationships to boys and men. Being female also means being given ambivalent messages. Parents and teachers rarely will tell a girl that she is less important than her brothers and other boys, for that would contradict the American ideal of equality and justice for all. The message of her inferiority will be communicated in more subtle ways: by lack of concern, by failure to fully nurture her potential for growth and development, by not expecting her to succeed at difficult tasks. And because the messages are mixed, a woman may feel that her mother's, father's, or teachers' lack of attention to her stems from some specific failing of her own. Internalizing the voices of her oppressors, the currents of her feelings of inferiority and self-hatred run strong and deep.

Women thus learn to doubt the value of their thoughts, their feelings, their creativity. They concede that the things women do are not valuable. They agree that making a home, rearing children, or being a nurse, secretary, or teacher are jobs requiring little creativity or skill—anyone can do them. And they believe that men's work, whether it is fixing cars, working on a factory line, building a house, or running a business, is more important than what women do. If they dare to challenge conventional patterns, they learn sooner or later that a woman's intelligence, creativity, and strength are not entirely acceptable. Qualities that are valued in men are deemed "too threatening" in women, whose attractiveness to men is based on nurturing men's creativity, not on expressing their own.

Women's feelings of inadequacy are epitomized in their feelings about their bodies. A woman can gain the approval and love of men by appearing beautiful. And yet she is also told by her mother, who communicates her own insecurities, and by the media that she is not beautiful. She must diet to rid herself of ugly fat; curl, straighten, or dye her hair; learn to apply make-up; learn how to dress; learn how to sit, stand, and walk in order to become acceptable. She must shave her legs and armpits, tweeze her eyebrows, bleach the hair on her arms and face in order to become acceptable. She must never forget perfume and deodorant. And then there is that dark space between her legs from which she bleeds each month. She must do everything she can to deny it exists. Each month she must hide the evidence of her bloody secret. She is even told to use douches or vaginal sprays to mask disgusting feminine odors. The message is clear: there is something wrong with being a woman, with her body, with being herself. Many women even learn to accept the battering of their bodies by husbands or lovers as the price they must pay to achieve acceptance. Though few women would state it so boldly, most women can understand what artist Judy Chicago meant when she wrote, "because I had a cunt, I was despised by society."

For many women the experience of nothingness is a vague sense of anxiety, or an uneasy feeling that their lives have not turned out as they expected them to. Other women experience their own nothingness so deeply that they begin to doubt the value of their own lives, to consider themselves mad, or to contemplate suicide. They do not know that their experiences are shared, even common, that they are not mad, that other women feel the same way. For just as women are excluded from autonomous significance and value in men's stories, so women must even read themselves sidewise into analyses of the experience of nothingness. Women need a literature that names their pain and allows them to use the emptiness in their lives as an occasion for insight rather than as one more indication of their worthlessness. Women need stories that will tell them that their ability to face the darkness in their lives is an indication of strength, not weakness.

Women's intense perception of their own nothingness sometimes gives them acute perceptions of the larger forces of nothingness, domination, death, and destruction that operate in men's world. They may have very clear visions of the ways in which the destructive power of men operates not only in their own personal lives, but also in the larger worlds of nature and society. Even when they cannot articulate them fully, women may sense connections between their own victimization and the relentless technological devastation of the environment, the exploitation of the poor, or the bombing of villages in foreign lands. Women's identification with the victims, combined with their own feelings of powerlessness, may explain why they often fail to get involved in conventional politics, but become involved in the struggles of oppressed groups. Women's sensitivities to the currents and forces of violence may also lead them to entertain apocalyptic visions of an ultimate destruction.

The experience of nothingness often has a different quality for women than for men. Men are not conditioned to think of themselves as worthless. For them the experience of nothingness often comes after they have taken their place in the world of male power and joined the traditional hierarchies that support men's dominance in family and society. After achieving power and respect, men may come to experience their power as illusory. They may then open themselves to a deeper experience of power "not as the world knows it." As literatures of both East and West indicate, the male mystic's quest is arduous and difficult. Men have often found it difficult to give up conventional power and ego gratification to open themselves to union with the powers of being. Women, in contrast, live in a male-defined world in which culture has, for the most part, denied them access to power. The ordinary experience of women in patriarchy is akin to the experience of nothingness. Women never have what male mystics must strive to give up. Mystic insight may therefore be easier for women to achieve than men. Women may need only to strip away the ideology of patriarchy that tells them they are fulfilled as wives and mothers in order to come face to face with the nothingness they know as lack of self, lack of power, and lack of value for women in a male-centered world. To open their eyes to the emptiness of their lives requires great courage, as Mary Daly has rightly noted, but it may be easier for women since they have less to lose.

"Awakening," the title metaphor of Kate Chopin's novel, is an appropriate term for describing change in women's consciousness. "Awakening" is a metaphor that mystics and seekers frequently use to describe the experience of enlightenment—the movement from conventional notions of the meaning of life to a more direct experience of the "really real" or ground of being, from ordinary to extraordinary consciousness, from bondage to freedom. Metaphors of sleep and waking, darkness and light seem particularly appropriate for describing this sort of spiritual experience because it involves a transition in consciousness and a new perception of reality. To one who has "awakened," conventional notions of reality seem as unreal and illusory as the world of dreams does to a person abruptly aroused from sleep. To one "enlightened," it is as if she had been trying to make out clear shapes in a dark room and suddenly the lights were turned on.

"Awakening" is perhaps a more appropriate term than "conversion" for describing women's mystical experience, because "awakening" suggests that the self needs only to notice what is already there. Awakening implies that the ability to see or to know is within the self, once the sleeping draft is refused. Conversion often seems to imply that one has turned from one source of authority to another, for example, from materialism to God. It seems to be characteristic of women's awakening that the great powers, while larger than the self, are within as well as without.

Awakening also takes a distinctive form in women's experience. As we have seen, "conversion," for men, means giving up conventional, worldly, egocentric notions of power, and trusting that genuine power is rooted in union with the powers of being. For women, awakening is not so much a giving up as a gaining of power. Women often describe their awakening as a coming to self, rather than a giving up of self, as a grounding of selfhood in the powers of being, rather than a surrender of self to the powers of being.

Women's awakening to their grounding in the powers of being often occurs through a specific *mystical experience*. By mysticism in women's experience I refer to a woman's direct experience of her grounding in the powers of being that sometimes, but not always, takes the form of identification between the self and the powers of being. Besides opening them to the experience of nothingness, traditional roles may encourage in women a habitual attitude of receptivity, thus opening them to the mystical experience of union or integration with powers. In this culture women are encouraged to be receptive to the needs of others—to please or nurture parents, children, spouses, lovers. The traditional work roles of women—such as teaching and nursing—require receptivity to others. This habitual orientation toward others often encourages women to fall into what two women theologians have called a uniquely female form of sin through self-negation. It is essential for women to move through self-negation and self-hatred to new affirmations of selfhood, power, and responsibility. But it is also important for women to name and cultivate the possible strengths that traditional roles have encouraged them to develop. If women's roles have made them open to certain kinds of spiritual experience, then this fact should not be denied, though neither should it be used to keep women in roles that are no longer meaningful for them. . . .

Simone de Beauvoir, a theorist of women's experience but not of mysticism, has noted that women often experience a transcendence in nature that is closed to them in society. "As a member of society she enters upon adult life only in becoming a woman; she pays for her liberation by an abdication. Whereas among plants and animals she is a human being; she is freed at once from her family and from the males." De Beauvoir rightly calls attention to women's exclusion from culture as one reason for their mystical experiences with nature. It should also be noted that traditional cultural associations of women with nature and the conventional limitation of their sphere to children, home, and garden also encourage women to be open to mystical experiences in nature. In almost all cultures, women's bodily experiences of menstruation, pregnancy, childbirth, and lactation, combined with their cultural roles of caring for children, the sick, the dying, and the dead have led to the cultural association of women with the body and nature, and men with culture, the spirit, and transcendence. Whether or not women really are closer to nature than men, cultural attitudes and cultural roles have encouraged women to develop a sense of their own affinity with nature. Poet Susan Griffin, who has explored many aspects of women's feelings of connection to nature, writes, "The earth is my sister; I love her daily grace, her silent daring . . . and I do not forget: what she is to me, what I am to her."

Women's mystical experiences in nature also provide them with a sense of authentic selfhood. Feminist literary critic Annis Pratt concludes that for many women "communion with the authentic self, first achieved by the heroine in early naturistic epiphanies, becomes a touchstone by which she holds herself together in the face of destructive roles proffered to her by society." Women's experiences in nature are extremely significant because they can occur in solitude when a woman feels isolated from other people and has nowhere to turn. When in the depths of despair and loneliness many women are rescued by sensing their grounding in nature.

While mystical experiences in nature frequently provide women with a sense of authentic selfhood, many also have mystical experiences in society or community. Many women writers also reflect a sensibility that I call social or communal mysticism. In this form of mysticism, the great powers to which women awaken are experienced through social groups or movements, rather than through nature. In this form of mystical insight, a specific social or political movement, such as the antiwar movement or the women's movement, is not deified or treated as the ultimate power. Instead it is recognized that great powers are revealed through such movements and that the quests for truth or justice or being which they embody are rooted in the powers of being. Social mysticism may be considered analogous to the Christian notion of "community of saints" or the Jewish "all Israel," images of a community united by its relationship to greater powers in which a mystical unity between the dead, the living, and those yet to be born is affirmed.

After a woman experiences the grounding of her quest in the powers of being, it is important for her to name her experience in words. When one woman puts her experiences into words, another woman who has kept silent, afraid of what others will think, can find validation. And when the second woman says aloud, "Yes, that was my experience too," the first woman loses some of her fear. "The dream of a common language," which Adrienne Rich has movingly depicted, is realized in the moment when two women acknowledge each other and themselves. Their act creates new possibilities of being and living for themselves and for all women. With the creation of a new language, the possibility that women will forget what they know is lessened.

Women have called the process of giving form to their experience through words a *new naming*. Mary Daly has spoken of the Genesis story of Adam's naming of woman and the animals as paradigmatic of a cosmic "false naming" in which women and the world have been named only from men's point of view. As women begin to name the world for themselves not only will they create new life possibilities for women, they will also upset the world order that has been taken for granted for centuries. "What would happen if one woman told the truth about her life?" asks poet Muriel Rukeyser. "The world would split open." Women's speech has the potential to transform the way people view the world. The subordination of women not only has been taken for granted by philosophers and poets whose writings have shaped Western consciousness, but the assumption of women's secondary status also has influenced philosophers' and poets' perceptions of the nature of authority and hierarchy, and of the relation of spirit and flesh, humanity and nature, body and soul. All of these subtle and not-so-subtle relationships will be challenged and, I hope, transformed as women begin to write out of their own experience. . . .

❖ LOUIS DUPRÉ ❖

The essential phenomenology of religion has also had a wider influence, most notably in the philosophical study of religion. In the following article Louis Dupré, a professor of religion at Yale University and the author of numerous books and articles on phenomenology and the philosophy of religion, applies phenomenological categories to problems in the philosophy of religion.

More specifically, he questions whether the phenomenology of religion can adequately express the transcendence and real existence of the religious object as attested by the religious believer. He also challenges the adequacy of any philosophical account of religious experience which is not squarely grounded in that experience but rather in autonomous reflection transcendentally divorced from that experience. Finally, he explores the contribution of Henry Duméry's phenomenological reflections on religion and praises his insights into the existence of the transcendent in the immanent. For Dupré phenomenology alone may be unable to provide the ultimate foundation for a satisfactory philosophy of religion. Nevertheless, no philosophy of religion will be satisfactory which does not incorporate a phenomenologically accurate account of religious experience.

❖

Philosophy of Religion and Revelation: Autonomous Reflection vs. Theophany

Limitations of Psychology of Religion

That Phenomenology was a reaction against psychologism is nowhere more evident than in the phenomenology of religion. Until recently its importance in this area lay more in the refutation of the psychological approach than in its positive contribution. It was obvious enough that behaviorism would never be able to comprehend a religious act in which the motivation is all-important. Yet, as Scheler pointed out, introspective psychology equally fails to grasp the essence of the religious phenomenon, for by limiting its investigation to the subject and its changes it excludes the object of the religious experience. Any claim of psychology to a full understanding of the religious experience, therefore, assumes that the religious act can be explained entirely as a subjective experience. Indeed, empirical psychology deals exclusively with the reality of the experience (i.e., its subjective, empirical aspect) and does not consider its intentional, ideal aspect.

If psychology ignores this limitation (which is not always the case—think of William James' *Varieties of Religious Experience*), it will interpret the religious experience entirely by its genetic process or by the partial elements of which the experience is composed. But to do this is to overlook the fact that the experience is determined by its objective intentionality. A psychological explanation may be instructive as regards the building material (the *Bausteine*) of the religious consciousness, but it never comes to grips with the religious consciousness as consciousness, i.e., as a subject ideally related to an object without ever coinciding with it. To "explain" the entire religious experience psychologically is to assume that religion is not more than the sum of some other, simpler experiences. Religion then is reduced to the non-religious: it is an expression of fear, a projection of the individual's feeling of inferiority with respect to the totality of the human race, or a sublimation of man's sexual drive. Psychological elementarism can easily be refuted, for the simple elements into which the religious experience is broken down are also conscious and, therefore, just as intentional as the total experience was.

The psychoanalytic interpretation, on the other hand, is more sophisticated in that it explains the religious experience by means of elements of a different nature (subconscious) rather than subordinating one conscious experience to another. Yet, even here the fact remains that wherever psychoanalysis pretends to possess a full understanding of man's religious activity, it dogmatically assumes that this activity can be explained through the real elements of the experience (which are different from the experience itself) rather than through its own ideal intentionality. We should not be surprised to learn that with this approach religion turns out to be an illusion. Accordingly, we would agree with Scheler when he writes:

The psychological processes which, as observed by introspection, are active within the praying subject, and the manner of their activity— these are matters as indifferent for the nature of the act of prayer as are a mathematician's indigestion or his fantasies, while he thinks a problem over, for the noetics of mathematics. The act of prayer can be defined only from the meaning of prayer.

But this verdict by no means excludes psychology from the study of religion. It is true that psychology is unable to explain why two plus two equals four, but it still has the task to determine how people reach this conclusion and, even more importantly, why some people do not. Psychology becomes an indispensable aid in discovering inauthentic elements in someone's religious experience. To do this the psychologist does not need to have a clear idea of what religion is in itself, for that does not belong to his domain. It suffices that, within the limits of his science, he is able to reduce alleged religious phenomena to pathological states of which one knows the symptoms and the origin (e.g., hysteria). Wherever he is able to do this one may safely conclude that the experience was neither entirely pure nor authentic. This task, however negative, is very important; for in the actual experience there is no such thing as "pure religion." The act may be authentic insofar as it has a noema and an intentionality of its own which it shares with no other act, but it is always given in a real experience determined by the totality of man's psychic life. To the extent that the real is the necessary condition of the ideal (the intentional), all religious activity is determined by a person's psychic constitution, and this is certainly the domain of psychology.

Limitations of the Phenomenology of Religion

Assuming, then, with the phenomenologists that empirical psychology deals with the real and phenomenology with the ideal, the question arises whether phenomenology itself is sufficiently equipped to provide an adequate explanation of the religious act. The discussion which started years ago and is still continuing today makes the answer to this question somewhat less than self-evident. There seem to be at least two requirements for an understanding of the religious act which phenomenology, insofar as it remains pure phenomenology, is hard put to fulfill: one is the maintenance of the transcendence of the religious object; the other, the insistence on its real existence (over and above its intentional being).

Problem I: Transcendence of the Religious Object

The first requirement could be summarized in the following way: if the specific character of the object of religion is to be transcendent, its essence remains hidden from autonomous reflection and can only be an object of faith. This creates a serious difficulty for the phenomenologist, who through his science claims to reach an intuition of the object of the experience. Scheler hardly seems to be aware of the problem. According to him, God is revealed symbolically in the world and its structure, and man knows him in these symbols through a direct, non-rational intuition. In spite of all his insistence on the negative character of this insight, Scheler seems to defend a *Wesensschau* of the divine which comes very close to compromising either the transcendence of the religious object or the purely natural character of phenomenology.

Van der Leeuw is more careful and makes a distinction between religion-as-experience and religion-as-transcendent (and therefore scientifically incomprehensible) revelation. Considered from the first point of view, religion is a search for the meaning of life in its totality:

But this meaning is never understood, this last word is never spoken; always they remain superior, the ultimate meaning being a secret which reveals itself repeatedly, only nevertheless to remain eternally concealed. It implies an advance to the farthest boundary, where only one sole fact is understood—that all comprehension is 'beyond'; and thus the ultimate meaning is at the same moment the limit of meaning.

This immanent experience does not contain the transcendent element of revelation, which can never be a phenomenon. At most, religion-as-experience points towards the necessity of revelation because of its own essential insufficiency. Phenomenology describes only this immanent experience of man's reaching toward a transcendent and phenomenologically unknown being.

However, it would seem that religion, in the proper sense, does not reach toward an unknown object (that is what the outsider sees in it); it attains its transcendent object; but precisely because the object is transcendent, it attains it only in faith. We would therefore conclude that for the religious man (and it is his experience which phenomenology describes) there is no distinction between an immanent reaching toward, and the attainment in fact of, a transcendent object. If the object of the religious act is transcendent, then it can only be an object of faith. The opposite is also true faith alone makes an object sacred. As Eliade shows, no particular object is sacred in itself; it is the religious attitude which converts the profane into the sacred by subsuming it under its own intentionality. This is true for the primitive man as well as for the Christian or Jew of our own age: only the religious attitude makes the acts and words of Christ or the prophets into sacred history and sacred doctrine. Now if the religious object is always an object of faith which can be grasped only in faith, the question becomes all the more urgent whether it does not altogether lie outside the boundaries of the phenomenological *epoché*. Moreover if the object falls beyond the scope of the phenomenologist's inquiry, the entire act which is specified by it becomes equally unknown.

To avoid such a conclusion, Van der Leeuw, who agrees that all religion is based on faith, distinguishes between theological faith (faith directly determined by a revelation) and the faith into which all understanding turns as soon as it realizes that the ground of understanding does not lie in itself but in some "other" all-comprehending being. Only the latter would be open to phenomenology. But even this distinction does not seem to be sufficient, for religious faith differs from any other form of belief in that it is directly specified by what the believer takes to be a transcendent revelation. It is always theological faith. Precisely because of this specification by its object, a correct understanding of the religious act cannot ignore altogether the revelation in which it originates. And this revelation is for the believer a revelation of the transcendent, which cannot be understood by autonomous reflection alone.

Of course, the phenomenologist will claim (and rightly so) that his own attitude is different from the believer's in that it abstains from all ontological value-judgment. He is concerned with what appears in consciousness: the transcendent object of the revelation interests him only to the extent that it is intended by an immanent experience. The notion of transcendence is phenomenologically relevant only insofar as it enters into the immanent experience. What the transcendent object is *in itself,* i.e., beyond its relation to the immanent being of consciousness, is un-important. Has God *really* spoken to man? Does the transcendent really communicate with the immanent being of consciousness? Those questions do not interest phenomenology.

It would be a mistake, however, to interpret this bracketing of the transcendent as if phenomenology considered only the logical coherence of the affirmations made in faith and not the modality of faith itself which inspired them, for this modality enters into the very meaning of the religious assertion. It is all too obvious that the meaning of an affirmation made in faith is different from the same affirmation made without faith. To illustrate this point we could compare it with the differences of meaning which an identical statement can have within and outside a poetic context. In the first case we will encounter secondary meanings, emotive import, and certain connotations which are absent from the second, and which can be grasped only by someone who is in the right disposition. We must disagree, therefore, with Dumery's thesis that the modality of faith belongs to the *credo* (the real experience) and not to the *creditum* (the ideal element of the experience, particularly the *noema*), which alone is being considered by the phenomenologist. The modality of faith is part of the ideal *noesis*: as such it profoundly influences the noema and may not be relegated to the existential part of the judgment which is bracketed in the phenomenological analysis. To abstract the terms from the modality of faith in which they are elicited is to take away the very element in which they make *religious* sense. To isolate the affirmation of the believer from his belief is to change the affirmation itself. Religious affirmations (and all religious acts are affirmations) have only one meaning: the meaning which they have for the believer.

But to place the religious affirmation in its own modality is to take it as a response to a transcendent (and, therefore, trans-phenomenological) call. A full understanding of the religious act, then, is impossible without taking into account a transcendent intervention (be it as subjective attraction or as objective revelation), since it is precisely this transcendent element which in the believer's mind gives its specific meaning to the religious act. To bracket the transcendent entirely is to interpret this act in such a way that no religious person will recognize it.

The conclusion, therefore, seems unavoidable that phenomenology can provide an authentic interpretation of the religious act only when it considers the immanent being of consciousness in its essential connection with the trans-phenomenological object of the act. To do this it must partly abandon its autonomy and share to some extent the faith which both contributes and preserves the transcendent character of the religious object. Of course, if this meant merely that there must be an intimate connection between the living religious experience and the phenomenological reflection upon this experience, phenomenology of religion would not be more difficult than that of other experiences. But other experiences bring their objects intentionally within the immanent realm of consciousness, whereas the religious act, although attaining its object, never possesses it. The paradox of the act of faith is that it makes its object immanent only by constituting it as entirely transcendent; it throws a bridge over a gap which it declares to be unbridgeable. The religious experience, therefore, never becomes completely immanent; its immanent being retains an essential incompleteness, due to the evasive and transcendent character of its object, which is unique in human experience. We may conclude, then, that no purely phenomenological analysis can adequately describe the religious act, because the object of this act never becomes sufficiently immanent in the experience to allow a complete analysis of the act without recurring to a transcendent and, therefore, transphenomenological datum.

This conclusion by no means denies phenomenology the right to deal with the religious experience nor does it deny that religion and its object have an immanent aspect as well as a transcendent. If there is a religious *experience* at all, it must obviously be immanent and, consequently, describable in a purely phenomenological fashion. But the immanence of the religious act is such that it constantly *transcends* itself in an intentionality which ultimately escapes the purely phenomenological analysis.

One cannot simply bracket the transcendent aspect of the religious object without losing the meaning of the act determined by this object. By its very nature, phenomenology is concerned merely with the immanent being of consciousness, but in the case of religion this immanent being itself can be understood only when seen in its essential connection with the transcendent. To see this connection requires some dependence upon faith.

This dependence, however, does not imply the need for a personal faith on the part of the phenomenologist, at least not during the phenomenological analysis. Even less does it imply that personal experience is a sufficient basis for phenomenological analysis: phenomenology is not introspection but description of consciousness as such. And this requires reflection upon much more than one's private experience. To discover the essence of the religious experience, the phenomenologist must familiarize himself with religious types of ages and civilizations so different from his own that a direct experience is excluded. Yet, without some personal religious experience he is unable to get any essential insight into the anthropological and historical material upon which he must necessarily rely, and the full meaning of the religious act remains closed to him.

Problem II: Real Existence of the Religious Object

The dependence of phenomenology on faith brings up the second problem: How can the phenomenological *epoché* be maintained when a principle of understanding is involved which is always committed to the *real* existence of the transcendent object? Unlike other thetic acts, the religious affirmation, because of its essential incompleteness, presents itself as *intrinsically* dependent upon a being other than the being of consciousness in which it takes place. To grasp the meaning of the act one must be able to share, at least ideally, in the believer's faith in a transconscious existence. How can this be done within the phenomenological *epoché*?

Scheler goes even further and claims that the religious act cannot be understood at all without an *actual* acceptance of its object's real existence. According to him, the intentional acts to which no finite object (nor a synthesis of finite objects) corresponds remain incomprehensible unless one accepts a transcendent realm of infinite being.

Only a real being with the essential character of divinity can be the cause of man's religious propensity, that is, propensity to execute in a real sense acts of that class whose acts, though finite experience cannot fulfill them, nevertheless demand fulfillment. The *object* of the religious acts is at the same time the *cause* of their existence. In other words, all knowledge of God is necessarily knowledge from God.

If religious acts form an essential class of mental acts, irreducible to any others, then we are obliged to assume a separate domain of reality corresponding to those acts. Not to do so would be to reduce one intentionality to another, as in the psychological fallacy.

The least one can say about this strange, ontological argument is that it oversteps the boundaries of the phenomenological method. To conclude from the fact that the religious act *intends* its object as *really* existent to the object's actual existence is to abandon all restrictions of the phenomenological *epoché*. Phenomenology deals with immanent being: it considers only the ideal being of consciousness. The intentional object is present only in its ideal aspect and the phenomenologist knows nothing of an existence beyond consciousness. To be sure, phenomenology uses the notion "transcendent being" in discussing consciousness' relation to the world, but this "transcendence" is no more than an indicator of immanent being: it refers to the sort of immanent being which is not revealed at once (as the object of introspection) but through an infinite series of perspective variations. Now, it may be possible on the basis of an analysis of the religious act or of consciousness itself to conclude to another sort of transcendence which—as opposed to that of the world which is not immanent because not given at once, hence defective— would be immanent *per excessum*, a ground of consciousness which could never be grasped in itself but only in its manifestations. Yet, again, within the limits of his method, the phenomenologist can never conclude to an existence independent of consciousness, and whatever transcendence he attains is restricted to the ideal order. This will not satisfy the believer, but if he wants to keep his method clean, the phenomenologist must abstain from all affirmations of *real* existence.

Why, then, did Scheler indulge in such an affirmation? It is inconceivable that he would have overlooked so basic a principle of the phenomenological method. I rather suspect that Scheler's position results from his awareness that the religious act cannot be understood unless we somehow follow the believer in his affirmation of the object's transconscious existence. Since phenomenology as pure science of immanent being is unable to do this, Scheler consciously ignores the restrictions imposed by its method and moves on into what he would call essential phenomenology and what is in fact an ontology of the religious act.

Limitations of Philosophy of Religion

Now, it is obvious that philosophy is able to cope with problems of existence. But this by no means diminishes the difficulty in understanding the religious act. Indeed, the question is not whether philosophy is able to cope with existence, but whether it is able to understand the religious act (including the fact that it affirms its objects as really existing) without invoking extra-philosophical principles. And here again it would seem to us that any autonomous philosophy of religion has proved to be a failure.

Looking at what philosophy of religion has actually accomplished in the past, one cannot but find its results disappointing. In most cases it turns out to be a substitute for religion which no religious person could accept. (The most illustrious example of this to my knowledge is John Dewey's *A Common Faith*.) The main reason for this failure lies in philosophy's desire to be autonomous. But if the object of the religious act is transcendent (and without the note of transcendence the believer will not consider it to be religious), then it is *given* from beyond and not *produced* by autonomous reflection. However, the very nature of philosophy makes it difficult for the philosopher to accept an experience which he is unable to explain in its totality. Rather than receive its object, philosophy of religion prefers to create it. The result is either an autonomous reflection in which the religious experience no longer recognizes itself—as in Kant's *Religion within the Limits of Reason Alone*—or a system which absorbs the transcendent elements of religion and then presents itself as an independent reflection (equally unacceptable to the believer and the philosopher)—as in Hegel's *Philosophy of Religion*.

The temptation to convert philosophy of religion into a religion of its own will always be strong, for two reasons. One is philosophy's ideal of constructing a coherent and self-supporting system. This remains true today, even though most philosophers have abandoned the nineteenth-century dream of bringing man's entire universe together in one vast synthesis. As much as his predecessors, the contemporary philosopher strives to understand the data on which he reflects to their utmost limit. Such is particularly the case with the object of religion, since it does not lie entirely beyond the scope of an autonomous philosophical investigation. Most metaphysical systems in the past have concluded to some sort of infinite being which, though itself beyond philosophical comprehension, must exist as the key to the comprehension of the world of experience. Throughout the ages great philosophers, such as Plato, Aristotle, Thomas, Descartes, Kant, and Hegel have found it necessary to provide a proof for the existence of an absolute being which they assumed to be the object of religion. From such a proof to a full and autonomous explanation of the religious experience is only one step—and, unfortunately, most philosophies of religion have taken that step.

The second reason why philosophy of religion all too often becomes a new religion is to be found in religion itself. Every religion has a Gnostic tendency which, if not carefully checked, transforms it into a philosophy. Reflection is an essential part of the religious experience: the religious act necessarily tends toward ever greater clarification. The *fides quaerens intellectum* is not an invention of philosophers but of theologians, and in the Christian tradition it has been practiced ever since the Fourth Gospel. However, if this desire for insight is not controlled by a strong sense of the transcendence of the *mysterium tremendum*, religion gradually abandons its original character and becomes philosophical speculation. Since religion claims its content to be in accordance with reason, philosophy of religion is entirely in order, but the moment religion is treated as if its content were merely rational it ceases to be religion and becomes something else.

In its study of what it takes to be the object of religion, an autonomous philosophy may well be able to conclude to the existence of an infinite and perfect being (which is more than phenomenology could ever do) but this insight is not directly relevant for the understanding of the object of the religious act. Unless philosophy studies this object from religion's own point of view, it will fall into the error, denounced by Scheler, of identifying two differently intended objects without proving that they are really identical. It is this gratuitous identification of a philosophical conclusion with the living object of man's religion, rather than any anti-intellectual bias, which made Pascal cry for the God of Abraham, Isaac, and Jacob—and not the God of the philosophers. The philosopher's conclusion is of no avail to the religious man who fails to recognize his God in this existing all-perfect being.

As long as philosophy of religion refuses to accept, in the words of Professor John Smith, that the religious content comes from beyond philosophy rather than being constituted by philosophical reflection, it does not take the religious content seriously but instead substitutes one of its own. To avoid this mistake, it is not sufficient merely that the philosopher work in close contact with religion (Hegel certainly did that); his philosophy itself must abdicate its autonomy. The content of faith can communicate itself only in the act of faith, and this act can be fully understood only by him who has had it. Rather than become a substitute for this act, philosophy of religion must make itself subordinate to it.

Philosophy of religion should be a critical reflection upon a *given* religious reality. Within the given context of faith it must analyze the meaning of the act and determine its various noetic structures.

What this implies has been described in Duméry's *Philosophy of Religion*, even though Duméry himself violates the restrictions which he set himself in his methodology.

A New Approach to Philosophy of Religion: Henri Duméry

Religion is always more than a mere speculative relation to the transcendent; it involves man's total existence in the world in its attempt to transcend this world. The religious consciousness projects its own intentionality on the world in liturgy, sacraments, sacred history, etc. It belongs to the philosopher's task to show how these projections have their origin in the religious impulse and remain related to it. But in doing this he should be on his guard against the temptation to create a "higher" religion in the form of a pure idea. The philosopher always has a tendency to *demythologize*, since he never finds the religious symbols adequate to express the surge of man toward the transcendent (precisely because the religious movement always goes beyond the symbols which it uses). Yet, if demythologizing means to replace archaic schemas and fossilized symbols by new ones, then it is not the task of the philosopher: religion alone can produce more adequate projections. The expression in schemas and symbols is an essential part of the religious act and only this act can give them their proper meaning and sense. Philosophy is not hierophanic; it can criticize but not create. If, however, demythologizing means to "purify" religion of its symbolic and imaginative elements altogether, then it should not be done at all, since these elements, however inadequate, are essential. Religion is never pure interiority, it involves man's total existence in the world. As Duméry writes, faith is the living conviction that there is more in time than time, more in man than man, but what surpasses time and what surpasses man cannot act and have meaning for us other than in time and in man. Religion discovers the transcendent in the immanent—it is active on all levels of human existence at once and integrates them all into one intentionality toward the transcendent.

The great quality of Duméry's philosophy of religion is to have shown that the religious experience is a total experience, irreducible to reason alone or to any single level of human experience. He thereby escapes the rationalism inherent in the interpretations of most of his predecessors. Unfortunately, he has not escaped their gnosticism. Although he does not restrict the religious activity to the requirements of reason, he reduces it to the immanent dynamism of consciousness as a *totality*. In order to maintain simultaneously the absolute transcendence of the religious object and the autonomy of the subject, Duméry interprets all determinations of the religious act—including the most basic ones of creation and salvation—as structures created by the mind itself in its dynamic ascent to a mystery which is neither determined nor determining. All his efforts to preserve the transcendence of the religious object are of no avail, since he ultimately sacrifices the transcendent aspect of the act itself: even though the religious impulse takes its origin in the transcendent ground of consciousness, the concrete determinations in which this impulse expresses itself are entirely immanent. These determinations merely function as constructions to carry the mind's dynamism toward the ground of its own creative activity. They are posited, rather than received, by the mind.

It is obvious that such a conception ultimately abandons the notion of a revelation as positive communication from the transcendent. The eternal object of the revelation, as well as its historical manifestations, is deprived of the very determinations which for the faithful make the religious experience more than an immanent striving of the mild toward the ground of all being. The Christian dogma of the Holy Trinity, for example, no longer attains the reality of God himself, since God, according to Duméry, is incommunicable; rather it is a logical construction, determined by a cultural tradition, which the mind *uses* in its surge toward an inaccessible transcendent.

The same is true for the historical events of religion. Duméry does not deny their historical authenticity nor the impact which they have had upon religion, but for him the historical character of the event remains entirely subordinate to the universal meaning which the religious mind bestows upon it. Duméry takes great pains to prove that this religious meaning is by no means an arbitrary one, left to the individual consciousness. The original interpretation of the Christ-fact was given by Christ himself and was developed by his early followers: later generations of Christians received rather than created the meaning of Jesus' life, death, and resurrection. Yet, the importance which the events themselves have for the believer is entirely shifted to the universal and a-historical meaning attributed to them by an autonomous consciousness. Christ thereby becomes more a genial interpreter of man's profoundest strivings than a transcendent savior. The distinction between myth and history all but disappears: in both cases the fact is incidental and the interpretation becomes all important.

But the believer cannot accept as autonomous structures religious determinations which he considers to be part of a heteronomous revelation. Faith is more than a profound attitude which expresses itself on the various levels of consciousness in myths, rites, schemas, and categories. As Jean Daniélou says:

It is the adherence to affirmations which are irreducible to rational necessity and which derive their certitude from the authority of the revealed word. It is clear that this appeal to authority appears to Duméry as the strengthening of external representations which should instead be reduced. But at once it is faith itself in its specificity that is eliminated.

One wonders whether Duméry's difficulties and those of philosophy of religion in general are not due to the nature of modern philosophy itself. Most philosophies of religion, for example, have been written within systems which make the acceptance of a revelation all but impossible. The concept of revelation requires a notion of intersubjectivity which until recently was entirely lacking in philosophy. Even more indispensable is a theory of the self's ontological connection with the transcendent. Unless the relation to the transcendent is from the beginning considered as essential, any later discussion of a communication between the transcendent and the self (which religion always implies) is bound to be arbitrary. A philosophy which first develops a notion of the self as a vertically closed entity is obviously unable to cope with the religious experience. But more than mere openness is required, for almost any philosophy has some notion of transcendence: the relation must be *constitutive* of the self. Only a philosophy which relates the self *essentially* to the transcendent can afford to be non-autonomous and allow for a transcendent communication with the self. It might be objected that for Duméry the relation to the transcendent *is* constitutive of the self. This is true, but his notion of an undetermined, undetermining transcendent is such that all real communication with the self is excluded. At least, then, on the level of action, the self for Duméry is an autonomous and totally immanent being.

To my knowledge, none of the major philosophical systems of modern times possesses both a notion of the self and a theory of intersubjectivity which would enable them to achieve an adequate reflection on the religious experience. We do find it, however, in less systematic thinkers, such as Schleiermacher, Kierkegaard, and Jaspers. They might be called *religious* philosophers, regardless of their personal beliefs, insofar as they make the relation to the transcendent into the very basis of the person. Yet, precisely because their whole philosophy is religious, these thinkers are less inclined to make religion a special object of study. Schleiermacher is an exception, but only because his whole philosophy has no other purpose than to justify an *a priori* accepted revelation. Strange as it may seem, the very fact that philosophers found it necessary to devote a special study to the religious experience was, in the past, almost always an indication that they had not considered man's relation to the transcendent where it must be considered in order to make a full understanding of this experience possible—in the beginning.

No satisfactory philosophy of religion exists today, and yet it is needed. The many data which the religious sciences have recently uncovered call for an ultimate foundation which phenomenology alone is unable to provide. The existence of these data is a challenge to any philosophy of religion in the future. It will no longer be possible to institute a reflection upon the religious experience without having studied carefully the positive elements of the experience itself. If philosophy persists in constructing an autonomous reflection which ignores the data of the real experience, it will be dismissed not only by the believer, as it was in the past, but also by the religious scientists.

❖

Social and Symbolic Forms of the Sacred

(Historical-Typological Phenomenology of Religion)

❖ C. J. ARTHUR ❖

C. J. Arthur, whose publications include *In the Hall of Mirrors*, is a professor in theology and religious studies at the University of Wales. The following essay makes a series of cogent methodological remarks about the past history and future prospects of the phenomenology of religion. Additionally, it discusses the fascinating phenomenological description of prehistoric religiousness developed in William Golding's novel, *The Inheritors*.

As Arthur shows, Golding portrays an encounter between Neanderthal and Cro-Magnon groups and by accepting their conceptual and linguistic limitations brilliantly depicts their consciousness and understanding. Moreover, Golding displays many important features of Neanderthal religious experience including cultic cannibalism, burial rituals, the cosmological and ecological meaning of fire in the social world of the Neanderthal, and the important role of women within their society. This essay, then, specifies features of prehistoric religion and raises them up for further historical and typological comparison with similar elements in other eras. Finally, this selection invites comparison with several other selections in this volume regarding the structures, dynamics, and mutability of religious meaning in human experience.

❖

Phenomenology of Religion and the Art of Story-telling: The Relevance of William Golding's 'The Inheritors' to Religious Studies

I. Introduction

One of the most extensive yet least conclusive methodological debates within religious studies revolves around the question of what, precisely, the phenomenology of religion is and what contribution it can make to the study of religion. I do not intend to answer this important question here. To do so satisfactorily would require a range of historical, philosophical and methodological inquiry which would go quite beyond the bounds of a single article. My intention in this paper is, by comparison, unambitious. It is to take one view of what phenomenology of religion is and to consider an area outside that usually explored by students of religion which can, nonetheless, shed some light on how religions might be studied in a way which is in accordance with the phenomenology of religion so understood. What follows will offer an answer to the question of what contribution one particular understanding of phenomenology might make to the study of religion, but no attempt will be made to establish whether or not this particular understanding ought to be regarded as normative.

It will be helpful in understanding what follows to note two assumptions which are being made. Firstly, much of the confusion about phenomenology of religion stems from too many statements about what it is, or ought to be, or will be, and not enough actual instances of its attempted application. If the debate is to proceed beyond the frustrations of untested methodology, a change of emphasis is needed such that less time is spent on theoretical discussions and more attention is given to how particular recommendations made by those who advocate a phenomenological approach can be applied to specific situations. Such a change of emphasis will occur in Section IV. Secondly, the seriousness and persistence with which phenomenology of religion is discussed, stems largely from the fact that the issues which it raises question the very nature of religious studies, a discipline notoriously unsure of its identity (witness the host of uneasy aliases: "comparative religion," "history of religion(s)," "science of religion," and of course "religious studies" and "phenomenology of religion" too). The confusion about phenomenology of religion is, to some extent, at least in its wider context, simply a confusion about how to study religion in a way that is non-partisan and non-theological, and it is indicative of deep-seated uncertainties about the intention, procedure and desired outcome of such an endeavor. Any contribution to the phenomenological debate may thus, without fear of undue digression, address some therapeutic comments to what has been termed the "profound methodological confusion" current in the general area of religious studies. Some such comments will be offered in Sections V and VI.

Before considering the particular view of phenomenology of religion on which our attention will be focused, the subject of Section III, I want first to look very briefly at something of the general confusion in this area.

II. The Phenomenology of Religion: A Confusion Observed

As Hans Penner has put it, anyone who wants to find out what phenomenology of religion is and how it is applied "will find the search a frustrating experience." To illustrate the cause of such frustration would not be difficult, for rather than any embarrassing silence it is the sheer number or conflicting replies to the question "what is phenomenology of religion?" which makes it so difficult to reach any satisfactory answer. Investigating the religious problems of man's nature and destiny, analysing the subjective manifestations of a religious sense in consciousness, conducting a systematic treatment of the history of religion in an attempt to arrive at an overview, and simply doing comparative religion under a new name—all these tasks have been presented as constituting the phenomenology of religion, and this is to abstract only a small sample of opinions from work in this field.

However, rather than presenting a lengthy catalogue of different views as to how phenomenology of religion might be seen, in order to show the extent of existing lack of agreement among scholars, I will take a short-cut which avoids going over too much old ground. By simply noting Penner's frustration and recording very briefly some similar reactions from others who have likewise been concerned with this topic, we can, I think, accept that there is considerable confusion here without having to survey that confusion in great detail or immerse ourselves in it directly.

Thus Eric Sharpe has suggested that "in potential scope and ambiguity" the term "phenomenology of religion" now equals the position once held by "comparative religion." Indeed, such is the confusion that it sometimes seems as if "even the scholars who use this term and claim to apply this method to their work, are not always sure as to its precise definition."

Now, of course, just because we cannot clearly define something does not necessarily mean that we do not know what it is ("religion" is a case in point, where though we might know quite adequately what the word means, formulating a satisfactory definition of it remains problematic). However, when it comes to a methodology as opposed to its subject matter, the lack of any satisfactory definitional formulation does seem to raise doubts about the extent to which we have a clear grasp of what we are trying to do. Accordingly, Klaus Klostermaier suggests that phenomenology of religion may, in fact, be little more than "a cover up for methodological confusion," and Charles Davis goes so far as to conclude that "the term 'phenomenology of religion' has no clear meaning and is better dropped because of misleading associations. It could be kept simply to refer historically to a number of writers who have used it." Obviously if such views expressed all that could be said about it, the phenomenology of religion would cease to be a problem—for it might then simply be jettisoned as misleading and our studies could proceed unencumbered by its troublesome vocabulary. However, although such comments as those of Penner, Sharpe, Klostermaier and Davis may well tempt us to ask if phenomenology of religion is worth the frustration and confusion which its manifold interpretations seem inevitably to cause, it is as well to re-member that underlying the whole discussion, even if it is now sometimes quite obscured by it, is the contention that phenomenology provides methodological guidelines of immense importance to the student of re-ligion. Thus Raffaele Pettazzoni, writing in 1954, suggested that "phe-nomenology represents the most important innovation which has come about in the realm of our studies during the last half century." And, more recently, Åke Hultkrantz has argued—*despite* his finding it immensely difficult to suggest any satisfactory definition of it—that phenomenology of religion is the methodological ideal towards which all empirical research in this area must aspire. Similarly, after noting the existing confusion and recommending a way of dealing with it, Michael Pye suggests that simply as a method which sets the discipline religious studies apart from its older sibling, Christian theology, phenomenology is quite essential.

Before the confusion about it can be properly resolved, some sort of clarifying genealogy for phenomenology of religion needs to be established in which its origins are identified, its development traced and the relationships between its various forms made clear. As Paul Ricoeur has observed with quiet understatement, the term "phenomenology" by itself is "not very illuminating," for since it has come to mean "science of appearances or appearings," "any inquiry or work devoted to the way anything whatsoever appears is already phenomenology." There is, however, no guarantee that order can be brought to the many interpretations allowed by such an understanding simply by returning to some original, authoritative source and setting it up as standard, for, as Herbert Spiegelberg notes in his definitive survey of the phenomenological movement, "in its early history the term 'phenomenology' seems to have been invented several times independently." Quite apart from the difficulties involved in firmly establishing their respective meanings, the relationship between the terms "phenomenology" and "phenomenology of religion" is far from clear. In particular, for those approaching the field today, there is a need to clarify the relationship between the philosophical phenomenology of Husserl and the phenomenology of religion. As things stand, there seems to be little doubt that to continue to speak of phenomenology of religion without careful qualification is to risk perpetuating, if not enlarging, the present unsatisfactory situation.

The task of clarification is, however, a large-scale one which extends far outside the boundaries of this paper. Returning to the smaller canvas which I wish to work upon here: from the tangle of phenomenologies of religion I wish to abstract a single thread. Once the features on this thread have been clearly identified we can proceed to an examination of its methodology in action and a consideration of what it can contribute to the study of religion.

III. Phenomenology of Religion as Imaginative Re-experiencing

In 1885 Friedrich Max Müller, editor of the epoch making *Sacred Books of the East*, remarked to one of his house guests who did not share the same teleological views, "If you say that all is not made by design, by love, then you may be in the same house but you are not in the same world with me." The sense of being worlds apart from people with whom we may otherwise, sometimes quite literally, be standing shoulder to shoulder, may arise through all manner of differences between us. Differences concerning religion, however, often seem to be the most distancing of all. Religious studies, which has been at least partially responsible for bringing to our notice the immense variety of religious worlds inhabited by humankind and the extent to which they appear to differ, has, increasingly, become concerned to provide an appropriate methodological vehicle for inter-global travel between them. The view of phenomenology of religion on which I want to focus gives phenomenology the role of providing just such a vehicle.

To use John S. Dunne's vocabulary, phenomenology of religion so conceived provides a means of effectively "passing over" into the religious situation which one wants to investigate and "coming back" with a clearer understanding of it. It is a means of passing over to someone else's religious world so that we may try to see how things appear when viewed through that perspective. It is an attempt to place us, so far as this is possible, in the other person's shoes, so that we might stand there and walk with them, observing and feeling what occurs with a closeness which would be impossible for an "external" descriptive study, where we stood rooted to the spot and made no attempt at passing over beyond the mere turning of an already judgmental gaze in the direction of the phenomena concerned.

Phenomenology of religion viewed as such seeks to offer to its sufficiently competent practitioner as non-secondhand an insight as it is possible to achieve into what animates the different vitalities and movements of meaning within any particular religious outlook. Its basic motivating idea is quite straightforward: to try to apprehend someone else's religion *as it appears to them*, rather than focusing attention on how that religion appears to us from a non-phenomenological viewpoint. To achieve this perspective it is necessary to maintain a deliberate open-mindedness, which postpones making any value judgments, and to let oneself be moved, if only temporarily, by the same currents of significance as stir the believer under study. Such a method thus relies to a great extent on the disciplined use of the imagination.

Winston L. King offers a clear statement of the goal of phenomenology of religion viewed in these terms. It is, he says, to observe all types of religiousness "from the veritable inside, and yet escape to tell all to outsiders including one's own outside ordinary self." Ninian Smart takes us a little further, pointing out that this sort of phenomenology of religion refers to "the procedure of getting at the meaning of a religious act or symbol or institution *for the participants*. It refers, in other words, to a kind of imaginative participation in the world of the actor." Phenomenology of religion thus rejects any picture of observer and observed facing each other across the inter-face of method, instead method becomes more like an encircling hoop which seeks to bind them close together for the duration of any period of inquiry. Gerardus van der Leeuw, considered by many to be one of the key figures in the phenomenological tradition within the study of religion, provides a further pointer towards what may be involved in this type of exercise. According to his analysis, phenomenology of religion necessitates "not only the description of what is visible from the outside, but above all the experience born of what can only become reality after it has been admitted into the life of the observer himself." In other words, the phenomenological observer is not to be seen as a white-coated diagnostician standing by the patient and noting every symptom—although part of his work *will* involve such meticulous observation. Rather, he seeks to move close enough to the subject of study so that the religious pulse makes itself felt against, or even within, his own skin.

The catalogue of statements portraying phenomenology of religion as an exercise in imaginative re-experiencing could be continued at some length, and the current of thought which advocates such deliberate and disciplined use of our imagination in the attempt to understand religion, extends beyond those who actually talk about phenomenology or term themselves phenomenologists. Rudolf Otto, for example, called for "penetrative imaginative sympathy with what passes in the other person's mind," and proceeded in *The Idea of the Holy* with what some have seen as a phenomenological exercise. Before Otto, James Haughton Woods suggested that a key task in the study of religion is "to reproduce, as if real to us, all the ideas which compose the mental picture present to the stranger, to repeat in our own imagination all the feelings or will-attitudes which are bound up with this experience." Whilst, more recently, Wilfred Cantwell Smith has cautiously suggested that by the exercise of "imaginative sympathy," cross-checked by various procedures, it may be possible to "infer what goes on in another's mind and heart." However, although it would be fascinating to trace the development within the study of religion of this emphasis on the importance of trying to see things from the other person's point of view, this is not a task which can be undertaken here. Suffice it to say that the single strand which has been abstracted from the tangled knot of interpretations which pronounce on what phenomenology of religion involves, is a thick one, with an interesting history which extends beyond the horizons of any purely phenomenological debate.

Clearly many objections can be cast in the path of envisaging phenomenology of religion as a careful exercise in imaginative re-experiencing. It might, for example, be argued that to call such an exercise "phenomenology of religion" is to isolate only the least fraction of what occurs under this heading and ignore other more important aspects of the phenomenological tradition. Moreover, even if the designation is allowed, how could it ever be possible to implement, for surely such a procedure immediately falls foul of what E. E. Evans-Pritchard aptly dubbed the "if I were a horse" fallacy?

To the charge of dealing with only a fraction of what occurs under the heading "phenomenology of religion," I plead guilty without reservation. It has been my intention to isolate (as it will be subsequently to concentrate on) a single view of what phenomenology of religion consists of, rather than to make pronouncements which might be applied across the whole range of work in this area. This is not to advocate a precisely specified methodology as the right way of seeing phenomenology of religion, nor is it to dismiss as erroneous or of no value to religious studies those varieties of phenomenology ignored by the selection of a single type. Such a narrow focusing as I am adopting simply has to do with keeping the discussion within manageable bounds. To the charge of advocating an impossible methodology, I would reply, "let us look beyond an abstract statement of what it involves before passing judgment on its effectiveness "—for I want to sidestep the theoretical circle of proposal, objection, counter-proposal, reformulation and so on, which tends to postpone any attempt at application indefinitely and render discussions about phenomenology of religion endlessly provisional. Instead of marshalling arguments for the defence of imaginative re-experiencing, I want to look straight away at a sustained attempt to put its principles into action.

IV. A Phenomenological Study of Prehistoric Religiousness

It is neither as allegory, myth or fable that I wish to consider William Golding's novel *The Inheritors* here, although I readily acknowledge that Golding's work can often be described in terms of these three categories. It is rather in terms of its possible role as exemplar for how phenomenology of religion might proceed with its task (phenomenology of religion being understood as an attempt to imaginatively re-experience whatever religious outlook happens to be under study) that I wish to spend some time looking at this book.

I choose *The Inheritors* because it "passes over" into a distant and alien religious world with great delicacy and effectiveness, and shows quite strikingly how open-mindedness, empathy and imagination can be brought to bear on the relevant information to enlarge our understanding of the facts. It provides a useful point of reference for the phenomenologist of religion poised to embark on some particular study.

In this book Golding deals with the confrontation between a small group of Neanderthal men and a larger group of Cro-Magnon men—the first true *Homo sapiens*. The Cro-Magnons, in the course of fleeing from their original homeland as the result of a tribal dispute, make a temporary stop in one of the Neanderthalers' established haunts. The book tells the story of the confrontation which follows. It is not, however, as an adventure story about a prehistoric clash of cultures that *The Inheritors* is relevant to religious studies. That relevance stems, rather, from its nature as a fictional study, based on a detailed knowledge of early man, in which Golding presents a picture of primitive religiousness in a way which seems to be in substantial accordance with calls to place ourselves in the thought-world of the other person. Let us see, then, how—from this admittedly rather unlikely source—the phenomenologist of religion who advocates imaginative re-experiencing can derive many important clues as to how he might go about his work.

Golding's chosen point of view, which the reader must adopt if he is to see anything beyond the most superficial and confused narrative level, is one wholly consonant with the idea of seeing another world of meaning as it appears to its own inhabitants—whilst still maintaining the status of observer. In *The Inheritors* we see from the inside out rather than remaining as merely external observers. But since the process of "passing over" is mediated through a special use of a language with which we are already familiar, a critical awareness of what is happening must be maintained if we are to be aware of what is going on in the first place. Without that critical awareness, the path to such a vantage point as Golding offers simply remains closed.

In a study of the theological dimensions of Golding's work, David Anderson has aptly remarked of *The Inheritors* that "Golding does not merely describe Neanderthalers from the outside, as an anthropologist would do; he attempts to enter their consciousness, to experience existence as they experienced it." Here we have an example of King's observing from the veritable inside, of Smart's imaginative participation in the world of the actor, of Otto's penetrative imaginative sympathy. Anderson goes on to suggest that we respond to Golding's skill by "recognizing the recess in our own being where we remember that reality was once unfractured, and our minds fill with echoes of primal innocence and lost Edens." Such a process of recognition, of becoming aware of resonances within ourselves which sound in sympathy with what occurs in the narrative, seems strongly reminiscent of van der Leeuw's notion of "systematic introspection."

But is the picture which Golding presents via imaginative re-experiencing a reliable one? If it is to be of any use as a model for the phenomenology of religion then clearly Golding's study must be *accurate*. There would be no point advocating as exemplar something which presented a wholly erroneous picture of the religiousness it deals with. Our task in this section must be to try to establish the authenticity of the book's factual foundations, and in the course of doing this to give some idea of the "flavour" of this extraordinary novel to those who are not acquainted with it.

To begin with, what sets the tone of the whole book is that Golding's Neanderthalers do not display the same intellectual/linguistic virtuosity as that found in *Homo sapiens*. The main reason why the book is difficult (and relevant to our discussion of phenomenology) is that much of the "action" is told from this standpoint. Golding strictly refuses to take short-cuts which would enable us to realize much more quickly what is going on. He does not resort to abstract descriptive statements telling us about a particular situation, but instead leads us to a first hand appreciation of it for ourselves. In *The Inheritors* we approach the Neanderthal world from the point of view of a Neanderthaler (what a Neanderthaler might have been being based on a painstaking reconstruction of available evidence). Mark Kinkead-Weekes and Ian Gregor sum up well the immense problems of style which Golding incurs by writing in this mode, for trying to express the experience of primitive man from his conceptually and linguistically limited point of view involves "continuous and severe self-denial." Indeed, Golding had to "deprive himself of all analysis, by himself or his characters, and of most of the possibilities of dialogue." He had, in other words, to sustain a disciplined empathy and open-mindedness throughout the book. He had to observe a holding back or bracketing out, familiar in the phenomenological vocabulary, which disallowed the intrusion of analyses, explanations, value judgments or clarifying comments from his own twentieth-century point of view. Of course Golding does allow himself one "compromise"—essential if the book was ever to have been written given what Mark Adriaens calls his "epistemic choice" of approaching things from the Neanderthalers' viewpoint—namely, that whilst acknowledging their conceptual limitations, their inability to put their experience into words, Golding does use all the resources of our language to convey such a situation. However, he uses such linguistic resources such that they are "exactly descriptive of what the Neanderthalers [might] see, feel, hear and touch." Thus, for example, when Golding describes Lok, one of the Neanderthalers, seeing a companion cry, we read: "Lok watched the water run out of her eyes. It lingered at the rim of her eye hollows, then fell in great drops on her mouth." But this only states accurately what Lok himself observes, even though it requires words totally beyond him to express it. We are not simply told that "the Neanderthalers had very limited linguistic ability" or that "she was crying," but are led to see how things might have appeared to one who could not express them in terms intelligible to us, or understand our descriptions.

To see how such a technique works in more detail and to see further the sort of intellectual/linguistic scope Golding grants his Neanderthalers, let us consider a slightly longer passage:

The man turned sideways in the bushes and looked at Lok along his shoulder. A stick rose upright and there was a lump of bone in the middle. Lok peered at the stick and the lump of bone and the small eyes in the bone things over the face. Suddenly Lok understood that the man was holding the stick out to him but neither he nor Lok could reach across the river. . . . The stick began to grow shorter at both ends. Then it shot out to full length again. The dead tree by Lok's ear acquired a voice. "Clop!" his ears twitched and he turned to the tree. By his face there had grown a twig: a twig that smelt of other, and of goose, and of the bitter berries Lok's stomach told him he must not eat.

Translating out of Lok's "understanding" of the incident and putting it in ordinary descriptive terms: Lok sees a Cro-Magnon man across the river who shoots a poisoned arrow at him but misses. The "lump of bone" in the middle of the "stick" are the man's knuckles grasping the bow, which, because they are, unlike his own, hairless, appear bone-like to Lok. Similarly, Lok thinks that cheekbones and forehead are "bone things" over the man's head, rather than a natural and integral part of his visage.

The limited conceptual and speech ability of Neanderthal man, the significance of which Golding seeks to make us aware of at first hand, has, in fact, been well evidenced by the research of Lieberman and Crelin, who have reconstructed the supra-laryngeal tract of a Neanderthal skull and from this reconstruction have established the range of sounds which such a creature could have produced. They conclude that Neanderthal man "did not have the anatomical pre-requisites for producing the full range of human speech." In developing this research, a comparison of the skulls of Neanderthal man, the new-born and adult human and the Chimpanzee was initiated in order to see more precisely how phonetic ability could be determined by related anatomy. The conclusion reached was that "the Neanderthal vocal tract cannot produce 'a', 'i', or 'u'. This may not seem to be particularly significant until we realize that human speech achieves its high information rate by means of an 'encoding' process that is structured in terms of the anatomic and articulatory constraints of speech production." The ability to produce vowel sounds appears to be precisely one of those factors which facilitate this encoding process. Moving from phonetics to survival, Ralph Solecki has suggested that articulate speech and the power of conceptualization which goes with it may, perhaps, be considered as the "new weapon" with which Neanderthal man's hominid replacement, i.e., *Homo sapiens*, was able to displace this older race.

Golding's overall style is, I think, compatible with such conclusions, for the confrontation he presents is very much one between a superior and inferior linguistic/conceptual ability. Of course we could not deduce from *The Inheritors* that the supra-laryngeal tract of *Homo neanderthalensis* was incapable of producing the vowel sounds "a," "i," and "u," but by showing us in a specific and appropriate setting what such conceptual shortcomings might mean in terms of an outlook on the world, Golding's work gives us an insight into what the significance of such facts might be, and how things might appear to a consciousness constrained by them.

On a more specific level we can, time and time again, confirm the technical accuracy underlying *The Inheritors*. For example, in the death and burial of Mal, the "old man" of the Neanderthal group, Golding's knowledge of prehistory is well evidenced on a number of points. Thus when Mal, aware that in his sickness he has misdirected the group, says, "Do not open my head and bones. You would only taste weakness," we are reminded of those archaeological finds of Neanderthal skeletons which strongly suggest some form of cultic cannibalism. Alberto Blanc, for example, describes an intentional mutilation on one of the Monte Circeo skulls which is "identical to the one presently produced by headhunters of Borneo and Melanesia with the object of extracting the brain and eating it for ritual and social purposes."

Such purposes are usually an attempt to benefit from the strength or wisdom or courage of the one who has just died (or been killed)—thus Mal's reluctance to pass on what he sees as his weakness.

When Mal finally does die, two of his companions "pushed the great gaunt bones of his knees against his chest, tucked in his feet, lifted his head off the earth and put his two hands under it." And this is in accordance with archaeological findings that, though by no means always, "Neanderthal skeletons were usually buried in the attitude of sleep." In digging the grave under the hearth around which the remaining members of the group still live, Golding is again "true to life." Thus Solecki notes that "the living abode was not shunned as a burial place by the Neanderthalers" and Rachel Levy notes "signs of continued habitation" above excavated graves. Moreover, in digging the grave, Lok passes through several "layers," several different hearth places and bones from previous generations of Neanderthalers who had occupied the same site. This was a phenomenon also found by Solecki at Shanidar (a cave site in Iraqi Kurdistan) and is evidence of the uniformity displayed over long periods of time by the culture of the Mousterian era. Finally, in having the Neanderthalers bury food and water with Mal, Golding is again quite accurate. And if the "mourners" do not add flowers too, it is doubtless because Solecki's extraordinary discoveries on this count were only made a decade or so after *The Inheritors* was written.

Many further examples of Golding's faithfulness to the facts could be given: his emphasis on the mystery and importance of fire to the Neanderthalers, who collect and use it rather than make it themselves, his casting of the old woman in the role of keeper and tender of the fire, his treatment of the numinous in the form of a pantheistic female energy, his account of Cro-Magnon rituals, all can claim to be in substantial accordance with what we know about this period. In short, judging from Golding's sustained application of its principles, there is no intrinsic flaw in the methodology of imaginative re-experiencing such that we would have to dismiss such a technique as necessarily misleading in terms of its treatment of the facts. In beginning his imagination from the inside and working out, in leading the reader around to discovering things for himself, rather than merely describing them, in building up a situation in which we can know imaginatively what it might be like to look through other eyes, to live in a different world of religious meaning, Golding does not rely on the fabrication of erroneous details. Its accuracy established—and something of its nature illustrated—it remains to consider what this kind of procedure has to offer religious studies which is not already available through a more straightforward descriptive approach.

V. Information and Insight in the Study of Religion

Accurate though it may be, *The Inheritors* could not be relied on as a source-book of information about the religiousness of early man. So what does Golding's study (and the imaginative re-experiencing it represents) have which a standard descriptive approach—on which after all it is based—does not? Why should we put forward *The Inheritors* rather than, say, J. G. Maringer's "The Gods of Prehistoric Man" as being relevant to the intending phenomenologist who is interested in early religion? What can such imaginative re-experiencing as Golding performs contribute to the study of religion, which is not already available through existing non-phenomenological approaches?

To answer this question I want to return to and fulfil an undertaking given in the opening section of this paper, namely that some therapeutic comments would be addressed to the methodological confusion current in religious studies. For it is largely as a way out of this confusion that we can see the value of the sort of imaginative re-experiencing which is available through story-telling of the sort found in *The Inheritors*. How this can offer a way out of existing confusion comes into focus when we pause to consider the part played in that confusion by the rapid growth of information about religion which has taken place over the last hundred years or so.

As early as 1905, Louis Henry Jordan noted that a particular characteristic of the study of religions was "the overwhelming mass of detail, still rapidly increasing, which controls every earnest investigator." By 1958, G. F. Woods had realized that "we are standing near an explosion of knowledge" which has left us somewhat shell-shocked and, some twenty years later, Eric Sharpe characterized religious studies as involving "rapidly increasing accumulations of material" in search of some method to make sense of it, whilst, in similar vein, Georg Schmid presented the contemporary situation of the subject as one of "boundlessly broadening acquaintance with religious data." Such comments are not intended simply to draw attention to the prodigious growth of a new discipline. They identify, rather, a heavy sense of perplexity which has emerged as such growth provides us with more and more information about religion.

Indeed the sheer extent and easy availability of information about different religious outlooks is a fact whose educational, philosophical and theological consequences are only beginning to make themselves fully felt. It is, for example, no longer clear what should be taught about religion in the schools when it has become a virtually impossible task, as Eric Johns has shown, "to state what knowledge the religiously educated person should finally possess." For the philosopher of religion, on the other hand, attempting to map out the boundaries of rational belief, the task of deciding what Swinburne has termed "the relative probabilities of creeds" involves the necessity of far more investigation in this century than it would have done at any other time in history. Meanwhile theologians are faced with searching questions about criteria of likeness and dissimilarity as the religious concepts of East and West intermingle and collide with each enlargement of our vocabulary for the sacred. The problems of holding fast to any particular form of religiousness or, indeed, of abandoning a religious outlook increase dramatically in the case of the individual who is aware of the vast accumulation of religious information which is now available to the serious thinker.

At least part of the profound methodological confusion which has been diagnosed within religious studies seems to stem simply from the vast *amount* of information now accumulated and the attendent difficulties which a diversity of religious data on this scale must inevitably pose. Until a way is found to resolve some of these difficulties, it seems counterproductive, if not pointless, just to continue with the production of further factual information. Ironically, where once the key factors standing in the way of understanding the religious experience of humankind were lack of information and prejudice, the problem has, in a sense, become inverted. What now seems to block understanding in many areas is a glut of information and a methodological insistence on distancing neutrality. Obviously we cannot dispense with the facts, but it seems that once we have acquainted ourselves with them to a certain level, a further step needs to be taken if our understanding is to advance.

There are, I know, many who would deny that there was any need for a further step here. The identification of an accumulation of information about religion as a locus of methodological confusion presupposes that we should do something with the facts beyond collecting them. But surely it could be argued that the academic study of religion is primarily concerned with laying bare the facts of the matter as accurately and as extensively as possible, that such study addresses itself precisely to the task of acquiring and disseminating reliable information about all the phenomena which ran within its vast and diverse field of study and if the resulting accumulation of information poses problems for educationalists, philosophers, theologians, or anyone else, well, that is *their* concern. Certainly this is one way of dealing with the methodological conclusion which arises from the sheer bulk of information gathered—simply to deny that it exists and carry on as before, arguing that the whole idea of there being any doubt about how to proceed arises from a misapprehension of the aims of this particular academic endeavor.

The dissatisfaction which many feel with viewing or practising religious studies according to these terms is not based on any unreasonable

desire to see it suddenly performing tasks better left to theology or philosophy. Rather, it stems from doubting that the factual, impersonal and
abstract approach which is taken by the discipline so conceived, can provide the most suitable basis on which to philosophize or theologize or try
to reach some decision about one's own individual religious stance. As
C. J. Bleeker has observed, although the extent and refinement of our
knowledge about religion increases yearly, "this does not mean that our
understanding of the innermost of these religions is proceeding in the
same proportion." There are still "many blindspots on the map of our
insight" and these occur not just because there is some factual material
yet to be collected—even were our information complete they would per-
sist. In similar vein, Eustace Haydon has condemned much of the last
quarter century's work in this field as providing only "great areas of
facts . . . without a soul." Although we may know more about religion
now than ever before, there seems to be something important which is
being missed out by our work, and the cure for its absence seems not to
lie in a straightforward pressing ahead with the descriptive endeavour
(indeed, such a pressing ahead might simply make its absence more
keenly felt). But what approach is left to us if we reject, as being in some
sense inadequate, such surely central methodological norms as factuality,
impersonality and abstraction?

I would suggest that it is this current of thought, discontented with
much existing practice and desirous of a new approach in religious studies, which finds expression in the advocation of phenomenology as imaginative reexperiencing. For if we really take seriously the various proposals involved in such an idea—proposals about penetrative imaginative
sympathy, participation in the world of the actor, seeing things from the
veritable inside, and so on, we will arrive precisely at a methodology
which might be described as being *non-factual, personal* and *holistic.*

VI. Phenomenology of Religion as Non-factual, Personal and Holistic

Granted, such a methodology might suggest some way of avoiding the
confusion and discontentment which seems to be generated by gathering
information from an impersonal and abstract perspective. The problem
is, of course, how an approach which claims to be non-factual, personal
and holistic can possibly offer us any insight into religion at all. For, on
first hearing at least, such terms sound anything but reassuring about the
provision of any legitimate means of knowing. I want therefore to con-

sider in more detail what they mean, whilst referring back to Golding's work as an example of such a methodology in action.

(i) *The Inheritors* may be seen as non-factual in that it does not supply us with any *new* facts about prehistoric religiousness beyond what is already available in existing descriptive studies. Although Golding's knowledge of prehistory is impressive—indeed he confessed to reading extensively in the subject before he started writing—*The Inheritors* does not seek to add to the facts nor simply to repeat them. Rather, it sets them in a particular context which enables us to see them from a new perspective. It animates the information by the imaginative construction of consciousnesses through which it can be seen "live" or "in action." Although such an approach supplies us with no additional factual material about this period, or about the types of religious practices associated with it—and is, indeed, reliant on such material to get underway—it *does* provide an opportunity for us to consider what, in one sense, we already know, in a way which may yet teach us something new about it. The various elements of our knowledge of prehistory are used to build up a picture of how such things might have been seen by those individuals whose lived experience of the world is what generated such elements in the first place. It is that lived experience which imaginative re-experiencing seeks to approach more closely, hoping in this way to come to a greater understanding of what particular forms of religiousness mean to those who live and think (or lived and thought) according to them.

Renford Bambrough has drawn attention to occasions when "we can achieve and convey knowledge and understanding by seeing and showing a pattern of relationships in between a set of items in which each separate item is already available for inspection." Imaginative re-experiencing is, or seeks to be, such an occasion, when an advancement in learning takes place without our acquiring any increase in itemizable bits of information which were not available to us before. It is concerned with the sense-giving patterns and relationships which individual experience imposes upon, derives from, or expresses through such environing information as is visible to an external descriptive study. As Bambrough went on to show, in reading a story we may learn something which is quite "disproportionate to the number of new facts we learn" or to whether we learn any new facts at all. Indeed, many works of literature can be said to teach us about things we might already claim to know all about. For example, Tolstoy's *Death of Ivan Illych* may tell us nothing about the facts of human mortality which we did not know already, but to say it taught us nothing about our finitude would surely be to risk confining knowledge to a somewhat superficial level. Likewise, *The Inheritors* may in one

sense tell us nothing about stone-age religion which is not already accessible in the existing literature, but to say that it can therefore offer no
insight into this area would surely be to risk equating understanding with
information, where clearly the two are not co-terminous.

Imaginative re-experiencing does not advocate an *abandonment* of
information in favour of some kind of factually unfounded exercise in
speculation. Rather, it sees being well informed as a pre-requisite for its
imaginative endeavour. Information is seen as the raw material for that
endeavour, it is not, however, accepted as the final product which is
sought.

(ii) *The Inheritors* is personal in the sense that it adopts particular
individual perspectives. Most of the book seeks to place us behind the
eyes of the Neanderthaler, Lok. We observe through his individual perspective, not by means of an objective, impersonal description. The individuals with whom we become concerned are, however, imagined within
carefully controlled guidelines, they are not the result of haphazard and
undisciplined invention. In one sense, of course, Lok and his fellows are
fragments of Golding's imagination, but in another sense—the one which
must be stressed for the purposes of imaginative re-experiencing—they
are intended as life-like constructs, individual (but not unrepresentative)
models born of a detailed knowledge of the facts and a sensitivity of
feeling which allows one individual to infer what it might be like to
experience life lived according to many quite different conditions. As
Wilfred Cantwell Smith has put it, in studying religions we have primarily
to do "not with religions, but with religious *persons*." Imaginative re-
experiencing provides a method of approach for work which wishes to
take such a remark seriously. It seeks not to focus on some such abstraction as "the things themselves," but rather on the way in which the world
appears when seen through particular religious outlooks.

(iii) *The Inheritors* is holistic in that it does not set before us a study
of pre-historic religiousness, but tells us a story of prehistoric life in
which religion has its place among other things. Golding does not abstract ritual, or the sense of the numinous, or the construction of symbolic images and so on for special attention. Instead we encounter these
in the context of Neanderthal existence as a whole. Such a holistic approach, which refuses to abstract beyond the minimal level necessary to
locate a particular area of study, seems necessary if we are not to let the
focus of attention slip back into the impersonal. Individuals live lives in
which religion plays a part, to abstract that part and deal with it alone is
to risk seeing it as some sort of separate entity which exists independently
and is intrinsically intelligible without reference to life as a whole. As
Cantwell Smith has put it, in the course of his powerful argument for a

shift in emphasis from "religion" to "faith," an argument which can, incidentally, be used to back a policy of imaginative re-experiencing, if we would understand the Buddhist or the Hindu or the Muslim we must not look at their religion so much as attempt to see how the world looks through their eyes. This is because, taking Hinduism as an example case, we may be sure that the Hindu, as he looks around him, "does not see 'Hinduism'. Like the rest of us he sees his wife's death, his child's minor and major aspirations, his moneylender's mercilessness, the calm of a starlit evening, his own mortality. He sees these things through coloured glasses, if one will, of a Hindu brand." Story provides a way for us to share his vision, we cannot be expected to see it simply by studying the colour and structure of the lenses. In a sense, much of religious studies has, to date, concentrated on religious lenses without trying to see what outlook appears through them, or, worse, has confused the lenses for what is seen through them. Phenomenology of religion, envisaged as imaginative re-experiencing, suggests a way of changing this emphasis.

There would seem to be no immediate reason, then, for rejecting a methodology which is non-factual, personal and holistic (in the senses described above) simply on the grounds that it could not provide any legitimate means of knowing. It might not be easy to specify precisely what we do learn from such an approach, since the nature of the knowledge it offers resists any process of itemization, but it seems clear that it can teach us something—perhaps a great deal—even in those areas where we may feel fully informed already. Whether such a methodology could help to fill in the blindspots which Bleeker identified in the study of religion, is difficult to say in advance, but providing it was carried out properly it would not seem unreasonable to hope that it could offer us a much richer insight into many forms of religiousness than would be possible were no process of imaginative re-experiencing attempted. At the same time, it is clear that Nobel prize-winners are hard to emulate—the imaginative exercise performed by Golding in *The Inheritors* is not something to be undertaken lightly. However, the degree to which he is successful in so difficult an area, about which we know very little, is surely encouraging for more accessible areas of study to which we have, nonetheless, not yet passed over.

VII. Conclusion

There are, of course, *many* objections which could be raised about the whole idea of phenomenology of religion as imaginative re-experiencing. The extent to which it is legitimate to term such an endeavour "phenomenology" may be challenged, as may the *possibility* of its suggested course of action. The need for such a methodological emphasis in religious studies may be denied altogether, as we have seen (if, that is, we are content to remain at an "informational" level), and even supposing that it *was* allowed as phenomenological, desirable and possible, it could be asked whether story-telling was the best mode of operation for imaginative re-experiencing to adopt. Would biography, or, indeed, fictionalized autobiography, not be more appropriate? It must also be clear that definitions, both of "imagination" and "story-telling," are needed to help us distinguish between those modes of them which might be suitable for the task and those which would not be. After all, William Golding is one thing, Mickey Spillane quite something else. Moreover, what has been said raises important questions about the relationship between information and insight, and this will almost certainly prompt us to ask for clarification of such associated terms as "interpretation," "explanation," "understanding" and so on. In other words, such a shift in methodology as imaginative re-experiencing seems to propose, raises some fundamental questions about the basic epistemology which is operative in this area of thought.

However, it has been my intention in this paper to suggest some large-scale methodological proposals for discussion, in a context where they could be referred to a particular example, rather than to engage in the more intricate business of critically exploring in detail the various pros and cons of adopting such a methodology throughout religious studies' field of interest. Such a task might, perhaps, constitute "Phenomenology and the Art of Story-Telling, Part II," but clearly it cannot be undertaken here.

Let us, in conclusion, try to imagine what the result might be if some of the proposals which I have made were taken seriously enough to be acted on. Suppose that religious studies developed into a discipline with "pure" and "applied" sides, the former concentrating on a descriptive and classificatory approach which sought to establish the facts about religion and to provide some sort of general typology for them, the latter concentrating on seeing how those facts are, or have been, or could be, applied in human lives so as to provide such lives with particular reference points of meaning. In what direction would such "applied" religious studies take us?

We can, I think, find a clue here by comparing the practitioner of such a discipline to the actor. As Mircea Eliade has remarked, through the voice of Bibiscescu, one of the characters in his novel *The Forbidden Forest*, the actor:

identifies himself in turn with innumerable human existences, and he suffers, if he is a good actor, just as the character he represents on stage suffers in his life. This means that he knows in a single life-time the passions, the hopes, the suffering and the revelations of fifty or a hundred lives.

In much the same way we might, perhaps, expect the phenomenologist of religion who followed a strategy of imaginative re-experiencing to know in a single life-time the passions, the hopes, the suffering and so on which are found in a wide range of human faiths.

Doubtless the process of exploration and discovery involved would reveal many quite fascinating phenomena, but, at the end of the day, would there be any point to such a phenomenologist's extensive repertoire of roles, beyond the fact that "playing" them was intrinsically interesting? Is the endeavour to pass over into a series of religious worlds of meaning merely some sort of sight-seeing trip with little more to offer than an exciting route, a collection of colourful souvenirs and a satisfied curiosity? We could, perhaps, take such a view were there no possibility of the phenomenologist's own outlook and opinions changing as a result of his studies. If all his painstakingly structured imaginative ventures could be supposed invariably to return him to the point from which he set out, and if this point of departure remained wholly unaffected by any of the cargoes his coming back contained, then it *would* be hard to see how such a process could make any real advance on the abstract, impersonal approach which concentrates on amassing religious facts yet seems eventually to become somewhat pointless.

However, unlike the actor, whose own identity is presumably not fundamentally challenged by the parts he plays, the process of imaginative re-experiencing introduces the phenomenologist of religion to material which has the potential at least to influence his own religiousness, perhaps to the extent that his outlook before and after such an exercise will be significantly different, for according to Eliade, "to the extent that you *understand* a religious fact (myth, ritual, divine figure, etc.) you *change*, you are modified, and this change is equivalent to a step forward in the process of self liberation." Precisely what Eliade means by "self liberation" is not entirely clear, but his assertion of change following understanding certainly runs counter to any idea that a neat dividing line separating commitment and neutrality may be drawn between religion and those who study it, such that the observer is quite separate from the subject of study and immune to any influence stemming from his examination of it. Perhaps some neat bisection of this type may be possible—indeed desirable—in "pure" religious studies so that the facts are not vitiated by what Jastrow termed the "personal equation," but it cannot be thought to operate in the same way in imaginative reexperiencing. Eliade's remark would suggest that when we approach religious phenomena closely enough to see their meaning, we are with material which may well affect our existing outlook on the world and, as such, would seem inevitably to introduce a critically evaluative element into our studies. If this is the case then perhaps imaginative re-experiencing might, in the end, be seen as purposeful in terms of exploring and defining our own religiousness, through a process of exploring the religiousness of others.

❖ W. BREDE KRISTENSEN ❖

In the historical-typological phenomenology of religion one of the most familiar categories of investigation concerns types of holy words. Words of creation, words of consecration, words of proclamation, and words of commission can all be phenomenologically differentiated within the category of holy words. Another important example within this category is that of words of trust or prayer. In the following selection W. Brede Kristensen (1867–1953) examines prayer. Kristensen held the Chair of History and Phenomenology of Religion at the University of Leyden in the Netherlands. His wide-ranging publications included specialized studies of the religions of antiquity in addition to several methodological essays. In this excerpt from his important study, *The Meaning of Religion: Lectures in the Phenomenology of Religion*, Kristensen draws on religious traditions as disparate as Native American, Babylonian, Hindu, and Christian among others to explore in a richly comparative manner that fundamental religious act of immediate relation to the sacred which is contained in all prayers. Acknowledging the complexity of this subject, Kristensen displays the range of types of prayers and highlights the importance of the attitude by the believer of surrender to and trust in the sacred. In Kristensen's work one not only finds an excellent example of the historical-typological approach to the phenomenology of religion but also an important contribution to the larger task of comprehending the experience of the sacred.

Prayer

Prayer is the most characteristic expression of religious life and the only religious act which takes place in all religions. In prayer man ceases all outward activity and enters into immediate relation to God: here the essence of religion comes to its purest expression. But just this central place of prayer in religious life raises peculiar difficulties for the phenomenological approach. Phenomenology has set itself the task of so grouping phenomena that they shed light upon one another and lead to a deeper insight into the essence of a whole group of similar phenomena. But prayer is not a phenomenon which can be easily observed. No religious act is so hidden and so difficult to evaluate as is prayer. The phenomena, which are the set forms in prayer, do not permit the motivating impulse to come so clearly to light, and they give more occasion for mistaken explanations than do the forms of sacraments, sacrifices, and consecrations.

The data are numerous enough, and they have been collected and classified by modern authors in overwhelming numbers. This is the case with Friedrich Heiler's *Prayer*. . . . His work is certainly an amazing accomplishment, and it is one, moreover, in which the reverent attitude of the writer towards so many alien ideas makes a very favourable impression. Nevertheless, the overwhelming quantity of data sometimes causes more confusion than clarification. In such a quantity the material cannot be analyzed with any prospect of success. We want to know the spiritual factors which are active in all prayer, but faced with such extensive material, we must also have the courage, relying on a certain amount of intuition, to separate what is important from what is not. Then we must give our attention exclusively to the data which can reasonably well be approached and understood, and which therefore hold out promise of yielding positive results. In any case, we must avoid that besetting sin of ethnographic literature, the recital of dozens of similar instances where a single example is sufficiently clear.

Most writers in assessing and arranging the facts make a comparison based on their evaluation of those facts, and they classify the data according to the degree of development which they see indicated in them. That which is considered the least developed prayer is "the naive prayer of primitive man" (Heiler), which is concerned only with security and outward prosperity. The highest type is that which is met within our own culture, which is generally called spiritual prayer. We must object to this kind of classification. All phenomenology is indeed based upon comparative observation. Phenomenology of Religion is the comparative study of the history of religion. But evaluative comparison does not come within its domain; that belongs in the provinces of philosophy and dogmatic theology. Phenomenology makes use of comparison only in order to gain a deeper insight into the self-subsistent, not the relative, meaning of each of the historical data. It wishes only to learn to understand the conception of the believers themselves, who always ascribe an absolute value to their faith. The construction of a history of prayer is obstructed by the fact that a separation between an unspiritual and a spiritual type of prayer cannot consistently be made; it is based solely upon external characteristics.

This fact is usually forgotten. We often consider prayer concerned with material desires to be simple and easy to understand. He who prays for good hunting, an abundant harvest, or a calm sea must surely have discovered that his prayer is often unfulfilled. Would not even primitive man come to realize in the long run that prayer is a useless means for exerting influence upon the course of nature? But it is nevertheless a fact that those discoveries do not cause him to abandon prayer; his conviction of its effectiveness always remains quite undisturbed. How is this to be explained if he is concerned only with the outward fulfillment of his wishes? This is evidently not the only important concern.

Prayer, even in its "primitive" form, cannot be compared to a request addressed to a human being. Such a request is meaningful only if one can reasonably count on its being granted. Every prayer, on the contrary, is a religious act, in which probability is not calculated, because the external data are conceived in an infinite relation. Edward Tylor gives many interesting examples of this. In addition to the simple, "give me bread for today," which is surely not an unusual prayer even for us, there is also this other type (among the Algonquins): "Thou, you Great Spirit, have made this lake, and you have made us your children; you can now cause

that the water shall remain smooth while we pass over in safety." Prayer
is thus based upon the conviction that nature is subjected to spirit, the
conviction of the spiritual source of outward phenomena. This type of
prayer is found among the Incas in Peru: "Thou who gavest life and
valour to man and woman, watch over them that they may live in health
and peace." Human existence is traced back to its spiritual source; it is
there that man's salvation must be found. The Zulus furnish another example. It is sufficient for them to pray to the spirits of their ancestors
without stating what it is they want; the spirits know. Their prayer is
simply, "People of our house," or "You know what is good for us, give it
to us!" Socrates has said that we only have to pray that the gods will give
us good gifts, for they know best what is good.

In all these cases, the basic attitude is one of surrender to and trust in
the leading of the Spirit, who created and governs man and cosmos. Must
this be called "primitive?" It is in any case clear how different this is from
a request made of a human being. Even the denial of a prayer's petition
has a mystical character.

Even in the simplest prayer present situations and possible future oc-
currences are conceived *sub specie aeterni*. They are understood not in
their finite and causal determination but in their absolute determination;
that is to say, as they have been willed and directed by an independent
spirit. The man in prayer has won a victory over the world, and has
realized in prayer his dependence on God alone. It is rightly said that
prayer is born out of life's distress, out of man's sense of dependence as a
finite being, and that its goal is liberation from this finite dependence.
And, indeed, the dependence as a finite being is taken up in prayer into a
new dimension: a dependence on the infinite, which contains all the finiteness of man and cosmos. Man withdraws to his spiritual foundation
and there attains his true freedom; the world has lost its hold on him.
This is the answer given to prayer; it is no problem for the man who is
praying, but a reality which he actually experiences. It sounds paradoxical, but it is nevertheless true that prayer, even the "primitive" and most
simple prayer, gives the one who is praying that power which enables
him to be indifferent as to whether the calm sea or good harvest for
which he prays actually results or fails to materialize. Definite favours are
asked, but the observable fulfillment is not more miraculous than the lack
of fulfillment, for in both cases the crucial point is the divine decision.
This is the infinite, not the finite, determination of the event. The definite
thing which prayer is about is really not "defined" or "determined," for
it is conceived in its infinite determination. Thus prayer is always answered, but perhaps in another way than we would conclude from the

words with which it is uttered. This explains why "primitive" man will never abandon prayer.

It is clear that at this point we touch upon the essential element in the religious relationship. Man does not resign himself to the superiority of brute force; in a deeper sense he is not dependent upon it. In all adversity he remains the innate victor. In the proud words of Pascal,

Man is only a reed, the weakest in nature, but he is a thinking reed. If the world destroys him, he remains nevertheless its superior; for he knows that he will die, and the world does not know how it has triumphed over him.

Spirit is dependent only on spirit. And there are not two kinds of spirit. The absolute spirit who rules the universe is not a power confronting man from outside, but forms the foundation of his existence, stretching far beyond him and yet recognized as his own essential being. Recognized, but not known, for no one knows his own essence. This is the meaning of the thought which can be found in every prayer, even the simplest: we know not what we must pray.

In prayer man engages in his highest spiritual activity, for in prayer he realizes his infinite being. We must, to be sure, remember that the terms in which we express the mystery of the religious relationship can never be adequate (for example, if we say that the man in prayer asks for something definite, which is nevertheless not "definite"). But provided we keep this in mind, we may also say that man in prayer possesses supernatural power and divine strength. Everything, we read, which rises from man to God, prayers, thoughts and deeds, have a divine origin; it is not the human self but the divine in man which prays.

Thou, my Righteousness (which yet is not my own), praise through me (divine) Righteousness; Thou Truth, praise Truth (through me).

Thy Logos (spiritual essence) praise Thee through me; receive from me through the Logos the universe as a spiritual sacrifice (*logike thusia*). Thus do the Powers (*Dynameis*) in me cry out.

The Logos, the divine wisdom and regulating power active in the one who prays, thus bring to God the universe which He has created as a sacrifice. The basic idea implicit in sacrifice (which is also the essence of prayer) cannot be more accurately expressed. Every sacrificial act is a realization and perpetuation of the sacredness of the offering; therefore the perfect offering is the universe, which reveals divine life in the broadest sense. This sacrifice cannot be made in an external way, but it occurs in a spiritual sense in prayer, because in prayer the divine determination of all events is, in principle, established, and in this way the sacredness of the entire creation is firmly indicated. The bond between God and man in prayer is also represented as a circular path: rays of divine light come down into man and rise above as prayers. "Thou life and light, from Thee comes the hymn of praise, and to Thee it returns. Prayer is not of our-selves, and yet it passes through us." With this we may compare Romans 8: 26 f.:

Likewise the Spirit helps us in our weakness; for we do not know how to pray as we ought, but the Spirit himself intercedes for us with sighs too deep for words. And he who searches the hearts of men knows what is in the mind of the Spirit.

We have thus considered a few examples both of simple prayer for material favours and of preeminently spiritual prayer, in which prayer itself is a divine gift to man. As we consider the widely divergent forms, the question returns as to whether prayer has not gone through a great many stages and does not show a process of growth.

To ask this question, one need not have in mind an historical connec-tion between the stages, with influences radiating from particular centers or persons. But cannot an ideal development be observed, in which we are fully aware of the creative but inexplicable power of religious life? Is it not true that the lasting significance and value of this religious act comes more clearly to light and is more clearly expressed in some forms than in others? The believer always takes refuge in the spiritual founda-tion on which both man and the world rest. Can the ideal development not be measured according to the degree in which this is recognized? Hegel answers these questions in the affirmative: history, including reli-gious history, is a process of growth governed and determined by spirit. He speaks of the dialectical development of the religious self-conscious-ness, and this growth is reflected in the many stages about which history teaches us.

But there are also important objections to such a history of prayer. If only it could be stated in which forms the spiritual content revealed itself more or less independently and consciously! The spirit (or the idea) must always have a body; only in theoretical reflection can the two be distin-guished. If we speak of the essence or the religious idea of prayer, we must nevertheless not forget that the essence or the idea is always hidden in a form. It is certain that where all attention is devoted to the essential core, as is the case in Hellenistic mysticism, reflection about practical life displaces practical life itself. There may be a one-sided "spiritualization" of religious life, which attests to religious poverty, although it may signify philosophical riches. Prayer for "daily bread" is never antiquated, and we should not say that it is a primitive or selfish prayer in one religion and a spiritual prayer in another. With equal justice it might be maintained that it is precisely the simple prayer for material goods which shows most clearly the superiority of spirit to matter. We cannot decide on the basis of the words which a man prays what is occurring within him; even he himself can give no explanation of it. The religious relationship is an inexpressible reality; no psychology or philosophy can penetrate the secret of the man in prayer. It is true that not every prayer is suitable for everyone, but in every prayer a miracle is prayed for or a miracle is assumed, and a miracle is, according to Schleiermacher's striking definition, only the religious term for an event which means an infinitely (i.e., spiritually) determined occurrence. Miracle is just as miraculous in the spiritual as in the material world.

The study of Phenomenology, therefore, provides no criterion for determining by comparison the religious value of the different forms of prayer. We must always try in our study to put ourselves in the position of the believer, because it is there alone that the religious reality is to be found which we wish to understand. But in that reality, prayer, or the trust which expresses itself in prayer, always has absolute validity, and absolute values are not subject to comparison with one another. Obviously the follower of one religion will always reject the prayer of adherents of other faiths. When that occurs, we are confronted with a religious reality which cannot be considered invalid. But it is just as certain that the believer does not see the true—namely the absolute—character of the alien faith, and this indeed is proved by his rejection of it. His rejection is a religious act and must be understood as such by the investigator. It is even true that in practice every religious man is always rejecting alien positions and points of view simply by virtue of the fact that he does not follow them. But the research of Phenomenology is not the practice of religion. The attempt to understand religious phenomena historically and psychologically is a reflective and intellectual activity, not a religious one. We can come to see the absolute character of particular religious data in an approximate way, but never more than approximately. And the absolute character of the data offers resistance to the construction of an "ideal history" of prayer.

There are numerous data which warn us against any evolutionary classification, whether historical or ideal, and against patterns which are forced on history and distort it. To mention only one point: in the realm of prayer the "highly" developed and the "primitive" repeatedly appear side by side. In hymns to such gods as Mazda, Ushas, Shamash, Marduk, etc., we sometimes see a glorification of wisdom, power and faithfulness, and protection of righteousness and truth—prayers which we would consider to be genuinely pious. Yet such hymns frequently turn into the most "primitive" prayers for material goods: "give us power, riches, swift horses, and all kinds of splendour" or "break the sorcerer's spell." Or consider this example in a Babylonian text: "May the tables of my sins and foolishness be broken, may I be pure for Shamash and live!" Immediately following this, however, come the prescriptions for all manner of magical ceremonies, such as smearing sacrificial blood on the door and pouring out all sorts of objects for the gods into water basins.

O Shamash, King of heaven and earth, ruler of all above and below, Thou who makest the dead to live again, who loosest the bound [the sick, for example], unbribeable judge, leader of men, creator of everything in heaven and earth, break the spell by which the sorcerer binds my head, my right and left side, break the spell over my house, door, hearth, chair . . . etc.

All sorts of religious thought are expressed in symbolic word and gesture: reconciliation for the house, and similar matters. This is magic, but undoubtedly of religious content and essence. It is difficult and sometimes almost impossible to understand such facts, but we do better to recognize this difficulty than to judge the data with standards which are alien to the believer himself.

There is a kind of "magic prayer," namely the invocation of God in different religious acts, in which a certain compulsion is exerted on the god. It is usually in connection with a sacrifice or another religious rite, such as purification, whose external appearance exhibits magical traits; it is not a favour which is asked. No, "man has done his part—now God must do His part too." God must do it in order not to endanger His own existence, or in order not to deny Himself. The world would perish if God's word, His will and law, did not remain effective. To help us to understand this coercion in prayer, we may compare what Luther said after a crisis of deep personal significance: "God could do nothing else; the pass was cut off for Him." This religious assurance is also to be found in magical coercion.

But this "coercion" of deity sometimes goes even further: if the god is not benevolent, he is punished. In China such gods are degraded. Augustine mentions that in the first circus games after the loss of their fleet, the Romans did not carry around the statue of Neptune. After the death of Germanicus temples were stoned and images overthrown. Fetishes are sometimes chastised. It is difficult to understand such cases; the term "primitive" by itself explains nothing. One wonders how anyone, while maintaining his faith in the deity, can treat him so contemptuously; how does he then imagine his god? The remarkable fact is that he does not doubt the god's existence, yet for an instant he feels himself his superior.

He believes that he is right, religiously, in the conviction that the power of the spirit must maintain itself and may not give way to the wicked and the accidental. In a surge of religious self-assurance he corrects the god. This type is pictured in such a vivid way in the Old Testament that we should hardly wish to call it "primitive." When Job in his despair challenged God to justify himself concerning his way of acting, he undoubtedly felt himself the superior. He is brought to repentance, not by his friends, but by God. His friends are not his superiors, and perhaps neither are we.

This step between feeling one's superiority and administering punishment is not so very great. In the latter we see so easily a grotesque element, but the matter undoubtedly has another aspect, even though we are not able to fathom it. The remarkable fact is that the faith in a god who is so treated does not disappear. Man comes to repentance and will propitiate his god, as Augustus propitiated Neptune.

We find personification of prayer in Brahmanaspati, "the lord of prayer" or of the holy word. He represents the infinite power of prayer, because prayer is a divine word. He sings the sacrificial hymns, repeats the prayers and pronounces the incantations "in which Indra, Varuna and Mitra find pleasure." Here there is really the conception that the government of the cosmos takes place by means of "divine prayer." Brahmanaspati places the "shining word" in the mouth of the sacrificial priest who sacrifices for rain. Brahmanaspati does everything which is otherwise ascribed to other gods; he becomes identical with Indra, as victor in the struggle. Brahmanaspati is the infinite cosmic power of the divine spirit which is active in the man at prayer. It is a quite remarkable hypostatization or personification of prayer, a remarkable view of the essence of prayer. It is comparable with what was taught in the Gnostic circles of Hellenistic philosophy about the divine source of man's prayer. It is not I who pray, but the divine within me. Prayer is a gift of God, a communication of divine power. Brahmanaspati is that divine energy by means of which all the gods possess power. Prayer is a god. It is remarkable in this connection that Brahmanaspati is a figure in the practical religion, a god who is worshipped active in the man (priest) who prays, but also outside him as the highest cosmic ruler.

Ludwig Feuerbach (1804–1872) tried to give a psychological answer to the question of how prayer originated and how it can be explained. His basic thesis is that man's desire, need and hope are what have created the gods; what man praises, glories in or desires is for him "god" (and therefore all ideas of deity are anthropomorphic). Whatever man rejects are considered to be hostile powers, "demonic beings." God is a projection of the human mind; God is created in the image of man, and not vice versa; theology is anthropology. The gods are "Wish beings" (*Wünschwesen*), "the wishes of men which are thought to be real; that is, wishes changed into real beings." Prayer is an act by means of which man tries to fulfill his wish, but the fulfillment of a wish, as long as it remains a wish, is an illusion. Religion, therefore, which is the objectivizing of man's own essence, "is worthless illusion." If he loses his religion, man loses nothing, since there is no new reality hidden for him in religion. This is indeed a remarkable sample of a psychological explanation which is extraordinarily unpsychological and in conflict with the experience of all ages. What leads man to represent his wish as a fulfilled wish? To put it even more forcibly, how can he come to feel dependent on a god who is merely a projection of his own wish and thus is his own creation? These are psychological riddles, not explanations. To say that men have always needed "illusions" in order to dare to live is a witticism which points only to a lack of real "wit" (in its old meaning of intelligence). Who is to decide what an illusion is? And what weighs more heavenly, a thousand years' experience or a theory about the origin of religion?

❖ J. M. KITAGAWA ❖

Pilgrimages to sacred spaces are widespread phenomena in the history of religions, ones that are familiar in Buddhism and Japanese religion as well as in Judaism, Christianity, and Islam. The form of the pilgrimage can range from the austere simplicity of the Buddhist monk with his food bowl and staff to the dramatic spectacle of the Muslim's expedition to Mecca. The objects of pilgrimage have been even more varied, including natural locations, such as mountains, grottos, or aquifers, and humanly constructed edifices, such as temples, stupas, and shrines as well as historical sites associated with holy persons and holy actions. Finally, following Harold W. Turner, one can differentiate between the temple and the meeting-house types of sacred space, and thus distinguish on phenomenological grounds between pilgrimage to a temple and weekly presence at congregational places of worship. Here one would attend to the meaning of spatial contexts (as sacred center, as microcosm of the cosmos, as intersection between the divine and human, as divine domicile), temporal patterns (weekly, annual, once-in-a-lifetime experiences), and intentional structures (house for the god versus house for the people of the god) in order to grasp the rich texture and challenging diversity contained in the category of pilgrimage to sacred space.

In the following selection Joseph M. Kitagawa, (1915–) the distinguished historian of Asian religions and author of such books as *Religions of the East, Understanding Japanese Religion*, and *The History of Religions*, explores three types of pilgrimage within Japanese religion.

His discussion focuses on pilgrimages to sacred mountains, to temples and shrines, and to places hallowed by their associations with holy persons. In so doing, Kitagawa sketches the ensemble of spiritual and mundane features, motives, and expectations contained within the pilgrimage experience and highlights the distinctive ethos of each pilgrimage, particularly as it concerns the soteriological path exhibited in each type.

Three Types of Pilgrimage in Japan

Gershom G. Scholem once stated that "there is no such thing as mysticism in the abstract . . . there is only the mysticism of a particular religious system." This is an important dictum which students of *Religionswissenschaft* can ill afford to forget. To be sure, it is the task of the historian of religions to delineate universal structures out of the multitude of varied and variable religious data and to telescope long and complex histories of religions by depicting certain significant events and their persistent characteristics. Yet, his conceptions and abstractions must be constantly re-examined in the light of the integrity and the unique cluster of meanings of particular religious systems or phenomena. With this in mind, I would like to depict three types of pilgrimage as expressions of the characteristic pieties of Japanese religious tradition, and hope that it will make a modest contribution to the growing literature on the universal phenomena of religious pilgrimage.

In every religious tradition, the pilgrimage combines more than other religious acts diverse and often contradictory features, which are both spiritual and mundane. Travelling a long distance, visiting holy mountains or shrines, involves physical hardship and endurance, but it also has pleasurable aspects, such as sightseeing and meeting new friends. Usually, pilgrims are motivated by religious objectives, such as adoration of the deities or saints who are enshrined at various sacred places, gaining merit for one's salvation, paying penance for annulment of sin, or praying for the repose of the spirits of the deceased, but these religious motives are often mixed with the desire to acquire healing, good fortune, easy childbirth, prosperity and other this-worldly benefits. Even the ascetic practices, which are usually imposed on the pilgrims, notably sexual abstinence and fasting or dietary restrictions are interpreted as necessary investments for the expected rewards. Besides, the pilgrimage provides welcome relief from the routine of the dull everyday life of the people. Furthermore, seen from a broader perspective, the pilgrimage, which cements the solidarity of religious groups, also stimulates trade and commerce, dissemination of ideas, and intercultural exchange. Notwithstanding these "universal features, which are shared by the pilgrimages of various traditions, each one tends to show a unique ethos of its own, which can be understood only within its religious and cultural contexts.

Historically in Japan, the development of the pilgrimage was greatly conditioned by the geographical and topographical as much as religious and cultural factors. According to Shinto, the whole world is permeated by the sacred (*kami*) nature, so that every mountain, river, tree, rock as well as human being is potentially an object of veneration. As far as the practice of pilgrimage is concerned, it had little place in early Shinto, because Shinto was closely related to the life of the clan (*uji*), which more often than not was settled in a particular geographical locality. To be sure, in many agricultural communities the *kami* of the mountains were believed to come down and become the *kami* of the rice field during the part of the year and then return to the mountains after the harvest. It is conceivable, therefore, that some people might have climbed the mountains in order to experience the mystique of the abode of the *kami*. But such practices were spontaneous and were not regularized as pilgrimages by early Shinto.

The introduction of Chinese civilization and Buddhism during the sixth century A.D. brought about far-reaching religious and cultural changes in the subsequent periods of Japanese history. Eventually, there developed three major types of pilgrimages out of the fusion of indigenous Shinto and folk religious beliefs and practices with Buddhist and Chinese—especially Taoist—elements. They are (1) the pilgrimage to the sacred mountain; (2) the pilgrimage to the temples and shrines, based on the faith in the divinities enshrined in those sanctuaries; and (3) the pilgrimage to sacred places based on the faith in certain charismatic holy men who are believed to have hallowed those places by their visits. It is the purpose of this paper to inquire as to how these types of pilgrimages developed in Japan and also to depict the basic similarities and dissimilarities among them.

Pilgrimage to the Sacred Mountain

We have already hinted at the importance of sacred mountains in the religious life of the early Japanese. It is significant to note in this connection that even after the introduction of Chinese civilization and Buddhism people in Japan continued to venerate mountains as the abodes of divinities, and to pay special respect to the "austerity man" (*gyo-ja*) who was believed to have acquired superhuman power by the rigorous ascetic training of the mountain (*sanrin-toso*). Among the Buddhists, too, there developed in the eighth century a movement called "Nature Wisdom School," which sought Enlightenment not by the traditional meditation and disciplines within the compound of the monasteries but by being close to Nature in the mountains. Besides, some of the monks and pious laity underwent austerity training in the mountains in order to acquire magical power (*siddhi*). Meanwhile, shamanistic diviners, healers and ascetics, who earlier had no connection with Buddhism, came under Buddhist influence. Their affiliation with Buddhism was very tenuous, but they were called "unordained Buddhist practitioners" (*ubasoku; upasaka*), and many claimed to have acquired power to work miracles by undergoing austerity training in the mountains. The combined effect of these movements was the emergence of the so-called Order of Mountain Ascetics (*Shugen-do*) which, despite its formal affiliation with the Tendai and the Shingon schools of Buddhism, retained many elements of Shinto and folk religious traditions.

The popularity of the mountain ascetics during the eleventh and twelfth centuries was greatly enhanced by the belief prevalent among the aristocrats that pilgrimage to sacred mountains, especially those of Kumano and Yoshino, would enable them to experience while on earth a foretaste of the Pure Land. It was also widely held by that time that the native Shinto *kami* of those mountains were in reality manifestations of Buddhist divinities. Thus, the pilgrimages to these mountains, accompanied and guided by the experienced mountain ascetics, were believed to bring favours from both the Shinto and Buddhist divinities simultaneously. With the decline of the court nobility in the latter part of the twelfth century, the mountain ascetics sought patronage among warriors and other non-aristocratic elements by establishing devotional confraternities (*ko-sha*) in various parts of the country. Most members of these confraternities belonged to local Buddhist and/or Shinto groups, but they found additional impetus in their devotion to the deities of the particular sacred mountains which were often far away from their homes. A number of such confraternities have continued to exist until our own times. Since the main function of these groups was pilgrimage to the sacred mountains, upon many of which women were not allowed, the membership of these confraternities was at first predominantly male. They considered the stiff mountain climbing, conducted by experienced guides, essential for spiritual and physical disciplines, and thus the pilgrimage was often considered an initiatory ceremony for boys who were entering the age of adult life. Eventually miniature models of sacred mountains were established in some parts of the country for the benefit of those who could not make real pilgrimages, and the mountain cult grew in popularity by attracting older people and women as well. It was estimated that in the latter part of the nineteenth century there were 17,000 "senior guides" to sacred mountains, which meant that a considerably greater number of mountain ascetics must have been functioning in various capacities.

The three so-called Sect Shinto denominations of our time—(1) Jikko-kyo ("practical conduct" religion), (2) Fuso-kyo (religion of Fuso, which is the classical name of Mt. Fuji), and (3) Ontake-kyo (religion of Mt. Ontake)—are direct heirs of the traditions of the mountain ascetics, while Fuji-ko (devotional confraternity of Mt. Fuji), later renamed as the Maruyama-kyo, became a sub-sect of another Sect Shinto denomination called Shinto Taikyo (the great teaching of Shinto). In addition, there are today many formal and informal mountain pilgrimage groups, ranging from those which follow strict disciplines to those whose activities border on the semi-recreational.

Pilgrimages Based on Faith in Certain Divinities

In the religious history of Japan, the popularization of pilgrimage was not confined to sacred mountains. Many pious clergy, laymen and laywomen, stimulated to be sure by the pilgrimage to the mountains, considered it also meritorious to visit less hazardous holy places in the plain, usually Buddhist temples or Shinto shrines where certain divinities known for their potencies are enshrined. Such pilgrimages are motivated not by the desire to undergo ascetic practices but by people's devotion to a certain Buddha, Bodhisattva or *kami*, to whom the pilgrims pay homage, offer thanksgiving or ask for special favours. Among the Buddhist divinities, the most sought after were Kannon (Avalokitesvara), the Buddhist counterpart of the "goddess of mercy"; Amida (Amitabha), who is believed to have vowed to save all creatures; Jizo (Ksitigarbha), the protector of souls in the realm of hell; Yakushi (Bhaisajyaguru), the "healing Buddha"; and Miroku (Maitreya), the Buddha of the future. The temples which enshrined the statues of these divinities attracted many pilgrims. The most organized of all is the so-called "Pilgrimage to the Thirty-three Sanctuaries in Western Japan" (*Saigoku sanju-san-sho*), which was based on devotion to Kannon (Avalokitesvara).

According to a pious legend, the Emperor Kazan (reigned 984–986), upon the death of his consort, abdicated the throne and in priestly attire visited the 33 sanctuaries dedicated to Kannon. Although this legend is not reliable, it is fairly certain that the practice of the "Zuda" (*dhuta*) pilgrimage to the 33 sanctuaries of Kannon was undertaken by two Tendai priests, Gyoson and Kakuchu, in the twelfth century. Both of them had previously undergone austere training in the mountains, and they appropriated some features of the pilgrimages to sacred mountains to the pilgrimages to the 33 sanctuaries of Kannon. Evidently, judging from the records of the thirteenth and fourteenth centuries, there were variations in the selection of sanctuaries, even though there was general agreement on the sacred number of 33. It was probably in the fifteenth century that the present arrangement of the pilgrimages to the "Thirty-three Temples in Western Japan" (*Saigoku sanju-san-sho*) was fixed by common consent. By that time, the pilgrimage was no longer the monopoly of the well-to-do and the clergy. Due largely to the activities of the leaders of new Buddhist movements that arose in the thirteenth century, i.e., the Pure Land, the True Pure Land, and the Nichiren schools, the poor as well as the rich came to accept the belief that they were living in the period of "degeneration of Buddha's law" (*mappo*), whereby they felt the sense of urgent need for the grace and mercy of divinities for their rebirth in the Pure Land after death. Undoubtedly this is why Mount Nachi, believed to be the model of Kannon's Pure Land on earth, was chosen as the starting point of the pilgrimage. Gradually, the attire of the pilgrim—wearing a large sedge-hat, hanging a rosary around the neck, carrying a walking stick, a ladle, a wooden pail and a bell—came to be accepted. On the road the pilgrims sing a rhythmic chant consisting of 33 verses, each referring to Kannon's mercy and miraculous power manifested at one of the 33 sanctuaries. Incidentally, they beg for food and alms which sustain them throughout the pilgrimage.

In the course of time, the pilgrimage to the 33 sanctuaries of Kannon also developed in the eastern and other parts of Japan. Also, many other forms of Buddhist pilgrimages came into existence, such as the pilgrimage to the 25 temples of the Pure Land School, the pilgrimage to the 100 temples of the Nichiren school, and the pilgrimage to the 100 temples in the Higashiyama section of Kyoto. Unlike pilgrimage to sacred mountains, which is taken as a group guided by an experienced mountain ascetic, pilgrimage based on devotion to certain divinities can be undertaken by individuals. Nevertheless, a number of devotional confraternities arose in connection with such pilgrimages, and their members form small groups of pilgrims for the sake of mutual support and encouragement.

In the Shinto tradition, which also developed the practice of pilgrimage during the last few centuries, the most prominent is the pilgrimage to the Grand Shrine of Ise, the sanctuary of the Shinto deity *par excellence*, Amaterasu-o-mikami, known as the Sun Goddess. It has been promoted by the Confraternity of Ise (*Ise-ko*), which selects by drawing lots certain members who then represent others in making the pilgrimage to Ise, usually in the spring or autumn. Their departure and return are celebrated by special ceremonies and feasts attended by all the members. Since their expenses are paid by the confraternity, which is supported by membership dues, the pilgrims to Ise—or other Shinto pilgrims for that matter—do not beg for food and alms on the road. Otherwise, the aim of the pilgrimage to Ise is similar to that of Buddhist pilgrimages, except that the object of devotion is the Shinto divinity.

Pilgrimage Based on Faith in Charismatic Persons

Next to pilgrimages to sacred mountains and those to sanctuaries of various divinities, there developed in Japan the pilgrimage based on faith in certain charismatic holy men. It is to be recalled in this connection that even before the introduction of Buddhism the Japanese venerated various types of charismatic persons as embodiments of superhuman powers. After the introduction of Buddhism, some of the outstanding Buddhists, such as Prince Regent Shotoku, who in the late sixth and early seventh centuries promoted Buddhism as the *de facto* state religion, and Gyogi, an eighth century popular Buddhist leader who because of his philanthropic activities and saintly character was called the living Bodhisattva, became the objects of adoration on the part of pious Buddhists. Similarly, many of the founders of Buddhist schools, e.g., Shinran (1173–1262), the founder of the True Pure Land School, and Nichiren (1222–1282), founder of the school bearing his name, came to be regarded as semi-saviours, and their writings became for all intents and purposes sacred scriptures comparable to the Tripitaka. It is interesting to note that Japanese Buddhism, unlike its Chinese counterpart, did not produce such men as Fa-hsien, Hsüan-tsang and I-ching who dared to visit India, crossing the desert or ocean, to set foot on sacred spots which were sanctified by the blessed memories of the historic Buddha. On the other hand, it became the accepted pattern for the Japanese Buddhists to make pilgrimages to mausolea of leading Japanese Buddhists, many of whom were known for their charismatic qualities. The most outstanding example in this respect is the cult which developed around the memory of Kukai or Kobo Daishi (774–835), systematizer of the esoteric Buddhist school called the Shingon-shu.

Little need be said about Kukai, whose real life has been buried under layers of pious legends. What is significant is the fact that he is remembered by pious followers as the itinerant holy man who visited many remote areas of Japan, digging wells, healing the sick and working various kinds of miracles to help the poor and the oppressed. Furthermore, it is widely believed that Kukai did not die, and that even today he is still walking around under the disguise of a pilgrim helping those who need his assistance. Understandably, the devotees of Kukai must have visited his birthplace in the island of Shikoku as early as the ninth century, and it is plausible that some sort of formalized pilgrimage in the "four provinces" (Shikoku) might have arisen in the twelfth or thirteenth century. However, the present practice of visiting 88 sanctuaries in Shikoku was not firmly established until about the seventeenth century.

As far as we can ascertain, the "Pilgrimage in Shikoku" is a complex phenomenon. In many ways, it has striking similarities to the "Pilgrimage to the Thirty-three Sanctuaries of Kannon in Western Japan" (*Saigoku sanju-san-sho*). In both cases, the pilgrims wear similar sedge-hats, carry bells and walking sticks, and their chants are similar in form and sound. In fact, among the "main buddhas" (*hon-zon*) enshrined in the 88 temples, those of Kannon are most numerous with 29, followed by Yakushi with 23 and Amida with 9. Ironically, Dainichi (Mahavairocana), the supreme Buddha of the Shingon school, which was established by Kukai, has only 6.

Upon closer examination, however, it becomes evident that the central motif of the "Pilgrimage in Shikoku" is not devotion to the divinities enshrined in the 88 holy sites, which no doubt has become a feature of it, but rather its main emphasis is on the act of "walking with Saint Kukai." That is to say, the "Pilgrimage in Shikoku" is based on faith in the memory of the charismatic holy man, Kukai, of whom the walking stick is the living symbol. Thus, even when a single individual undertakes the pilgrimage, it is called the pilgrimage of two (*dogyoni-nin*), meaning Saint Kukai and himself. According to the established tradition, the pilgrimage to Shikoku begins at Mt. Koya, the seat of the Shingon monastic centre established by Kukai. The pilgrims are expected to pay homage to Kukai's mausoleum, where he is believed to be sleeping until such time when he returns to this world with the future Buddha, Maitreya. From Mt. Koya, the pilgrims go to one of the ports and cross the strait to Shikoku by boat.

The 88 holy places are scattered unevenly among the four provinces that constitute Shikoku. Historically, the Awa province, which has 23 holy sites, has been called the "exercise arena for the spiritual awakening" (*Hosshin no dojo*), the Tosa province with 16 holy sites has been called the "exercise arena for ascetic discipline" (*Shugyono dojo*), the Iyo province with 26 holy sites has been called the "exercise arena for enlightenment" (*Bodai no dojo*), and the Sanuki province with 23 holy sites has been called the "exercise arena for the state of Nirvana" (Nehan no dojo). The holy sites are numbered from No. 1 to No. 88. Of them, Nos. 19, 27, 60, and 66 are considered to be "barriers" (*seki-sho*), and those who have done misdeeds are said to receive at one of these barriers omens, such as the appearance of a certain bird. Such omens indicate that they have displeased Saint Kukai, and they must terminate their pilgrimage and start again. Incidentally, the normal course of the pilgrim is to start from No. 1 and end at No. 88, but, after completing the regular course, one might undertake additional pilgrimage, this time reversing the course from No. 88 to No. 1. It is believed that the chance of encountering Saint Kukai walking in the disguise of a pilgrim is greater when one follows the reverse course. It is taken for granted that the complete pilgrimage is most meritorious. However, even such partial courses as the "ten holy sites" (*jukka-sho mairi*), the "seven holy sites" (*nanaka-sho mairi*) and the holy sites in "one of the four provinces" only (*ikkoku mairi*) are believed to be quite beneficial.

As in the case of the Pilgrimage to the Thirty-three Sanctuaries of Kannon, the Pilgrimage in Shikoku is often undertaken by individuals or by small family groups. But there are also many kinds of formal and informal groups, which sponsor group pilgrimages, such as the Daishi-ko (Confraternity for the devotion to Kobo Daishi) and the Kongo-ko (Confraternity of the Shingon devotees). Equally noteworthy is the development of the confraternities which are dedicated to the task of offering hospitality and assistance to the pilgrims (*set-tai-ko*). Members of these confraternities believe that by offering hospitality to the pilgrims they are in fact serving Saint Kukai. Some of these hospitality groups come from distant places, chartering boats to carry food and other items, and set up hospitality centres at various spots along the main course of the pilgrimage.

The popularity of the Pilgrimage in Shikoku was such that from the eighteenth century onward several "miniature eighty-eight sanctuaries of Shikoku" were established in various parts of the country, such as Edo (Tokyo), Chita (near Nagoya), Soma (in the present Chiba prefecture) and the island of Shozu in the Inland Sea. These small scale pilgrimages are of course not so meritorious as the pilgrimage to the real holy sites in Shikoku, but they have provided opportunities to many people who otherwise would not have been able to "walk in faith with Saint Kukai."

Even such a brief portrayal of the three types of pilgrimages in Japan makes it clear that there are many similarities as well as significant differences among them. The first type, namely, the pilgrimage to the sacred mountains may be characterized by its corporate activities under the supervision of an expert guide. Its emphasis on ascetic and physical disciplines implies a soteriological path based on self-power (*jiriki*), even though there is in it an element of faith. And the notion that the sacred mountains are the models of Paradise gives strong impetus to the pilgrims to seek the religious meaning of life within the realm of phenomenal existence. The second type, namely, the pilgrimage based on faith in certain divinities tends to be more individualistic and also lacks rigorous ascetic emphasis because its soteriological path relies on the saving power of the divinities (*tariki*). Even though the pilgrims seek immediate experience of some degree of salvation here on earth, they accept the existence of the future realm as the only real arena of salvation. Finally, the third type, namely, the pilgrimage based on faith in charismatic holy men has some of the features of the first and the second. But its own unique character is demonstrated in the notion that the saving power has been already actualized in the life of the charismatic holy man, who thus combines the roles of the deity and of the guide. In other words, the pilgrim relies on the other-power (*tariki*), but the other-power is not far away in a transcendental realm, either in space or in time. The saving power, fully actualized in a person, shares every step of the earthly pilgrimage as the real "fellow pilgrim."

It goes without saying that the task of the historian of religions involves many difficulties especially when one deals with a complex phenomenon such as the development of religion in Japan which has homologized diverse features of Buddhist, Taoist, Shinto and folk religious beliefs, symbols, cults and practices. In such a situation, one meaningful approach may be to study a significant form of religious cult which has developed out of the fusion of various elements. On this score, it is our hope that this preliminary study of the three types of pilgrimage might throw some light on the characteristic pieties of Japanese religious tradition.

❖ MIRCEA ELIADE ❖

Mircea Eliade (1907–1986) served on the faculty of the University of Chicago as professor of the history of religions. During his career he earned an international reputation for his many publications including *Shamanism, Patterns in Comparative Religion*, and *The Quest*. In the following essay, Eliade examines the topic of sacred space and notes several distinctive features. Sacred space enables the religious believer to live in an intelligible world. Sacred space orients the believer toward realms of meaning by reduplicating the work of the gods. In sacred space, Eliade suggests, images of the cosmos are found in the symbols, the geography, the constructions, and the associations which are contained in the sacred space. Eliade's analysis of sacred space complements Kitagawa's earlier description of pilgrimage to sacred spaces and together they illustrate the rich insights into the structures and ethos of particular religious traditions available through phenomenological examination.

❖

The World, the City, the House

Living in One's Own World

Years ago, one of my professors at the University of Bucharest had the opportunity to attend a series of lectures given by the famous historian Theodore Mommsen. At that time, in the early 1890s, Mommsen was already very old, but his mind was still lucid and harbored a memory that was astonishingly complete and accurate. In his first lecture, Mommsen was describing Athens during the time of Socrates. He went to the blackboard and sketched, without a single note, the plan of the city as it was in the fifth century; he then proceeded to indicate the location of the temples and public buildings and to show where some of the famous wells and groves were situated. Particularly impressive was his vivid reconstruction of the environmental background of the *Phaedrus*. After quoting the passage in which Socrates inquires where Lysias is staying, and Phaedrus replies that he is staying with Epicrates, Mommsen pointed out the possible location of Epicrates' house, explaining that the text states that "the house where Morychus used to live" was "close to the temple of Olympian Zeus." Mommsen continued by graphically mapping the route that Socrates and Phaedrus took as they walked along the river Ilissus, and he then indicated the probable place where they stopped and held their memorable dialogue at "the quiet spot" where the "tall plane tree" grew.

Awed by Mommsen's amazing display of erudition, memory, and literary insight, my professor was reluctant to leave the amphitheater immediately after the lecture. He then saw an elderly valet come forward and gently take Mommsen's arm in order to guide him out of the amphitheater. At this point, one of the students still present explained that the famous historian did not know how to go home alone. The greatest living authority on fifth-century Athens was completely lost in his own city of Wilhelminian Berlin!

For what I intend to discuss in this article I could hardly find a better introduction. Mommsen admirably illustrates the existential meaning of "living in one's own world." His *real* world, the only one that was relevant and meaningful, was the classical Greco-Roman world. For Mommsen, the world of the Greeks and Romans was not simply *history*, that is, a dead past recovered through a historiographical *anamnesis*; it was *his* world—that place where he could move, think, and enjoy the beatitude of being alive and creative. I do not really know whether he always required a servant to guide him home. Probably not. Like most creative scholars, he probably lived in two worlds: the universe of forms and values, to the understanding of which he dedicated his life and which corresponds somehow to the "cosmicized" and therefore "sacred" world of the primitives; and the everyday "profane" world into which he was "thrown," as Heidegger would say. But then, in his old age, Mommsen obviously felt detached from the profane, nonessential, and for him meaningless and ultimately chaotic space of modern Berlin. If one can speak of an amnesia with regard to the profane space of Berlin, one has also to recognize that this amnesia was compensated for by incredible *anamnesis* of all that concerned Mommsen's existential world, i.e., the classical Greco-Roman universe. In his old age, Mommsen was living in a world of archetypes.

Perhaps the closest parallel to this experience of feeling lost in an unknown, chaotic space is found among the Achilpas, one of the Australian Aranda tribes. According to their mythology, a divine being called Numbakula "cosmicized" their territory, created their ancestor, and founded their institutions. Numbakula fashioned a sacred pole out of the trunk of a gum tree, climbed up to the sky on it, and disappeared. This pole represents the cosmic axis, for it is around it that the land becomes habitable and is transformed into a "world." For this reason its ritual role is a considerable one. The Achilpas carry it with them in their wanderings and decide which direction to take according to the way it leans. This allows them, in spite of their continual moving about, always to find themselves in "their world" and at the same time to remain in communication with the heaven into which Numbakula has vanished. If the pole is broken, it is a catastrophe; in a way, it is the "end of the world" and a regression into chaos. Spencer and Gillen relate a legend in which the sacred pole was broken and the entire tribe fell prey to anguish. The people wandered haphazardly for a time and finally sat down on the ground and allowed themselves to perish. This is an excellent illustration of the necessity for "cosmicizing" the land which is to be lived in. The "world," for the Achilpas, becomes "their world" only to the degree that it reproduces the cosmos organized and sanctified by Numbakula. They cannot live without this vertical axis which assures an "opening" toward the transcendent and at the same time makes possible their orientation in space. In other words, one cannot live in a "chaos." Once this contact with the transcendent is broken off and the system of orientation is disrupted, existence in the world is no longer possible—and so the Achilpas let themselves die.

No less dramatic is the case of the Bororos of the Matto Grosso in Brazil, which is brilliantly discussed by Claude Lévi-Strauss in his book *Tristes tropiques*. Traditionally, the Bororo village was organized in a rough circle around the men's house and the dancing ground; and it was also divided into four quarters by two axes—one running north to south and the other east to west. These divisions governed the whole social life of the village, especially its system of intermarriage and kinship. The Salesian missionaries who first dealt with this tribe thought that the only way to help them was to persuade them to leave their traditional village and settle in a new one. These charitable and well-meaning missionaries established what they thought to be a more convenient and practical village of rectangular huts set out in parallel rows. This reorganization completely destroyed the complex Bororo social system, which was so closely bound to the layout of the traditional village that it could not survive transplantation into a different physical environment. What was even more tragic was that the Bororos, in spite of their quasi-nomadic way of life, felt completely disoriented in the world once they were removed from their traditional cosmology depicted in the village plan. Under these conditions, they accepted any plausible explanation offered by the Salesians for their new and confusing universe.

Ultimately, for the man of archaic society, the very fact of *living in the world has a religious value*. For he lives in a world which has been created by supernatural beings and where his village or house is an image of the cosmos. The cosmology does not yet possess profane, protoscientific values and functions. The cosmology, that is, the cosmological images and symbols which inform the habitable world, is not only a system of religious ideas but also a pattern of religious behavior.

The Cosmogonic Model of City-Building

But if living in the world for archaic man has a religious value, this is a result of a specific experience of what can be called "sacred space." Indeed, for religious man, space is not homogeneous; some parts of space are qualitatively different. There is a sacred and hence a strong, significant space; and there are other spaces that are not sacred and so are without structure, form, or meaning. Nor is this all. For religious man, this spatial nonhomogeneity finds expression in the experience of an opposition between space that is sacred—the only *real* and *really* existing space—and all other spaces, the formless expanse surrounding it. The religious experience of the nonhomogeneity of space is a primordial experience, comparable to the founding of the world. For it is the break effected in space that allows the world to be constituted, because it reveals the fixed point, the central axis for all future orientation. When the sacred manifests itself in any hierophany, there is not only a break in the homogeneity of space; there is also a revelation of an absolute reality, opposed to the nonreality of the vast surrounding expanse. The manifestation of the sacred ontologically creates the world. In the homogeneous and infinite expanse, in which no point of reference is possible and hence no *orientation* can be established, the hierophany reveals an absolute fixed point, a *center*.

So it is clear to what a great degree the discovery—that is, the revelation—of a sacred space possesses existential value for religious man; for nothing can begin, nothing can be *done*, without a previous orientation—and any orientation implies acquiring a fixed point. It is for this reason that religious man has always sought to fix his abode at the "center of the world. "*If the world is to be lived in*, it must be *founded*—and no world can be born in the chaos of the homogeneity and relativity of profane space. The discovery or projection of a fixed point—the center—is equivalent to the creation of the world. Ritual orientation and construction of sacred space has a cosmogonic value; for the ritual by which man constructs a sacred space is efficacious in the measure in which *it reproduces the work of the gods*, i.e., the cosmogony.

The history of Rome, as well as the history of other cities or peoples, begins with *the foundation of the town*; that is to say, the *foundation* is tantamount to a *cosmogony*. Every new city represents a new beginning of the world. As we know from the legend of Romulus, the ploughing of the circular ditch, the *sulcus primigenius*, designates the foundation of the city walls. The classical writers were tempted to derive the word *urbs* ("city") from *urvum*, the curve of a ploughshare, or *urvo*, "I plough round"; some of them derived it from *orbis*, a curved thing, a globe, the world. And Servius mentions "the custom of the ancients [which decreed] that, as a new town was founded by the use of a plough, so it should also be destroyed by the same rite by which it was founded."

The center of Rome was a hole, *mundus*, the point of communication between the terrestrial world and the lower regions. Roscher has long since interpreted the *mundus* as an *omphalos* (i.e., navel of the earth);

every town possessing a *mundus* was thought to be situated in the center of the world, in the navel of *orbis terrarum*. It has also been rightly proposed that *Roma quadrata* is to be understood, not as being square in shape, but as being divided into four parts. Roman cosmology was based on the image of a *terra* divided into four regions.

Similar conceptions are to be found everywhere in the Neolithic world and the Early Bronze Age. In India the town, as well as the temple, is built in the likeness of the universe. The foundation rites represent the repetition of the cosmogony. In the center of the town there is symbolically located Mount Meru, the cosmic mountain, together with the high gods; and each of the four principal gates of the town are also under the protection of a god. In a certain sense, the town and its inhabitants are elevated to a superhuman plane: the city is assimilated to Mount Meru, and the inhabitants become "images" of the gods. Even as late as the eighteenth century, Jaipur was built after the traditional model described in the *Silpa-sastra*.

The Iranian metropolis had the same plan as the Indian towns, that is, it was an *imago mundi*. According to the Iranian tradition, the universe was conceived as a wheel with six spokes and a large hole in the middle, like a navel. The texts proclaim that the "Iranian country" (*Airyanam vaejah*) is the center and heart of the world; consequently, it is the most precious among all the other countries. For that reason, Shiz, the town where Zarathustra was born, was regarded as the source of royal power. The throne of Chosroes II was constructed in such a way as to symbolize the universe. The Iranian king was called "Axis of the World," or the "World's Pole." Seated on the throne, in the middle of his palace, the king was symbolically situated at the center of the cosmic town, the Uranopolis.

This type of cosmic symbolism is even more striking with regard to Angkor in Cambodia:

The city with its walls and moats represents the World surrounded by its chains of mountains and by the mythical oceans. The temple in the center symbolizes Mt. Meru, its five towers standing up like the five peaks of the sacred Mountain. Its subordinate shrines represent the constellations in their courses, i.e. the Cosmic Time. The principal ritual act imposed on the faithful consists in walking round the building in the prescribed direction, so as to pass in succession through each stage of the solar cycle, in other words to traverse space in step with time. The temple is in fact a chronogram, symbolizing and controlling the sacred cosmography and topography of the Universe, of which it is the ideal center and regulator.

With some variations, we find the same pattern everywhere in Southeast Asia. Siam was divided into four provinces, with the metropolis in the middle; and in the center of the town stood the royal palace. The country was thus an image of the universe; for according to the Siamese cosmology, the universe is a quadrangle with Mount Meru in the middle. Bangkok is called "the celestial royal city," "the city of the Gods," and so forth. The king, placed in the center of the world, was a *cakravartin*, a cosmocrator.

Likewise, in Burma, Mandalay was built, in 1857, according to the traditional cosmology, that is, as an *imago mundi*—quadrangular and having the royal palace in the center. We find in China the same cosmological pattern and the same correlation among cosmos, state, city, and palace. The world was conceived as a rectangle having China in the middle; on the four horizons were situated four seas, four holy mountains, and the four barbarian nations. The town was built as a quadrangle, with three gates on each side and with the palace at the center, corresponding to the Polar Star. From this center, the perfect sovereign was able to influence the whole universe.

The House at the Center of the World

It is a mistake to think that this cosmological symbolism was restricted to palaces, temples, and royal capitals and that such symbols were intelligible only to the learned theologians and the rich and powerful sovereigns, administrators, and aristocrats. For obvious reasons I have referred to some of the most famous examples of architectural construction; but we find the same cosmological symbolism in the structure of any house, hut, or tent of traditional societies, even among the most archaic and "primitive."

As a matter of fact, it is usually not possible to speak of the house without referring to the city, the sanctuary, or the world. In many cases, what can be said of the house applies equally to the village or the town. The multiple homologies—among cosmos, land, city, temple, palace, house, and hut—emphasize the same fundamental symbolism: each one of these images expresses the existential experience of *being in the world*, more exactly, of being situated in an organized and meaningful world (i.e., organized and meaningful because it was created by the supernatural beings). The same cosmological symbolism, formulated in spatial, architectonic terms, informs house, city, and universe. To understand the symbolism of a Dyak house, one must know the cosmogonic myth, namely, that the world came into being as a result of a combat between two polar principles, the supreme deity, Mahatala, and the primordial water snake. For every house is a replica of the primeval exemplary house: it is symbolically erected on the back of the water snake, its roof corresponds to the primeval mountain on which Mahatala is enthroned, and an umbrella represents the tree of life. In the same way, the cosmological dualism characteristic of Indonesian religion, culture, and society is clearly seen in the structure of every Indonesian house, with its ritually consecrated "male" and "female" divisions.

The traditional Chinese house is similarly informed by a cosmic symbolism. The opening in the roof, called "window of heaven," assures communication with heaven. The Chinese applied the same term to the opening at the top of the Mongolian tent. This term—"window of heaven"—also means, in Chinese, "chimney." The Mongolian tent is constructed with a central pole, which emerges through this upper hole. This post is symbolically identified with the "Pillar of the World," i.e., with the *axis mundi*. In many parts of the world this *axis mundi* has been concretely represented either by the central pillar that supports the house or in the form of isolated stakes called "World Pillars." In other words, *cosmic symbolism is found in the very structure of everyday habitations.* The house is an *imago mundi*. Because the sky was conceived as a vast tent supported by a central pillar, the tent pole, or the central post of the house, was assimilated to the Pillars of the World and was so named.

Similar conceptions are found among many North American Indian tribes, especially the Algonquins and the Sioux. Their sacred lodge, where initiations are performed represents the universe. The roof symbolizes the dome of the sky, the floor represents the earth, the four walls the four directions of cosmic space. The ritual construction of the sacred space is emphasized by a threefold symbolism: the four doors, the four windows, and the four colors all signify the four cardinal points. The construction of the sacred lodge thus repeats the cosmogony, for the lodge represents the world. We may also add that the interdependence between the cosmos and cosmic time ("circular" time) was so strongly felt that in several Indian languages the term for "world" is also used to mean "year." For example, certain California tribes say that "the world is past" or that "the earth has passed" to mean that "a year has passed." The Dakotas say: "The year is a circle around the world," that is, a circle around the sacred lodge.

Perhaps the most revealing example of house symbolism is that of the Fali, a people of the North Cameroun. The house is the image of the universe and consequently of the microcosm represented by man; but it reflects at the same time all the phases of the cosmogonic myth. In other words, the house is not a static construction but has a "movement" corresponding to the different stages of the cosmogonic process. The orien-

tation of the separate units (the central pole, the walls the roof), as well
as the position of the tools and furniture, is related to the movements of
the inhabitants and their location in the house. That is to say, the members of the family change their places inside the habitation in respect to
the seasons, the time of day, and the various modifications of their famil-
ial or social status.

I have said enough about the religious significance of human dwelling
places for certain conclusions to have become almost self-evident. Exactly like the city or the sanctuary, the house is sanctified, in whole or in
part, by a cosmological symbolism or ritual. This is why settling some-
where—by building a village or merely a house—represents a serious
decision, for the very existence of man is involved; he must, in short,
create his own world and assume the responsibility of maintaining and
renewing it. Habitations are not lightly changed, for it is not easy to
abandon one's world. The house is not an object, a "machine to live in";
*it is the universe that man constructs for himself by imitating the para-
digmatic creation of the gods, the cosmogony.* Every construction and
every inauguration of a new building are in some measure equivalent to
a new beginning, a new life. And every beginning repeats the primordial
beginning, when the universe first saw the light of day. Even in modern
societies, with their high degree of desacralization, the festivity and re-
joicing that accompany settling in a new house still perserve the memory
of the festive exuberance that long ago, marked the *incipit vita nova.*

Israel, the Sacred Land

I do not think that we can dismiss all these beliefs and experiences on
the ground that they belong to the past and have no relevance for modern
man. The scientific understanding of cosmic space—a space which has
no center and is infinite—has nothing to do with the existential experience of living in a familiar and meaningful world. Even such a *history*-
oriented people as the Jews could not live without a cosmological framework comparable to some of the patterns I have been discussing. The
Jews also believe that Israel is located at the center of the world and that
the foundation stone of the Temple in Jerusalem represents the foundation of the world. The rock of Jerusalem reached deep into the subterra-
nean waters (*tehom*). The Temple was situated exactly above the *tehom*,
the Hebrew equivalent of the Babylonian *apsu*, the primeval waters before Creation. The *apsu* and the *tehom* symbolize the aquatic chaos, the
preformal modality of cosmic matter, and, at the same time, the world of
death, of all that precedes and follows life. The rock of Jerusalem thus

designates the point of intersection and communication between the lower world and earth. Moreover, this vertical image is homologized to horizontal space, as the lower regions can be related to the unknown desert regions that surround the inhabited territory; that is, the underworld, over which the cosmos is firmly established, corresponds to the chaos that extends beyond the city's frontiers.

Consequently, Jerusalem is

that one place on earth which is closest to heaven, which is horizontally the exact center of the geographical world and vertically the exact midpoint between the upper world and the lower world, the place where both are closest to the skin of the earth, heaven being only two or eighteen miles above the earth at Jerusalem, the waters of *Tehom* lying only a thousand cubits below the Temple floor. For the Jew, to journey up to Jerusalem is to ascend to the very crucible of creation, the womb of everything, the center and fountain of reality, the place of blessing *par excellence*.

For that reason Israel is, as Rabbi Nachman of Bratislava puts it, the "real center of the spirit of life and therefore of the renewal of the world . . . the spring of joy, the perfection of wisdom . . . the pure and healing power of the earth." The vital power of the land and the Temple is expressed in a variety of ways, and the rabbis often appear to vie with one another in contests of exaggeration. In the same sense, a rabbinical text asserts that "when the Temple was ruined, the blessing departed from the world." As the historian of religions Jonathan Z. Smith interprets this rabbinical tradition,

The Temple and its ritual serve as the cosmic pillars or the "sacred pole" supporting the world. If its service is interrupted or broken, if an error is made, then the world, the blessing, the fertility, indeed all of creation which flows from the Center, will likewise be disrupted. Like the Achilpas' sacred pole . . . the disruption of the Center and its power is a breaking of the link between reality and the world, which is dependent upon the Sacred Land. Whether through error or exile, the severing of this relationship is a cosmic disaster.

Contemporary Jewish scholars and writers as different as Chaim Raphael, David Ben-Gurion, Richard L. Rubenstein, and Jonathan Smith utilize similar cosmological images when they try to express what the Exile meant for the Jews. "While the exile is an event which can be located chronologically as after A.D. 70," writes Jonathan Smith, it is above all a thoroughly mythic event: "the return to chaos, the decreation, the separation from the deity analogous to the total catastrophe of the primeval flood." The loss of Jerusalem, writes Chaim Raphael, meant more than the historical event of the Jews driven into exile: "God himself was in exile. The world was out of joint. The destruction was the symbol of it." Of course, the "homeless God," the presence of God exiled, are images previously used by Rabbi Akiba in the first century; but it is highly significant that they are so popular today. Jonathan Eibschutz, an eighteenth-century Talmudist, writes: "If we do not have Jerusalem . . . why would we have life? . . . Surely we have descended from life unto death. And the converse is true. When the Lord restores the captivity of Zion, we shall ascend from death unto life." It is striking that

even among the so-called atheistic, secularist, deeply Marxist Zionists who founded the first *kibbutzim*, their religion of "land and labor" is a resurgence of the old language of a recovered center, of life shared with the land. Thus, for example, A. D. Gordon, understood by many to be the leader of the secular communitarians in the early twentieth century, describes their experience in a language resplendent with overtones of cosmic trees, world navels, and so forth: "It is life we want," writes A. D. Gordon, "no more, no less than that, our own life feeding on our vital sources, in the fields and under the skies of our Homeland. . . . We come to our Homeland in order to be planted in our natural soil from which we have been uprooted. . . . It is our duty to concentrate all our strength on this central spot. . . . What we seek to establish in Palestine is a new re-created Jewish people."

Cosmic Religions and Biblical Faiths

I could easily multiply quotations, and, of course, I could add many comparable examples from other modern cultures. I have stressed Jewish cosmological symbolism because it is less familiar; as a matter of fact, Judaism and, to a certain extent, Christianity are generally regarded as being almost entirely *historical*, that is, time-oriented, religions. The land of Israel, with Jerusalem and the Temple in the center, is a sacred country because it has a sacred history, consisting of the long and fabulous series of events planned and carried out by Yahweh for the benefit of his people. But this is true for many other religions, primitive as well as Oriental. The land of the Arandas, of the Dyaks, and of the Bororos is sacred because it was created and organized by supernatural beings: the cosmogony is only the beginning of a sacred history, which is followed by the creation of man and other mythical events.

I do not need to discuss here the similarities and differences between so-called primitive, *cosmic* religions and *historical*, biblical faiths. What is relevant for our theme is that we find everywhere the same fundamental conception of the necessity to live in an intelligible and meaningful world, and we find that this conception emerges ultimately from the experience of a sacred space. Now one can ask in what sense such experiences of the sacred space of houses, cities, and lands are still significant for modern desacralized man. Certainly, we know that man has never lived in the space conceived by mathematicians and physicists as being isotropic, that is, space having the same properties in all directions. The space experienced by man is *oriented* and thus anisotropic, for each dimension and direction has a specific value; for instance, along the vertical axis, "up" does not have the same value as "down"; along the horizontal axis, left and right may be differentiated in value. The question is whether the experience of oriented space and other comparable experiences of intentionally structured spaces (for example, the different spaces of art and architecture) have something in common with the sacred space known by *Homo religiosus*.

This is, surely, a difficult question—but *who* can be expected to offer an answer? Certainly not someone who is unaware of what sacred space means and who totally ignores the cosmic symbolism of the traditional habitation. Unfortunately, this is very often the case.

I would like to conclude by reminding you of that famous lawsuit which followed Brançusi's first exhibition at the Armory Show in New York. The New York customs officials refused to admit that some of Brançusi's sculptures—for example, *Mlle Pogany* and *A Muse*—were really works of art and so taxed them, very heavily, as blocks of marble. We must not be overly harsh in our judgment of the New York customs agents, for, during the subsequent lawsuit over the taxation of Brançusi's works, at least one leading American art critic declared that *Mlle Pogany* and *A Muse* were mere pieces of polished marble!

Brançusi's art was so new that, in 1913, even some art specialists could not *see* it. Likewise, the cosmic symbolism of sacred space is so old and so familiar that many are not yet able to recognize it.

❖ ÅKE HULTKRANTZ ❖

Typological phenomenology of religion has had an impact in other academic modes of inquiry, particularly in the historical and anthropological study of religion. Åke Hultkrantz (1920–   ) is professor of the history of religions and director of the Institute of Comparative Religion at the University of Stockholm, Sweden. He has written extensively on the religious traditions of North American Indians and his publications include *Conceptions of the Soul Among North American Indians, The Religions of the American Indians,* and *Belief and Worship in Native North America.*

In the following essay, Hultkrantz employs a "regional phenomenology," which he describes as "comparative within certain geographical limits," in order to examine the phenomena of the cult of the dead among North American Indians. He defines this cult as "ideological premises and acts of worship concerned with dead persons or groups of (presumably) deceased persons, who may bestow some benefit upon their devotees." Upon this basis he then gives an overview of these beliefs and practices in North America. He concludes with a discussion of Kachina ideology and suggests relevant connections to such phenomena as potlatch ceremonies and guardian spirit concepts. Beyond his specific contribution to the understanding of Native American religious traditions, Hultkrantz's work clearly demonstrates the usefulness and importance of historical-typological phenomenological investigations for other scholarly approaches to religion.

❖

The Cult of the Dead among
North American Indians

The following investigation takes up a theme which at first sight may appear outmoded and little rewarding. Outmoded, because this theme belonged with the evolutionistic approaches of fifty years ago, and practically no more modern works treat it; little rewarding, because North American Indians in general have had little inclination toward a pronounced cult of the dead. However, the latter circumstance presents us with some clues to an understanding of why and where such a cult may occur. In a wider perspective, from phenomenological points of view, the cult of the dead, or ancestor worship, may be referred to as an important aspect of the study of death. In certain cases it also represents a dimension of the study of theism. It seems less apparent, however, that it constitutes a stepping-stone to the belief in gods, as Spencer and Karsten thought.

Very little has been written on the cult of the dead in North America, presumably because of its restricted importance. There are some generalizations in Schoolcraft's famous work on North American Indians, but they concern death customs rather than the cult of the dead. Daniel Brinton adequately remarked that "ancestral worship . . . is a branch of the religion of sex, for only when the ties of relationship are somewhat strongly felt, can it arise. In America it existed, but was not prominent." The observation of the role played by social structure is quite correct and has in later days been emphatically stressed by A. R. Radcliffe-Brown. At the turn of the century Miss Laetitia Moon Conard discussed the possible existence of a cult of the dead among the Algonkian-speaking peoples of eastern North America. She found that, generally speaking, there was no such cult. The deceased appear to us as feeble beings, just shadows of men, she says; they need the assistance of the living in order to procure nourishment and clothes, tools and weapons, even fire. This is indeed the reverse of a cult of the dead.

The first more general appreciation of the cult of the dead in America appeared in the *Encyclopaedia of Religion and Ethics* in 1908. In a general article on the subject W. Crooke said that ancestor worship existed in various forms throughout America—but then, he included reincarnation ideas and carved grave posts to such worship. Stansbury Hagar conceded that the dead as a rule could return to earth to warn, protect and instruct the living. However, "strictly speaking, instances of true worship of ancestors or of the dead in America are rare. The dead are seldom confused or identified with the various deities, whose attributes, with few exceptions, clearly reveal their origin in the personification of natural phenomena." Hagar added that information was all that was asked of the dead, seldom anything else. The evidence is moreover slight that the dead were regarded as superior beings. We must, of course, realize that Hagar's account was written before there was any thorough knowledge of American archeology and ethnology.

Later pronouncements are short statements, nothing more. Hartley Burr Alexander simply declared, in his survey of North American mythology, that Indians performed rites to secure the assistance of the dead—a sweeping statement. Ruth Benedict remarked that the idea that one may seek guardian spirits among the dead is nearly absent in North America. She pointed out that the association of masked gods with impersonal dead in the Pueblo area is unusual in America, "and even that is slightly developed." K. Th. Preuss found a main distinction between North and South American religions in the fact that in the latter continent guardian spirits are usually identical with dead persons, in particular shamans, and thus we have a cult of the dead here. Wilhelm Schmidt, again, considered real ancestor worship to be rare in all of America with the exception of Peru during Inca time. His view that such worship belongs with agricultural societies and other societies influenced by them was shared by Walter Krickeberg. In his comprehensive work on the fear of the dead Sir James Frazer arrived at the conclusion that American aborigines had some worship of the dead, although it was far less important and extended than the same sort of worship in Africa—a rather trivial conclusion. About the same time Robert Lowie succinctly wrote that ancestor cults "are rarely typical of American Indians, hence they are not an inevitable stage in religious evolution."

Here, then, Spencer's evolutionism is refuted with the aid of the American evidence. Paul Radin for his part assigned a rather late date to the rise of ancestor worship. He strongly insisted (like Father Schmidt earlier) that there were no well-authenticated traces of this worship among food-gathering, fishing, and hunting peoples.

There has been little written on our subject during the last forty years. One notable exception is, however, Ruth Underhill's short characteristic in a paper on American religions. She states that the spirits of the dead did not play the important part sometimes found in the Old World. Certainly, they could cause illness, act as guardian spirits, or become reincarnated. However, only a few might be elevated to powerful spirits and gods. The present author has discussed the poor development of North American Indian ancestor worship in some papers, but only briefly.

This negative appreciation of the role of ancestor worship in North America is well founded in the materials at hand. With the exception of particularly the Pueblo area, a real cult of the dead is scarcely mentioned in our sources. There are even direct denials. John Chapman, contrasting ideas and customs among the Ingalik of Alaska with the Batak of Sumatra, says that ancestor worship is found among the former "only in a rudimentary form, if it is to be found at all." We have seen Moon Conard's conclusion, built upon the perusal of a vast material, that Algonkian Indians lacked cult of the dead. David Mandelbaum tells us that Algonkian Plains Cree did not believe that the dead souls bestow power on man, but it was possible to beseech them to petition the higher powers to render aid to mortals. A bit confusingly, Lowie gives the information that among the Crow ghosts occasionally occurred as spiritual patrons, although ancestor worship in any form was totally lacking. Similarly, James Owen Dorsey disclaims for the southern Sioux Indians—Omaha, Ponca, Kansa, and Osage—all worship of the ancestors. The Yana Indians of northern California were apparently also devoid of such worship.

A particular reaction against anything associated with death, the dead person, his belongings, the lodge in which he died, characterizes Athapascan and, to a certain degree, Shoshoni-Paiute, Yuman, and Piman peoples in western North America. The Southern Athapascans in Arizona, New Mexico, and Texas, have a fright of death which ascends to morbid proportions. Writing about the Lipan Apache "death complex," Morris Opler states that its extensions "involve almost every aspect of Lipan thought and life." The fear of ghosts penetrates Apache and Navajo existence. No wonder, therefore, that the latter could not be induced to adopt the Ghost Dance or the Christian religion with their resurrection themes. In such a milieu there is, of course, no qualification for the existence of a cult of the dead. Considering the many loans the Navajo have made from the Pueblo peoples, not least in the area of ceremonialism, the distance between their fear of the dead and the ancestor worship of the Pueblo groups is striking.

Specification of the Subject

Before turning to a closer investigation of the evidence certain clarifications must be made. My investigation is a case of regional phenomenology (typology), which means that it is comparative within certain geographical limits. The area of investigation, North America, is indeed most extensive, and this circumstance calls for certain restrictions of the theme. Firstly, I have deliberately concentrated the account on the cognitive aspects of the cult of the dead which, in a comparative perspective, are of paramount theoretical interest. Of course, a closer study and systematization of such behavioristic facets as offerings, cult groups, prayers, and dances would have increased the value of this investigation, but considerations of space have prevented this operation. Secondly, the margins of the cult have been restricted to cases in which attitudes of veneration and accomplishment are unequivocal.

By *cult of the dead* or *ancestor worship* I mean ideological premises and acts of worship concerned with deceased persons, or groups of (presumably) deceased persons, who may bestow some benefit upon their devotees. The difference between cult of the dead and ancestor worship *stricto sensu* is that the former concept is more inclusive, also taking in other dead persons than the subject's own ancestors, whereas ancestor worship only refers to the latter.

Now, some students define ancestor worship in the same way as I have but reserve the term "cult of the dead" for ideas and actions connected with the disposal of the dead, and include observances directed against malevolent ghosts in "ancestor worship." This seems less advisable. A cult is a set of notions and rites aiming at the veneration of a supernatural being (cf. Latin *cultus*). Neither funeral concerns nor apotropaic rites against dangerous ghosts seem to fall within this definition. And since worship is a direct translation of "cult" the same rule holds in that case.

In order to make the record straight I shall discuss these points a little closer.

1. Burial gifts are no real offerings to the dead. It is a well-known fact that gifts for the dead are placed at (or in) the grave, or burned at the grave in order to release their spiritual essence. Such gifts may be made even long after death had occurred. Thus according to the Nootka of Vancouver Island, it may happen that the dead visit the living with good intentions. It is the practice of many families before going to bed to place a meal of dried fish and potatoes beside the fire for the refreshment of the dead visitors. Now, some authors have called such customs instances of a death cult. For example, Schoolcraft notes that North American Indi-

ans "worship the spirits of their ancestors. They both place cakes on their graves and sepulchres, and pour out libations." Moon Conard makes use of the (French) word "offrande" in order to characterize a gift to the dead. Although the boundary line between worship of, and gifts to, the ancestors is not clear-cut, as will be shown in sequence, in the vast majority of cases we are facing two different classes of phenomena. Already seventy years ago Hagar pointed out, with reference to American Indians, that the customs of burying clothing and tools with the body and leaving food and drink upon the grave expressed the service of love seeking to provide for the material wants of the dead. "It was not worship." Although not only love, but also fear of contamination with the dead or the death substance may lie behind these customs, the conclusion seems to be correct. The same differentiation between cult of the dead and grave gifts has been drawn by theoreticians like Reidar Christiansen and Marcel Mauss.

2. Preventive rites directed against dangerous ghosts are not included in the cult of the dead. Out of the enormous material on such apotropaic and propitiatory rites I select the following for illustration. Like most North American Indians the Blackfoot believe that ghosts may appear as owls. In order to ward off the evil the owls may bring, the Blackfoot use black paint on their faces. Schoolcraft's informant on the Dakota of Minnesota, Philander Prescott, reported that these Indians ascribed bad luck in hunting to some misconduct such as neglect of honoring the spirits of the dead. The Northern Paiute living close to Pyramid Lake, Nevada, "offered" to the dead food, beads, and other objects while an old man said, "Don't come back, stay away, we don't want you."

These precautionary measures cannot always be grouped together with apotropaic rites associated with death (such rites aim at getting rid of the dead person's soul, or ghost). Nevertheless, their general negative import precludes me from counting them to the cult of the dead. I am aware that other authors would accept them as part of ancestor worship. However, there is no veneration of the ancestors involved, no information that they might be resorted to, no hint of their permanence in belief or ritual. If we talk of a cult of the dead we certainly mean a cult with some permanence, and with not only negative but also positive aspects.

3. Ancestor worship in a proper sense is as we saw part of the cult of the dead. However, "ancestor worship" may be used as a term for the cult of the dead as well. If the dead whom the Indian turns to in prayer are looked upon as a collective, it is not reasonable to expect that they are his own ancestors unless they are explicitly identified as belonging to his lineage, and that is not commonly the case. From a tribal point of

view all dead in the past are common ancestors, and the distinction is therefore mostly of purely academic interest. (The case is, of course, different in the homeland of ancestor worship, Africa.)

Some of the ancestors are portrayed as clan-founders and have as such an enhanced prestige. (It is another matter whether they really once existed as humans or are mythic figures.) There is also the figure of the Ancestor, or First Man, who is sometimes identified as the culture hero, or some other cosmic divinity. However, although Father Schmidt has played on the importance of First Man in American Indian mythology this figure is too little investigated to be discussed in this article. He definitely belongs primarily to mythology, not to the cult and practical religion, and therefore should not be mixed with other ancestors.

As we observed earlier, Lowie and Underhill made a clear distinction between ghosts as spiritual patrons and ancestor worship. If we talk of a cult of the dead instead of ancestor worship, this distinction should fall away. One could object that the cult or worship feature is less apparent in man's attitude to guardian spirits, but then, as Underhill extravagantly formulates it, "worship is not an Indian custom." In other words, the gap is smaller than we think. It is therefore natural to include guardian-spirit beliefs in this investigation.

Some words should be said about the place of scalping customs in North American cults of the dead. Whatever the origins of scalping—and it is doubtful that they should be looked for on the American continent—the custom was primarily a means of procuring war trophies. At the same time the scalp preserved an identity with the scalped man that made it the object of religious beliefs. In several cases the scalp achieved the same status as the deceased in the cult of the dead. It is therefore necessary that also these cases will be observed in the following survey.

Finally, the Ghost Dance and other modern movements will not be discussed here. There is certainly no "cult of the dead" present in the Ghost Dance, although the deceased relatives are called in for aid: their return is thought as restoration to life, not as a visit of spiritual apparitions.

General Presentation of Facts Outside of the Pueblo Area

We shall now study the occurrence of a cult of the dead in the different North American Indian culture areas, in the tense of the "ethnographic present."

Alaska and western Canada is the home of Athapascan-speaking tribes and, as we have found earlier, they shun death and pollution from the dead. Nevertheless, some notices indicate that they are not indifferent to the power of the dead. Each autumn the Ingalik in western Alaska offer salmon and biscuits at the grave boxes of the dead. The dead are supposed to eat the food and bless the givers. It is also known that power may be had from a tree that springs up from a powerful shaman's disintegrated coffin. Among the Coyukon dead shamans are prayed to and their help is besought in difficult situations by the people among whom they once lived. A woman whose husband was moribund offered presents such as moccasins to deceased shamans and prayed at the fire, "Here I am giving you presents; I give you the things with which we make you thrifty, that you may come to my assistance." When the husband died her offerings ceased.

Another northern Athapascan people, the Hare at the Mackenzie River delta, offer food into the fire for the dead so that they will not disturb the people's hunting luck. We hear that the dead belong to the following of the thunderbird which returns each spring to the north after its winter séjour down in the south. The Beaver in northern Alberta offer food for the dead into the fire, asking them "to give us more of what we have put in the fire."

The North Pacific Coast tribes have long been considered having traces of ancestor worship. Duncan Strong found thirty years ago archeological evidence of a "ghost cult" on the Columbia River. Joyce Wike locates to the Northwest Coast "widespread, important, and systematized beliefs concerning the relationship of the living to the dead." To her, this is most natural in view of the extremes of status differentiation and hierarchical ranking found in this area.

The Tlingit of the southern Alaskan coast invest the drowned and departed shamans with power. According to a tradition, the spirit of a drowned man dwells in an underwater hole at Hazy Island. People go to the island to put food in the water and ask the spirit for good weather and a safe journey. The spirit helps those who show respect for wild life but persecutes those who disregard the laws of food conservation. H. J. Holmberg mentions that the shaman candidate seeks up the grave of a shaman and cuts out one of the latter's teeth, or he cuts off one of his little fingers. In this way he attracts the guardian spirits he needs—presumably those of the deceased shaman. We are also informed by Holmberg that each time a Tlingit in his canoe passes a shaman's grave he throws some tobacco into the water in order to receive the benignity and favor of the shaman. Occasionally ordinary dead can also grant powers, at least indirectly, through the influence of the sun. If we may believe John Swanton a dead person who is very much thought of is, at sunset on the day of the funeral, attended by his clansmen in festive blankets and with canes in their hands. As the sun sinks closer to the horizon they stretch out their canes toward it and utter some prayers like these: "Let me be rich," "Let me come across sea otter sleeping," "Let me kill seal," "Let me kill land otter."

If Haida Indians on Queen Charlotte Islands are poverty-stricken, their dead kinsmen are supposed to send them property. On the other hand, we are told that the Bella Coola on the British Columbia mainland make offerings to their dead without the hope of receiving favors from them. It is not quite clear if the Kwakiutl immediately south of them understand the dead as helping, benevolent beings. It is certain that their dead can be malevolent. The southern neighbors of the Kwakiutl, the Nootka, think that the spring salmon are sent up from the underworld by the spirits of the departed. An early Spanish source imparts the information that among the Nootka the dead are most important in controlling the food supply. The amount of mummies and skulls from dead people in Nootkan ceremonial houses has been described in several works. After a successful whale hunt the chief goes to the ceremonial house where he offers part of his catch to his ancestors.

The idea that the salmon come from the land of the dead reappears among the Quinault south of Mount Olympus. Here, however, the dead may prevent their coming; they do not, it seems, facilitate it. On the other hand, it is said that before the season of whaling a whaler had to rub himself with the bones of one of his male ancestors, "probably the one who had the whaler's guardian spirit." Furthermore, we are informed that most personal guardian spirits are spirits of the dead.

The interference of the dead with the living on the Northwest Coast is clearly expressed in the idea that the dead are present at the give-away feasts, or potlatches. We learn that only one motive underlies the custom of arranging potlatches among the Tlingit, regard for and respect for the dead. And among the Bella Coola the most important feature is the return of a dead ancestor or ancestors. Similar examples could be had from other tribes within the area. Indeed, Kaj Birket-Smith emphasizes that the one reason for giving a potlatch found everywhere is the memorial feast for the dead. He concludes that originally the potlatch institution was therefore probably connected with the death feasts.

There is also some evidence that the Plateau tribes, adjoining the Indians of the North Pacific Coast, believe in the protection of the dead. "Some powerful shamans of the Lower Lillooet had the dead as their guardian spirits, and obtained from them their knowledge. To this end they trained by sleeping in burial-grounds at intervals extending over several years." The Shuswap pray to powers like the earth, the sun, the guardian spirits, etc., but also to the chief of the dead and the dead themselves. James Teit who has given this information maintains that the custom of killing an enemy whenever a close relative had been slain was motivated by the wish to send an offering to the dead relative. The argument is scarcely convincing. The shaman of the Thompson Indians places the skull of a dead person in his sweat-house and sings and prays to him all night, asking him to impart his knowledge. In this way the dead person becomes the shaman's guardian spirit. The Nez Perce in Idaho assured Herbert Spinden that ghosts, which to some extent are held in fear, are never called upon for help of any kind. There is certainly talk about a "day ghost" as a special tutelary spirit good for laying a ghost, but the character of this spirit is not described. The Flathead of the Bitterroot Valley imagine that ghosts warn the living.

We now turn to the Algonkian Indians of eastern North America. In some older documents from the last century there is mention of prayers directed to the dead at their funerals. Thus at an Ojibway funeral an old man praises the virtues of the deceased person, prays for his blessing, and asks him to interfere, in favor of his living relatives, by sending game in abundance. Similarly, among the Ottawa (neighbors of the Ojibway close to Sault Sainte Marie) the headman of the family speaks at a funeral, calls on the deceased of the family group, and implores them to accept food prepared for them and "to assist him in the chase." Moon Conard who quotes these two instances finds it improbable that such prayers are directed to the dead on the occasions of funerals. Her reservation is understandable. However, two similar accounts could scarcely be wrong. It seems reasonable to postulate that occasionally such events have taken place. There is other evidence that the deceased took care of the food supply. The Jesuit Father Allouez clearly states that the Ottawa thought the departed governed the fishes.

The best analysis of the Ojibway idea of ghosts as spiritual helpers emanates from Hallowell. The Ojibway group investigated by him are the Berens River Saulteaux, east of Lake Winnipeg. He notes their general custom of throwing food and tobacco for the dead in the fire. The dead will then report this to the master of the dead (an instance of the "boss" concept so typical for the Ojibway), and the living will then receive some kind of blessing, such as long life. Hallowell also found that the Saulteaux, in performing the Dream Dance—which had been given them by the ancestors long ago—expected blessings from the dead. In the so-called ghost dance (not to be confused with the famous Ghost Dance of 1890) the drum is a medium of communication between the living and the dead. The dead also occur in the role of personal guardian spirits investing their clients with their power or skill. It seems that in the latter capacity they only appear in spontaneous dreams, not in deliberately sought visions. Furthermore, according to Hallowell, it is the master of the dead that functions as a guardian spirit, not anyone from the mass of the dead. The author insists that the spirits of the dead are not central in Saulteaux religious ideology but are peripheral to other spiritual beings with whom they tend to coalesce, such as the guardian spirits.

It is interesting to study the relations to the dead among the Plains Cree, close neighbors and relatives of the Ojibway. Their dead do not appear in visions, nor are they able to bestow power on human beings. No offerings are made to them. They are, however, asked to petition the higher powers to render aid to living men. Also the Plains Ojibway assert that the dead are never seen in visions and can impart no power. However, as we shall presently see these statements do not exhaust the possibilities.

One trait characteristic for both the Ojibway and the Plains Cree is the custom of addressing the dead as intermediaries for prayers to the high supernatural beings. The same custom prevails among the Fox, southwest of the Ojibway. The ruler of the land of souls receives a newly dead person as visitor. The dead person tells him the names of the persons who have made tobacco offerings at his demise. The ruler of the dead is pleased, listens to their prayers, and brings to pass the things they ask. If a person has become adopted into a family as a substitute for a recently dead person, he enacts the transmission of the gifts and prayers in a particular ceremony.

Whilst we hear of offerings to the dead among other Algonkian groups, without knowing however if such procedures invoke their positive interference in human life, the idea of the dead as intermediaries seems to have its center among the Algonkian tribes around the Great Lakes. Its southernmost occurrence may be found among the Shawnee where the living send maize and meat to the Creator through an old dying woman, thus causing the Creator to give them help. Among the Lenape or Delaware, again, the dead person can become a guardian spirit in the vision-quest.

Also the Siouan Winnebago, neighbors of the Fox, partake in the "middleman complex." At the burial one of the mourners throws some tobacco behind himself and exhorts the dead person to act as a mediator. Arrived at his destination, the deceased person asks Earthmaker (or a supernatural old woman) to send war honors, food, and long life. As a Winnebago Indian testifies, "Always, in the past, has the request of a ghost been successful."

The idea of the dead man as a mediator between man and the spirits may reflect influences from the Spirit Lodge seances (cf. below).

Archeologists have shown that the Southeast was a center of developed mortuary customs in pre-Columbian days. We know now that the advanced Hopewell culture, with roots in southern Illinois some centuries B.C., was characterized by complex burial ceremonies at huge burial mounds. The Hopewell culture was succeeded by the Mexican-inspired Mississippian culture about 700–800 A.D. Although primarily noted for its rectangular temple mounds, this culture retained the rites around prominent dead. This was demonstrated by the Natchez on the Lower Mississippi: they still represented the temple mound tradition in the eighteenth century, and their elaborate death rituals with executions of human beings at the death of the ruling prince were noted by the French. There are hints that the sacred chiefs of the Tekesta and Biloxi Indians received offerings and adoration after their death. There is no such evidence concerning the Natchez king, however, and we are on the whole little informed of what the dead chiefs could do for their people.

The Prairie and Plains Indians are usually known for their great fear of ghosts. The picture varies, however: the Dakota evince features that remind one observer of Chinese ancestor cult, whilst the Lipan and Kiowa Apache fear everything having to do with death. These differences mirror the mixed ethnic composition of the central grassland area. We have seen how the dead relatives of the Plains Cree are thought of as being able to help, indirectly, their living kinsmen. Another Algonkian group, the Blackfoot, have the belief that a dead husband may impart power to his widow if she wears a lock of his hair. The Gros Ventre, also Algonkian, say that occasionally a dead person becomes the guardian spirit of a surviving relative. Father Cooper, who is our authority here, points out however that "no cult of ghosts existed, and no prayers or food offerings were made to them." As said before, the guardian-spirit relationship is *de facto* cultic in character.

Passing over to the Siouan Prairie and Plains Indians, we notice that the Mandan of the northern Missouri bring back the skulls of those who have died away from their village. Such a skull "was considered sacred and was prayed to. Young men who addressed it as father would request permission to fast near it." A similar custom has prevailed among the Hidatsa. Although Lowie did not attribute ancestor worship to the Crow he found one exception: the medicine-man Big Iron told the Crow to lay down beads at his tree-burial, then he would fulfill their prayers; and they did so. One Crow family owned a bundle containing the skull of Braided Tail. It was an oracle in matters of warfare, hunting, and disease, and it located lost property.

The westernmost Assiniboin (Stoney) in Alberta can meet ghosts who promise them success in hunting and keep their word. The Assiniboin chief, Tchatka, was buried in a big tree to which, when passing, the Indians made offerings. They believed he could provide them with buffalo and other animals, or drive the animals from the country. Edwin Denig has recorded an Assiniboin prayer to the spirits of a person's dead relatives in which the petitioners ask for successful buffalo hunts, long life, aid in wars, and revenge on the enemy. The prayer is associated with a feast for the dead.

The Dakota Indians pray to their dead and give them offerings, and the dead listen to them. More specifically, Philander Prescott assures us the Dakota pray to their dead to show them where to find a deer or bear or other game. Also other things, for instance, good weather are asked for. The famous Dakota interpreter George Bushotter gives the information that at the so-called ghost feast offerings are given to the dead, whereupon a woman asks for many horses and a long life.

Although James Dorsey insists the Omaha on the middle Missouri do not venerate their dead, he mentions that they pour out some of their sacred meals as offerings to the ghosts. Alice Fletcher and Francis La Flesche interpret the Omaha attitude as reverence, not worship. The Ponca apparently embrace the idea that the dead promote the welfare of the living. Consequently, the manes receive offerings of food.

If we turn to the Shoshonean groups on the western Plains they, too, despite their fear of ghosts, have favorable dealings with them. The Wind River Shoshoni in Wyoming have sometimes ghosts as their guardian spirits. Thus a man who buried the scattered bones of a dead person once received ghost power. Also the Comanche on the southern Plains have medicine-men with such power.

Our impression that the worship of the dead has been more diffused in the Plains area than imagined before is strengthened by the wide occurrence of ghost controls in the Spirit Lodge ceremony. This ceremony, model for the so-called spiritualistic seances in the modern western world, is really a shamanistic performance in which the acting conjurer divines the unknown with the help of a main spirit and other lesser spirits. On the Plains the main spirit is most often a ghost or an owl, the latter embodying a ghost. The ghost imparts information but does not bestow power on the medicine-man. Since the ghost is the central spirit also in the Siberian Spirit Lodge, and the two areas of distribution are evidently linked with each other, it seems probable that we are facing an original dependence here on the craft of ghosts.

In the Basin area west of the Rocky Mountains, offerings of food, tobacco, etc., to the dead occur but mostly only with a preventive aim. However, the Paviotso include ghosts among the spirit-patrons of the vision-quest.

In spite of all mourning anniversaries, ghost personifications, and ghost dances, the California Indians do not give us much positive evidence of a cult of the dead. There are exceptions, however. The Patwin, northeast of the San Francisco Bay, celebrate a so-called *hesi* ceremony with impersonifications of ghosts. The latter appear "for the purpose of bettering the crops," "they named the various kinds of acorns in order to promote their growth." The kuksu cult in North Central California revolves around a mythical ancestor, but the latter is more a divinity than a dead person.

Of the nomads in the Southwest, the Apache are known as particularly ghost-fearing. And yet, at the turn of the century a Western Apache medicine-man declared that the ghosts who dance around Chromo Butte "to whom we always pray," and the gods of the dead would one day come and help the Indians against the whites. Since this pronouncement is so atypical for the Apache we may surmise here an influence from the Ghost Dance doctrine, in spite of everything that can be said against it.

We proceed to the southwestern village tribes. The Papago medicine-man may enter into contact with dead relatives appearing as owls. By offering tobacco to the ghost, the medicine-man receives from him news about enemy strategy, etc. The Pima are said to have offered prayer-feathers and prayer-sticks to the dead at ruins in old times, this being a Pueblo custom. Offerings of food and water on Pima and Papago graves are, however, recent. Expressions of veneration for deceased "matrons" are, in vague terms, reported from the Seri of northwestern Mexico. The Cahita, southern neighbors of the Seri, know some people who pray to the dead for assistance and are known to talk to the dead. In the acculturated Mayo society of the same region, the dead ancestors, or santos (saints), look after the interests of the villagers. In October or November, when the dead visit the places of the living, they bring the first cold rains of the season, which are followed by colds and diseases.

Far to the south in western Mexico, the Cora and Huichol make prayer-sticks for the dead, like the Pueblo Indians. These sticks are among the Cora used for the supplication of slain enemies in times of drought, for the dead enemy is a rain-maker. The association between rain and the cult of the dead shows both affinities to Pueblo rain ideology and Meso-american ancestor worship. The Huichol furthermore believe that departed relatives may give luck in hunting.

Evidence from the Pueblo Area

The main area of ancestor worship in North America is, as has been indicated, the Pueblo area in New Mexico and Arizona. Says Ruth Bunzel, "The worship of the dead is the foundation of all Zuni ritual. The dead form part of the great spiritual essence of the universe, but they are the part which is nearest and most intimate." Similarly, Mischa Titiev means that the cult of the dead is "one of the most essential elements in the religious mosaics of the Hopi." These pronouncements from two of the foremost students of Pueblo Indian religion are, however, in conflict with some other statements. Thus Alexander hesitates to talk about an ancestor worship since the spirits of the dead have been identified with divine rain-makers. Also Paul Radin sees here an "illegitimate extension of the concept ancestor-worship." According to Elsie Clews Parsons, there is little recognition of the deceased relatives in Hopi ritual, for they are rare or never prayed to. Perhaps it would be safest to say that the majority of Pueblo Indians had a cult of the dead which, however, had a weak anchoring in Hopi culture—not because the latter had been influenced by the Navajo, as Parsons thought, but because its historical roots are in the death-fearing desert culture.

In the Pueblo area the cult of the dead has become mixed with the kachina ideology, and this to such a degree that the connections are difficult to analyze. The kachina are in general identified as rain spirits, or as representatives of rain spirits; they are said not to bring rain themselves, but to interfere with the rain gods on behalf of the humans. Some examples will illustrate the complicated patterns. The importance of the rain for the crops is most obvious in the arid western part of the area, whereas in the eastern part the Rio Grande holds vast resources of water. In one respect the kachina cult differs from all other cults of the dead in North America: it is a collective cult organized by a society. The collectivism of the agrarian Pueblo culture is also expressed in the fact that the dead are addressed without distinctions, although single kachinas may carry individual (mythical) names.

If we start with the Zuni who—together with the Keres Pueblos—by some are identified as the main originators of the kachina cult, we notice that Bunzel observes three classes of dead people who receive the cult: (1) the newly dead, who may produce rain after their decease; (2) the ancestors, identified with the clouds and the rains, and to whom the Zuni pray for life, old age, health, power, rain, and fecundity; (3) the kachinas (here called *koko*), originally, in the mythological age, children who had died following a taboo contamination, and later on, a concept taking in the dead at large. Bunzel emphasizes that the identification of the dead with the kachinas is not complete: prayer-sticks are offered to the old people and the kachinas, and their sticks are different. The kachinas are especially associated with clouds and rain but may also stand for other activities. The kachina worship is expressed through dances in which male Zuni don their masks and costumes.

Turning to the westernmost Pueblo people, the Hopi, we learn that according to J. W. Fewkes "ancestral worship plays a not inconspicuous part in the Hopi conception of a Katcina." The person who dies becomes a kachina and is asked to bring the rain and intercede with the gods to fertilize the fields. The dead person is addressed "by the same name as that given to the ancestral personations," the kachinas. Furthermore, the kachinas are better described as general rather than as specific ancestors. There is the complication, however, that not all kachinas are spirits of the deceased. Animal deities, stars, and other powers appear among the kachinas. Even sun worship is part of the Hopi kachina cult. The latter is, in fact, more developed and refined than the Zuni kachina cult. Of course, the dancing of the masked kachina impersonators is also in the Hopi Pueblo the major trait, and acts promoting fertility and curing diseases are included.

As Edward Dozier has pointed out, the Western Pueblo rituals revolve around the kachina cult, whereas among the Eastern Pueblo Indians, where water is easily accessible (Rio Grande), this cult is less important. In the Keresan-speaking pueblo Cochiti, the kachinas are called *shiwanna* and consist of dead persons. They make rain and thunder, and give health and life. By putting on the sacred mask the men take on the personality of the *shiwanna*. The Tanoan-speaking inhabitants of Taos, the northernmost of the Rio Grande pueblos, travel each summer to their sacred Blue Lake to worship the kachinas, "the ones that send all what they get." They are the "cloud boys," who come with rain and thunder but are not identical with ordinary dead; only good chiefs, their wives, and men dying in the mountains become kachinas after their death. The restricted occurrence of kachina dancing and the maskless dancing point to the recency of the kachina complex in Taos.

The emergency of the kachina cult has been vividly discussed in the past. The theory that the kachina are basically clan totem beings has been vindicated from Fewkes to Titiev. Parsons found it probable that the kachina cult had partly developed out of the Catholic cult of the Saints, and pointed to the several parallels between them. This would in her opinion explain the differences between "ancestors" (the dead in general) and "kachinas" (the Saints). The other component of the kachina complex would have been indigenous rain spirits. In her last great publication on Pueblo Indian religion, Parsons assumes, more cautiously, a stimulation from the Spanish worship of the Saints. Increasingly archeological evidence has shown that the kachina cult is pre-Columbian (Mogollon) in origin. A suggestive background is given in Parsons' observation that the cultic performances of the kachina dancers had their close counterparts in Aztec religion. The general pattern against which the kachina worship should be seen is furnished by the fertility idea: like in other agricultural preindustrial areas the powers of fertility and the spirits of the dead are located in the same region, the underworld. Thus it is not surprising, writes H. K. Haeberlin, "that in a culture like that of the Pueblo, where almost every cultural phenomenon seems to be focused on the idea of fertilization, the deceased and especially the ancients should likewise have become associated with this idea."

The cult of the dead in the Southwest also affected the scalping complex in the old days. The scalps, as representatives of the dead, are thought to execute the powers of the latter. Among the Zuni the scalp passes through a cleansing ceremony and is thereafter prayed to as a rainmaker. Parsons writes that presumably in all the pueblos scalps have been rain-senders. They also have curative powers, as in Isleta, or promote population growth, as in Taos. Similar conceptions prevail outside the Pueblo area. Pima and Papago scalps are supposed to bring rain and cure diseases, and are nourished with tobacco smoke. Beals's hypothesis that the Acaxee of Mexico took the skulls of enemies for rain-making is without foundation.

The southwestern cult of the scalps may have been an intensification of a cult pattern of a somewhat wider occurrence. The Kiowa (who are, certainly, linguistic relatives of the Taos Indians), a southern Plains people, pray to a certain shield to which scalps are attached. Those who give offerings to it may achieve safety in war or cure for sickness. The Caddo in approximately the same area offer tobacco to scalps. The reason is not known.

Conclusions

It is obvious that in one form or another a cult of the dead has existed over most of North America. The Great Basin and California (at least the desert part) seem to be the great exceptions on our map. The sources on the Southeast are not sufficient for a clear judgment, and the same could be said about our source material on the Coast Algonkian groups. The general impression is that there are faint traces of, and a vague tendency to, a cult of the dead in all areas except those where the fear of the ghosts has been too strong (Southern Athapascans, Desert Numic). All over North America the ghosts are feared, and yet, their power and protection is sought.

This general, vaguely supplicating attitude, often expressed in simple prayers by single individuals and accompanied by small offerings of tobacco or meat in the fire, stands halfway between respect and reverence for the dead person at burial and an institutional cult of the dead. At times it is formalized in more fixed patterns, some recurrent, others localized.

Recurrent patterns are:

1. The dead are conceived as personal guardian spirits. This idea is noticeable here and there, on the Plateau, among the Algonkian Indians (Ojibway, Lenape), on the Plains (Gros Ventre, Shoshoni, Comanche, etc.). These are also the areas where the guardian-spirit ideology has its strongest anchoring. In other words, the nondescript cult of the dead has been reinterpreted within this domineering belief complex. Contrary to Radin's assumption, the cult of the dead seems to have given in to the guardian-spirit ideology, not the other way round. The fear of ghosts has probably precluded a wider distribution of the ghost-tutelary idea. In places, as among the Ojibway, there is a tendency for the ghost helper to coalesce with spirits of nature.

2. The dead are conceived as masters of the game. Such notions are found on the north Pacific Coast where they are mostly coupled to the salmon run (Nootka, Quinault?), among the Algonkian Indians (Ojibway, Ottawa), and on the Plains (Assiniboin, Dakota). That is, the dead are not specialized masters of the game, as the true animal bosses are, but they meet such desires as are usually directed to the masters of the game. In my opinion this function of the dead has become possible because the idea of a master of the game has become eclipsed by the guardian-spirit complex. This interpretation might be contested, but I offer it as a hypothesis.

3. Occasionally, the cult of the dead appears as tied up with a symbol of the dead person, his skull (cf. Nootka on the Northwest Coast, Crow, Mandan, and Hidatsa on the Plains and Prairies), his hair (Blackfoot, Siouan tribes), his scalp (different groups in the Southwest). This feature has not been exhaustively treated here. It deserves an investigation of its own.

Localized patterns are:

4. The "ghost cult" of the North Pacific Coast is difficult to assess, but there is no doubt that an emphasis on the presence of the dead in potlatch ceremonies is current in this area. The prevalent x-ray art, possibly connected with the death and life rites of shaman candidates and members of secret societies, should also stress the importance of the death motif. The dead live mixed with the spirits of nature; indeed, the Quinault may have thought there were more ghosts than natural spirits in the supernatural realm. Consequently, ghosts are sometimes responsible for natural phenomena, as among the Kwakiutl. In this general atmosphere the dead person is a natural resource of help and power.

5. The dead function as intermediaries between man and the powers above in the Central Algonkian area, including the Siouan Winnebago. The powers which help man are different but usually either the Supreme Being and the guardian spirits or the master of the dead. The dead are often the recently dead, and the petitions are delivered at their funeral ceremonies. The rich ritualism around the latter among, for instance, the Fox may have paved the way for the development of the complex. However, I also find it possible that the elaboration of the role of the ghost helper in the conjuring or Spirit Lodge could have stimulated the central idea, the dead as intermediary beings.

6. Ghosts of their transformations (owls) act as informants and spirit controls in the Spirit Lodge complex on the Plains. Here we evidently face an idea and a rite complex that has historical connections with Siberian practices. The fact that ghosts are informing spirits on the Plains, but not so much in surrounding areas where this ritual complex occurs may be ascribed to conservatism, but also to the intense interests in ghosts on the Plains. As has emerged, the idea of the dead as helpers is more distributed in this area than in any other area, excepting the Northwest Coast and the Pueblo Southwest.

7. A real cult of the dead is present among the Pueblo Indians where the dead are more or less interpreted as cloud and rain spirits. This cult, with a pronounced collectivistic character and direct association with the demands of the agriculturist, probably originated with the Keres Indians in the Mogollon culture (about A.D. 500) in the southwestern corner of New Mexico. Here, large ceremonial structures (kivas) formed the scenes of the kachina dances. Whether this cult of the dead is entirely a product of the requirements in an agricultural environment, or has also been stimulated from other sources—Central Mexico in the first place—will not be discussed here. I lean toward the last interpretation.

The North American materials give rise to several observations. One is that the cult of the dead is only rarely, and then primarily in the Central Algonkian and Plains areas, combined with rituals at graves. The Algonkians honor the dead at mortuary services, the Plains people give homage to particularly great persons at their graves. Another observation is that the dead are almost always conceived as anonymous collective spirits, except where rites are tied up with their burials and graves or great leaders are venerated. Certainly, we hear about individual cases here and there where personal ancestors have been prayed to; but they are less representative. It is therefore impossible to say if there is generally any difference in attitude between the cult of the ancestors and the cult of the vast host of the dead. A third observation is that large rituals of petition including dancing primarily occur among the Algonkians of the woods and the Pueblo Indians. The most important rituals take place among the latter.

The North American data demonstrate in an interesting way the rise of a cult of the dead from inchoate beginnings. I am thinking here of evolutionary levels as these may be defined in conjunction with social structures, not of historical developments in a strict sense. Terrence Tatje and Francis Hsu have suggested that there is a connection between certain kinship contents and ancestor cults. We have reasons to suspect that the cult of the dead tends to belong with unilinear societies. A quick glance at the North American ethnographic map will show that the main zones of the cult of the dead, the northern Northwest Coast, the Central Algonkian area, and the western Pueblo area, are all characterized by lineage systems. The trouble is, however, that in the important Pueblo area the Eastern Pueblos are primarily bilateral in social structure, and unilinear only with regard to moiety membership. Fred Eggan interprets this so that there had once been a unilinear social structure which in the east changed to bilateral due to migrations. In view of this hypothesis we might say that the complex, unilinear societies of the Pueblo Indians should have provided the right soil for the growth of a worship of the dead, whereas the more loosely, bilaterally organized societies of many hunting tribes rather precluded such a development.

The path of evolution seems clear. There is everywhere, also among the Pueblo Indians, a fear of the dead tempered by their affection for them. The conviction is spread that the dead help, destroy, or master one's existence in some mysterious way. People remember their achievements during life, their care, their wrath. As dead they continue to exert the same influence, but now in a supernatural nimbus. Unpremeditatedly, the living turn to them, talk to them, pray to them. By and by this attitude is strengthened and patterned. Institutional forms develop, particularly in unilinear societies. In North America where classical nomadism fails, it is primarily in the tightly settled agricultural areas that such changes have taken place.

❖

Levels of Meaning in the Religious Life-World

(Existential-Hermeneutical Phenomenology of Religion)

❖ PAUL RICOEUR ❖

Paul Ricoeur (1913–) studied with Gabriel Marcel and currently teaches at the University of Chicago. He is the author of several works including *The Symbolism of Evil, Freud and Philosophy, The Conflict of Interpretations*, and *Time and Narrative*. In the following selection Ricoeur examines the question of guilt by probing its meaning in semantic, ethical, and religious discourse. His exploration reveals a phenomenology of confession expressed as defilement, as wounded relationship, and as consciousness of being overwhelmed. Beyond that, it discloses a series of connections between the themes of freedom, obligation, and evil, and, finally, it uncovers the structures and significances of a religious language of hope. Sensitively pursuing these different discourses about guilt, Paul Ricoeur shows why he is widely regarded as one of the foremost practitioners of the existential-hermeneutical phenomenology of religion.

❖

Guilt, Ethics and Religion

I. Guilt: Semantic Analysis

I propose, first, to consider this term, not in its psychological, psychiatric or psychoanalytic usage, but in the *texts* where its meaning has been constituted and fixed. These texts are those of penitential literature wherein the believing communities have expressed their avowal of evil; the language of these texts is a specific language which can be designated, in a very general way, as "confession of sins," although no particular confessional connotation is attached to this expression, not even a specifically Jewish or Christian meaning. Some decades ago, Professor Pettazzoni of Rome wrote a collection of works covering the entire field of comparative religions. He called this precisely *Confession of Sins*. But it is not from the comparative point of view that I take up the problem. My point of departure is in a *phenomenology of confession* or avowal. Here I understand by phenomenology the description of meanings implied in experience in general, whether that experience be one of things, of values, of persons, etc. A phenomenology of confession is therefore a description of meanings and of signified intentions, present in a certain activity of language: the language of confession. Our task, in the framework of such a phenomenology, is to re-enact in ourselves the confession of evil, in order to uncover its aims. By sympathy and through imagination, the philosopher adopts the motivations and intentions of the confessing consciousness; he does not "feel," he "experiences" in a neutral manner, in the manner of an "as if," that which has been lived in the confessing consciousness.

But with which expressions shall we start? Not with expressions of confessions that are the most developed, the most rationalised, for example, the concept or quasi-concept of "original sin" which has often guided philosophical thought. On the contrary, philosophical reasoning should consult expressions of the confession of evil which are the least elaborated, the least articulated.

We should not be embarrassed by the fact that behind these rational-ised expressions, behind these speculations, we encounter myths, that is, traditional narratives which tell of events which happened at the origin of time and which furnish the support of language to ritual actions. To-day, for us, myths are no longer explanations of reality but, precisely because they have lost their explanatory pretension, they reveal an ex-ploratory signification; they manifest a symbolic function, that is, a way of expressing indirectly the bond between man and what he considers sacred. Paradoxical as it may seem, myth thus demythologised in its con-tact with physics, cosmology and scientific history becomes a dimension of modern thought. In its turn, myth refers us to a level of expressions more fundamental than any narration and any speculation. Thus, the narrative of the fall in the Bible draws its signification from an experience of sin rooted in the life of the community: it is the cultural activity and the prophetic call to justice and to "mercy" which provide myth with its sub-structure of significations.

Therefore it is to this experience and to its language that we must have recourse; or rather, to this experience *in* its language. For it is the lan-guage of confession which elevates to the light of discourse an experience charged with emotion, fear, and anguish. Penitential literature manifests a linguistic inventiveness which marks the way for existential outbursts of the consciousness of fault. Let us, therefore, interrogate this language.

The most remarkable characteristic of this language is that it does not involve expressions which are more primitive than the symbolic expres-sions to which myth refers. The language of confession is symbolic. Here I understand by symbol a language which designates a thing in an in-direct way, by designating another thing which it directly indicates. It is in this way that I speak symbolically of elevated thoughts, low senti-ments, clear ideas, the light of understanding, the kingdom of heaven, etc. Therefore, the work of repetition as applied to the expressions of evil is, in essence, the explicitation, the development of different levels of di-rect and indirect significations which are intermingled in the same sym-bol. The most archaic symbolism from which we can start is that of evil conceived as defilement or stain, that is, as a spot which contaminates from the outside. In more elaborated literatures, such as that of the Baby-lonians and especially of the Hebrews, sin is expressed in different sym-bolisms, such as to miss the target, to follow a tortuous path, to rebel, to have a stiff neck, to be unfaithful as in adultery, to be deaf, to be lost, to wander, to be empty and hollow, to be inconstant as dust.

This linguistic situation is astonishing; the consciousness of self, so intense in the sentiment of evil, does not, at first, have at its disposal an abstract language, but a very concrete language, on which a spontaneous work of interpretation is performed.

The second remarkable characteristic of this language is that it knows itself as symbolic and that, before any philosophy and theology, it is en route towards explicitation; as I have said elsewhere, the symbol "invites" thought; the myth is on the way towards logos. This is true even of the archaic idea of defilement or stain: the idea of a quasi-material something which contaminates from the outside, which harms by means of invisible properties—this idea possesses a symbolic richness, a potential of symbolisation, which is attested to by the very survival of this symbol under more and more allegorical forms. We speak even today, in a non-medical sense, of contamination by the spirit of monetary profit, by racism, etc.; we have not completely abandoned the symbolism of the pure and the impure. And this, precisely because the quasi-material representation of stain is already symbolic of something else. From the beginning it has symbolic power. Stain has never literally signified a spot, impurity has never literally signified filth; it is located in the "clear-obscure" of a quasi-physical infection and of a quasi-moral indignity. We see this clearly in rites of purification which are never just a simple washing; ablution and lustration are already partial and fictive actions which signify, on the level of body, a total action which addresses itself to the person considered as an undivided whole.

The symbolism of sin such as is found in Babylonian and Hebraic literature, in Greek tragedies or in Orphic writings, is certainly richer than that of stain, from which it is sharply distinguished. To the image of impure contact, it opposes that of a wounded relationship, between God and man, between man and man, between man and himself; but this relation, which will be thought of as a relation only by a philosopher, is symbolically signified by all the means of dramatisation offered in daily experience. So too the idea of sin is not reduced to the barren idea of the rupture of a relation; it adds to this the idea of a power which dominates man. Thus it maintains a certain affinity and continuity with the symbolism of stain. But this power is also the sign of the emptiness, of the vanity of man, represented by breath and by dust. So the symbol of sin is at one and the same time the symbol of something negative (rupture, estrangement, absence, vanity) and the symbol of something positive (power, possession, captivity, alienation). It is on this symbolic foundation, in this network of images and nascent interpretations that the word guilt should be resituated.

If we want to respect the proper intention of words, the expression guilt does not cover the whole semantic field of "confession." The idea of guilt represents the extreme form of interiorisation which we have seen sketched in the passage from stain to sin. Stain was still external contagion, sin already the rupture of a relation; but this rupture exists even if I do not know it; sin is a real condition, an objective situation; I would venture to say, an ontological dimension of existence.

Guilt, on the contrary, has a distinctly subjective accent: its symbolism is much more interior. It describes the consciousness of being overwhelmed by a burden which crushes. It indicates, further, the bite of a remorse which gnaws from within, in the completely interior brooding on fault. These two metaphors of burden and of biting express well the arrival at the level of existence. The most significant symbolism of guilt is that which is attached to the theme of tribunal; the tribunal is a public institution, but metaphorically transposed into the internal forum it becomes what we call the "moral consciousness." Thus guilt becomes a way of putting oneself before a sort of invisible tribunal which measures the offence, pronounces the condemnation, and inflicts the punishment; at the extreme point of interiorisation, moral consciousness is a look which watches, judges, and condemns; the sentiment of guilt is therefore the consciousness of being inculpated and incriminated by this interior tribunal. It is mingled with the anticipation of the punishment; in short the *coulpe*, in Latin *culpa*, is self-observation, self-accusation, and self-condemnation by a consciousness doubled back on itself.

This interiorisation of guilt gives rise to two series of results: on the one hand, the consciousness of guilt marks a definite progress in relation to what we have described as "sin"; while sin is still a collective reality in which a whole community is implicated, guilt tends to individualise itself. (In Israel, the prophets of the exile are the artisans of this progress [Ezek. 31: 34]; this preaching is a liberating action; at a time when a collective return from exile, comparable to the ancient Exodus from Egypt, appeared impossible, a personal path of conversion opened itself to each one. In ancient Greece, it was the tragic poets who assured the passage from hereditary crime to the guilt of the individual hero, placed alone before his own destiny.) Moreover, in becoming individualised, guilt acquires degrees; to the egalitarian experience of sin is opposed the graduated experience of guilt: man is entirely and radically sinner, but more or less guilty. It is the progress of penal law itself, principally in Greece and Rome, which has an effect here on moral consciousness: the whole of penal law is actually an effort to limit and to gauge the penalty in function of the measure of the fault. The idea of a parallel scale of crimes and sins is interiorised, in its own turn, in favour of the metaphor of the tribunal; moral consciousness becomes itself a graduated consciousness of guilt.

This individualisation and this gradation of guilt surely indicate a progress in respect to the collective and unqualified character of sin. We cannot say as much for the other series of results: with guilt there arises indeed a sort of demand which can be called scrupulosity and whose ambiguous character is extremely interesting. A scrupulous consciousness is a delicate consciousness, a precise consciousness enamoured of increasing perfection; it is a consciousness anxious to observe all the commandments, to satisfy the law in all things, without making an exception of any sector of existence, without taking into account exterior obstacles, for example, the persecution of a prince, and which gives equal importance to little things as to great. But at the same time scrupulosity marks the entrance of moral consciousness into its own pathology; a scrupulous person encloses himself in the inextricable labyrinth of commandments; obligation takes on an enumerative and cumulative character, which contrasts with the simplicity and sobriety of the commandment to love God and man. The scrupulous consciousness never stops adding new commandments. This atomisation of the law into a multitude of commandments entails an endless "juridisation" of action and a quasi-obsessional ritualisation of daily life. The scrupulous person never arrives at satisfying all the commandments, or even any one. At the same time even the notion of obedience is perverted; obedience to a commandment, because it is commanded, becomes more important than love of neighbour, and even love of God; this exactitude in observance is what we call legalism. With it we enter into the hell of guilt, such as St. Paul described it: the law itself becomes a source of sin. In giving a knowledge of evil, it excites the desire of transgression, and incites the endless movement of condemnation and punishment. The commandment, says St. Paul, "has given life to sin," and thus "hands me over to death" (Rom. 7). Law and sin give birth to one another mutually in a terrible vicious circle, which becomes a mortal circle.

Thus, guilt reveals the malediction of a life under the law. At the limit, when the confidence and tenderness, which are still expressed in the conjugal metaphors of Hosea, disappear, guilt leads to an accusation without accuser, a tribunal without judge, a verdict without author. Guilt has then become that irreversible misfortune described by Kafka: condemnation has become damnation.

A conclusion of this semantic analysis is that guilt does not cover the whole field of the human experience of evil; the study of these symbolic expressions has permitted us to distinguish in them a particular moment of this experience, the most ambiguous moment. On the one hand, guilt expresses the interiorisation of the experience of evil, and consequently the promotion of a morally responsible subject—but, on the other hand, it marks the beginning of a specific pathology, wherein scrupulosity marks the point of inversion.

Now the problem is posed: what do Ethics and the Philosophy of Religion make of this ambiguous experience of guilt and of the symbolic language in which it is expressed?

2. Ethical Dimension

In what sense is the problem of evil an ethical problem? In a twofold sense, it seems to me. Or rather, by reason of a double relationship, on the one hand with the question of freedom, and, on the other hand, with the question of obligation. Evil, freedom, obligation constitute a very complex network, which we shall try to unravel and to order in several stages of reflection. I shall begin and end with freedom, for it is the essential point.

In a first stage of reflection, I say: to affirm freedom is to take upon oneself the origin of evil. By this proposition, I affirm a link between evil and liberty, which is so close that the two terms imply one another mutually. Evil has the meaning of evil because it is the work of freedom. Freedom has the meaning of freedom because it is capable of evil: I both recognise and declare myself to be the author of evil. By that fact, I reject as an alibi the claim that evil exists after the manner of a substance or of a nature, that it has the same status as things which can be observed by an outside spectator. This claim is to be found not only in the metaphysical fantasies, such as those against which Augustine fought—Manicheism and all sorts of ontologies which conceive of evil as a being. This claim can take on a positive appearance, or even a scientific appearance, under the form of psychological or sociological determinism. To take upon oneself the origin of evil is to lay aside as a weakness the claim that evil is something, that it is an effect in a world of observable things, whether these things be physical, psychic or social realities. I say: it is I who have acted: *ego sum qui feci*. There is no evil-being; there is only the evil-done-by-me. To take evil upon oneself is an act of language comparable to the performative, in this sense, that it is a language which does something, that is to say, that it imputes the act to me.

I said that the relationship was reciprocal; indeed, if freedom qualified evil as a doing, evil is that which reveals freedom. By this I mean to say, evil is a privileged occasion for becoming aware of freedom. What does it actually mean to impute my own acts to myself? It is, first of all, to assume the consequences of these acts for the future; that is, he who has acted is also he who will admit the fault, who will repair the damages, who will bear the blame. In other words, I offer myself as the bearer of the sanction. I agree to enter into the dialectic of praise and blame. But in placing myself before the consequences of my act, I refer myself back to the moment prior to my act, and I designate myself as he who not only performed the act but who could have done otherwise. This conviction of having done something freely is not a matter of observation. It is once again a performative: I declare myself, after the fact, as being he who could have done otherwise; this "after the fact" is the backlash of taking upon oneself the consequences. He who takes the consequences upon himself, declares himself free, and discerns this freedom as already at work in the incriminated act. At that point I can say that I have committed the act. This movement from in front of to behind the responsibility is essential. It constitutes the identity of the moral subject through past, present, and future. He who *will* bear the blame is the same who *now* takes the act upon himself and he who *has* acted. I posit the identity of him who accepts the future responsibilities of his act, and he who has acted. And the two dimensions, future and past, are linked in the present. The future of sanction and the past of action committed are tied together in the present of confession.

Such is the first stage of reflection in the experience of evil: the reciprocal constitution of the signification of *free* and the signification of *evil* is a specific performative: confession. The second moment of reflection concerns the link between evil and obligation. I do not at all want to discuss the meaning of expressions such as "You ought" nor their relation with the predicates "good" and "evil." This problem is well known to English philosophy. My contribution to a reflection on evil will be limited to this problem: let us take as our point of departure the expression and the experience "I could have done otherwise." This is, as we have seen, an implication of the act by which I impute to myself the responsibility for a past act. But the awareness that one could have done otherwise is closely linked to the awareness that one *should* have done otherwise. It is because I recognise my "ought" that I recognise my "could." A being who is obligated is a being who presumes that he can do what he should do. We are well aware of the usage to which Kant put this affirmation: you must, therefore you can. It is certainly not an argument, in the sense that I could deduce the possibility from the obligation. I would rather say that the "ought" serves here as a detector: if I feel, or believe, or know that I am obligated, it is because I am a being that can act, not only under the impulsion or constraint of desire and fear, but under the condition of a law which I represent to myself. In this sense Kant is right: to act according to the representation of a law is something other than to act according to laws. This power of acting according to the representation of a law is the will. But this discovery has long-range consequences: for in discovering the power to follow the law (or that which I consider as the law for myself) I discover also the *terrible* power of acting *against*. (Indeed, the experience of remorse which is the experience of the relation between freedom and obligation is a twofold experience; on the one hand, I recognise an obligation, and therefore a power corresponding to this obligation, but I admit to having acted against the law which continues to appear to me as obligatory. This is commonly called a transgression.) Freedom is the power to act according to the representation of a law *and* not to meet the obligation. ("Here is what I should have done, therefore what I could have done, and look at what I did." The imputation of the past act is thus morally qualified by its relation to the "ought" and "can.") By the same fact, a new determination of evil and a new determination of freedom appear together, in addition to the forms of reciprocity which are described above.

The new determination of evil can be expressed in Kantian terms: it is the reversal of the relation between motive and law, interior to the maxim of my action. This definition is to be understood as follows: if I call a maxim the practical enunciation of what I propose to do, evil is nothing in itself; it has neither physical nor psychical reality; it is only an inverted relationship; it is a relation, not a thing, a relation inverted with regard to the order of preference and subordination indicated by obligation. In this way, we have achieved a "de-realisation" of evil: not only does evil exist only in the act of taking it upon oneself, of assuming it, of claiming it, but what characterises it from a moral point of view is the order in which an agent disposes of his maxims; it is a preference which ought not to have been (an inverted relation within the maxim of action).

But a new determination of freedom appears at the same time. I spoke a moment ago of the terrible power of acting against. It is, indeed, in the confession of evil that I discover the power of subversion of the will. Let us call it the *arbitrary*, to translate the German *Willkür*, which is at the same time free choice, i.e. the power of contraries, that which we recognised in the consciousness that one could have done otherwise, and in the power not to follow an obligation which I simultaneously recognise as just.

Have we exhausted the meaning of evil for Ethics? I do not think so. In the "Essay on Radical Evil" which begins *Religion within the Limits of Reason Alone*, Kant poses the problem of a common origin of all evil maxims; indeed, we have not gone far in a reflection on evil, as long as we consider separately one bad intention, and then another, and again

another. "We must conclude," says Kant, "from many, or even from a
single conscious evil action, a priori to an evil maxim as its foundation,
and from this maxim to a general foundation inherent in the subject, of
all morally bad maxims, a foundation which in its own turn would be a
maxim, so that finally we could qualify a man as evil."

This movement towards greater depth which goes from evil maxims
to their evil foundation is the philosophical transposition of the movement of sins to sin (in the singular) of which we spoke in section 1, on
the level of symbolic expressions, and in particular of myth. Among other
things, the myth of Adam signifies that all sins are referred to an unique
root, which is, in some way or other, anterior to each of the particular
expressions of evil, yet the myth could be told because the confessing
community raised itself to the level of a confession of evil as involving all
men. It is because the community confesses a fundamental guilt that the
myth can describe the unique coming-to-be of evil as an event which
happens only once. The Kantian doctrine of radical evil is an attempt to
recapture philosophically the experience of this myth.

What qualifies this re-examination as philosophical? Essentially the
treatment of radical evil as the foundation of multiple evil maxims. It is
therefore upon this notion of foundation that we should bring to bear
our critical effort.

Now, what do we mean by a foundation of evil maxims? We might
well call it an a priori condition in order to emphasise that it is not a fact
to be observed or a temporal origin to be retraced. It is not an empirical
fact, but a first disposition of freedom that must be supposed so that the
universal spectacle of human evil can be offered to experience. Neither is
it a temporal origin, for this theory would lead back to a natural causality. Evil would cease to be evil, if it ceased to be "a manner of being of
freedom, which itself comes from freedom." Therefore, evil does not
have an origin in the sense of an antecedent cause. "Every evil action,
when pushed back to its rational origin, should be considered as if man
had arrived at it directly from the state of innocence." (Everything is in
this "as if." It is the philosophical equivalent of the myth of the fall; it is
the rational myth of the coming-to-be of evil, of the instantaneous passage from innocence to sin; as Adam—rather than in Adam—we originate evil.)

But what is this unique coming-to-be which contains within itself all
evil maxims? It must be admitted that we have no further concept for
thinking of an evil will.

For this coming-to-be is not at all an act of my arbitrary will, which I
could do or not do. For the enigma of this foundation is that reflection

discovers, as a fact, that freedom has already chosen in an evil way. This evil is already there. It is in this sense that it is radical, that is anterior, as a non-temporal aspect of every evil intention, of every evil action.

But this failure of reflection is not in vain; it succeeds in giving a character, proper to a *philosophy of limit*, and in distinguishing itself from a philosophy of system, such as that of Hegel.

The limit is twofold: limit of my knowledge, limit of my power. On the one hand, *I do not know* the origin of my evil liberty; this non-knowledge of the origin is essential to the very act of confession of my radically evil freedom. The non-knowledge is a part of the performative of confession, or, in other words, of my self-recognition and self-appropriation. On the other hand, I discover the *non-power* of my freedom. (Curious non-power, for I declare that I am responsible for this non-power. This non-power is completely different from the claim of an outside constraint.) I claim that my freedom has already made itself not-free. This admission is the greatest paradox of ethics. It seems to contradict our point of departure. We began by saying: evil is what I could have not done; this remains true. But at the same time I claim: evil is this prior captivity, which makes it so that I must do evil. This contradiction is interior to my freedom, it marks the non-power of power, the non-freedom of freedom.

Is this a lesson in despair? Not at all: this admission is, on the contrary, the access to a point where everything can begin again. The return to the origin is a return to that place where freedom discovers itself, as something to be delivered—in brief to that place where it can *hope* to be delivered.

3. Religious Dimension

I have just attempted with the aid of the Philosophy of Kant to characterise the problem of evil as an ethical problem. It is the twofold relation of evil to obligation and to freedom, which has seemed to me to characterise the problem of evil as an ethical problem.

Now, if I ask what is the specifically religious way of speaking about evil, I would not hesitate for a moment to answer: the language is that of Hope. This thesis requires an explanation. Leaving aside for a moment the question of evil to which I shall return later, I would like to justify the central role of hope in Christian theology. Hope has rarely been the central concept in theology. And yet we now know, since the work of Johannes Weiss and Albert Schweitzer, that the preaching of Jesus was concerned essentially with the Kingdom of God; the Kingdom is at hand;

the Kingdom has drawn near to us; the Kingdom is in your midst. If the preaching of Jesus and of the primitive church thus proceeds from an eschatological perspective, we should rethink all of theology from this eschatological view-point. But this revision of theological concepts, taking its point of departure from the exegesis of the New Testament, centred on the preaching of the Kingdom-to-come, finds support in a parallel revision of the theology of the Old Testament. Thus Martin Buber contrasts the God of the promise—God of the desert and of the wandering—with the popular gods who manifest themselves in natural epiphanies, in the figure of the king or in the idols of the temple. The God who comes is a name, the god who shows himself is an idol. The God of the promise opens up a history, the god of epiphanies animates a nature. But the New Testament did not put an end to the theology of the Promise, for the Resurrection itself, which is at the centre of its message, is not only the fulfilment of the promise in an unique event, but the confirmation of the promise which becomes for all the hope of final victory over death.

What follows from this for freedom and for evil, which ethical consciousness has grasped in their unity? I shall begin by a discussion of freedom, for a reason which will become clear in a moment. It seems to me that religion is distinguished from ethics, in the fact that it requires that we think of freedom under the sign of hope.

In the language of the gospel, I would say: to consider freedom in the light of hope, is to re-situate my existence in the movement, which might be called, with Jurgen Moltmann, the "future of the resurrection of Christ." This "kerygmatic" formula can be translated in several ways in contemporary language. First of all, with Kierkegaard, we could call freedom in the light of hope the "passion for the *possible*"; this formula, in contrast to all wisdom of the present, to all submission to necessity, underscores the imprint of the promise on freedom. Freedom, entrusted to the "God who comes," is open to the radically new; it is the creative imagination of the possible.

But, in a deeper dimension, freedom *in the light of hope* is a freedom which affirms itself, *in spite of* death, and in spite of all the signs of death; for, in a phrase of the Reformers, the Kingdom is hidden *sub contrario*, under its contrary, the cross. Freedom in the light of hope is freedom for the denial of death, freedom to decipher the signs of the Resurrection under the contrary appearance of death.

Likewise, the category of "in spite of . . ." is the opposite or reverse side of a vital thrust, of a perspective of belief which finds its expression in the famous "how much more" of St. Paul. This category, more fundamental than the "in spite of," expresses what might be called the logic of superabundance, which is the logic of hope. Here the words of St. Paul to the Romans come to mind:

But the free gift is not like the fault, for, if many died through one man's fault, *how much more* have the grace of God and the gift conferred by the grace of that one man, Jesus Christ, abounded for many. . . . If because of one man's fault, death reigned through that one man, *how much more* will those who receive the abundance of grace, the free gift of righteousness, reign in life through the one man, Jesus Christ. . . . Law came in to increase the fault; but where sin increased, grace abounded all the more. . . . (Rom. 5: 15, 17, 20)

This logic of surplus and excess is to be uncovered in daily life, in work and in leisure, in politics and in universal history. The "in spite of . . ." which keeps us in readiness for the denial is only the inverse, the shadow side, of this joyous "how much more" by which freedom feels itself, knows itself, and wills itself to belong to this economy of superabundance.

This notion of an economy of superabundance permits us to return to the problem of evil. It is from this point of departure, and in it, that a religious or theological discourse on evil can be held. Ethics has said all it can about evil in calling it: (i) a work of freedom (ii) a subversion of the relation of the maxim to the law (iii) an unfathomable disposition of freedom which makes it unavailable to itself.

Religion uses another language about evil. And this language keeps itself entirely within the limits of the perimeter of the promise and under the sign of hope. First of all, this language places evil *before* God. "Against you, against you alone have I sinned, I have done evil in your sight." This invocation which transforms the moral confession into a confession of sin, appears, at first glance, to be an intensification in the consciousness of evil. But that is an illusion, the moralising illusion of Christianity. Situated before God, evil is installed again in the movement of the promise: the invocation is already the beginning of the restoration of a bond, the initiation of a new creation. The "passion for the possible" has already taken possession of the confession of evil; repentance, essentially directed towards the future, has already cut itself off from remorse which is a brooding reflection on the past.

Next, religious language profoundly changes the very content of the consciousness of evil. Evil in moral consciousness is essentially transgression, that is, subversion of the law; it is in this way that the majority of pious men continue to consider sin. And yet, situated before God, evil is qualitatively changed; it consists less in a transgression of a law than in a pretension of man to be master of his life. The will to live according to the law is, therefore, also an expression of evil—and even the most deadly, because the most dissimulated: worse than injustice is one's own justice. Ethical consciousness does not know this, but religious consciousness does. But this second discovery can also be expressed in terms of promise and hope.

Indeed, the will is not constituted, as we have seemed to believe in the context of the ethical analysis, merely by the relation between the arbitrary and the law (in Kantian terms, between the *Willkür* or arbitrary will and the *Wille* or determination by the law of reason). The will is more fundamentally constituted by a desire of fulfilment or achievement. Kant himself in the dialectical part of the *Critic of Practical Reason* recognised this intended goal of totalisation. It is this precisely which animates the *Dialectic of Practical Reason*, as the relation to the law animates the *Analytic*. Now this tendency toward totalisation, according to Kant, requires the reconciliation of two moments which Rigorism has separated: "virtue," that is, obedience to pure duty, and "happiness," that is, satisfaction of desire. This reconciliation is the Kantian equivalent of hope. This rebound of the philosophy of will entails a rebound of the philosophy of evil. If the tendency toward totalisation is thus the soul of the will, we have not yet reached the foundation of the problem of evil so long as we have kept it within the limits of a reflection of the relations of the arbitrary and the law. The true evil, the evil of evil, shows itself in false syntheses, i.e. in contemporary falsifications of the great undertakings of totalisation of cultural experience, that is, in political and ecclesiastical institutions. In this way, evil shows its true face—the evil of evil is the lie of premature syntheses, of violent totalisations. Evil "abounds" wherever man transcends himself in grandiose undertakings, wherein he sees the culmination of his existence in the higher works of culture, in politics and in religion. And so these great simulacra, the cult of race, the cult of the State, and all forms of false worship, are the very birth of idols, substituted for the "Name," who should remain faceless.

But this greater deepening of our understanding of evil is, once again, a conquest of hope: it is because man is a goal of totality, a will of total fulfilment, that he plunges himself into totalitarianisms, which really constitute the pathology of hope. As the old proverb says, demons haunt only the courts of the gods. But, at the same time, we sense that evil itself is a part of the economy of superabundance. Paraphrasing St. Paul, I dare to say: Wherever evil "abounds," hope "super-abounds." We must therefore have the courage to incorporate evil into the epic of hope. In a way that we know not, evil itself co-operates, works toward the advancement of the Kingdom of God. This is the viewpoint of faith on evil. This view is not that of the moralist; the moralist contrasts the *predicate* evil with the predicate good; he condemns evil; he imputes it to freedom; and finally, he stops at the limit of the inscrutable; for we do not know how it is possible that freedom could be enslaved. Faith does not look in this direction; the origin of evil is not its problem; the end of evil is its problem. With the prophets, faith incorporates this end into the economy of the promise, with Jesus, into the preaching of the God who comes, with St. Paul, into the law of superabundance. This is why the view of faith on events and on men is essentially benevolent. Faith justifies the man of the *Aufklärung* for whom, in the great romance of culture, evil is a factor in the education of the human race, rather than the puritan, who never succeeds in taking the step from condemnation to mercy, and who thus remains within the ethical dimension, and never enters into the perspective of the Kingdom which comes.

Such are the three "discourses" which may be held about guilt: the semantic discourse is mainly a phenomenology of confession by means of an interpretation of symbolic expressions; the ethical discourse is an explanation of the relation between freedom, obligation and evil (it relies on the performatives through which I take on myself the origin of evil and constitute myself as a responsible will); the religious discourse is a re-interpretation of freedom and evil in the light of hope—in Christian terms, of hope in the universal resurrection from the dead.

If I consider these three discourses as a whole, they offer a kind of progression, which could be compared to the progression from the aesthetic stage to the ethical and the religious stage in Kierkegaard's philosophy. I should accept this comparison, if I did not find it disparaging and discouraging.

❖ JOHN E. SMITH ❖

John E. Smith (1927–   ) teaches at Yale University and is the author of several books, including *Reason and God, Experience and God,* and *The Spirit of American Philosophy.* The following essay focuses on the experience of the holy and its relationship to the historically specific idea of God. Refining Rudolf Otto's distinction between the holy and the profane, Smith concentrates on the contexts of encounter with the holy, those turning points or crises in life which pose the problematic nature of our existence. Exploring these experiences of sacred encounters in time and space leads Smith to conclude that even if there is no necessary transition from the experience of the holy to the Judeo-Christian concept of God, there is still the possibility of a logical relation between such experiences and a general concept of God as an object of supreme devotion and worship. Combining materials from the history of religions with issues derived from existential philosophy and western religious thought, Smith makes an important contribution to an existential phenomenology of the holy.

The Experience of the Holy
and the Idea of God

The phenomenological approach to any philosophical problem means an approach through the analysis of primary experience and the reflective grasp of what we actually encounter. This view, though positive, implies the negation of certain other views. First, it means that experience is not to be understood either as a way of transforming reality into mere phenomena devoid of power and otherness, or of reducing reality to the data of sense; second, it means that experience is not to be identified with an exclusively private or "mental" content confined to an individual mind; third, it means that ingredient in experience is a real world of things, events, and selves transcending the encounter I had by any one individual or any finite collection of individuals. The general assumption behind these negations is that experience is neither a substitute for reality nor a veil that falls between us and what there is, but rather a *reliable medium of disclosure* through which the real world is made manifest and comes to be apprehended by us.

Our task here is to seek an understanding of the experience of the Holy, to mark out distinctive features of the situations which the presence of the Holy is felt, and then to express the relation of these features to the idea of God as the supremely worshipful being of religion. Rudolf Otto, in his well-known study *The Idea of the Holy*, began with the record of certain experiences or encounters with God which played a special role in the foundation of the Hebraic-Christian religion. The question might be raised, however, whether instead of beginning with the special experiences that are recorded and interpreted in the biblical, especially the Old Testament, literature, it would be more in accord with a phenomenological approach to start from a broader base and consider certain recurrent situations that are to be found universally in experience. In this way we can face more directly the difficult problem of passing from the experience of the Holy to an historically specific idea of God.

Let us approach the Holy by the method of contrast. A distinction to be found in some form in every culture known to us is the distinction between those persons, objects, events, and places that are said to be "Holy" and those that are called "profane." The most distinctive and yet most abstract characteristic of the Holy is that it is *set apart* from what is ordinary in human life, because of the sense that the Holy is powerful, awe-inspiring, dangerous, important, precious, and to be approached only with fitting seriousness and gravity. The Holy stands over against the profane, which is, by contrast, open, manifest, obvious, ordinary, and devoid of any special power to evoke awe and reverence. The profane belongs to the ordinary or customary course of events and harbors no mysterious depth within itself. Whereas the Holy can be approached only with due preparation, profane existence is readily available and is taken for granted without evoking much thought or concern.

The initial contrast that enables us to make the fundamental identification of the Holy is a distinction—not a separation or total disconnection. The Holy is "other than" the profane but not "wholly other." In order to avoid separating the two spheres so that they are severed of all intelligible connections, it is important to notice the dual nature of their relations. On the one hand, the Holy is set apart from the profane, but on the other hand, its disconnection from the profane is not the final fact about its being. Otto tended to emphasize their separation and the "wholly other" character of the Holy because he was trying to present it as an ultimate and irreducible feature of reality, and also to avoid the reduction of the Holy as a religious reality to the sphere of morality. But the Holy must impinge upon and become ingredient in life, including the activities of profane or ordinary existence; it cannot be merely set apart. The Holy is not to break through life or destroy it as if life were of no account, but rather to consecrate and sustain human existence. In addition, therefore, to the awe and reverence expressing our sense that there is a *gulf* between the Holy and our ordinary life, there is also the concern on our part to have communion with the Holy, to partake of its power and thereby elevate profane existence to a new level of importance.

In the course of experience we discover that the situations we encounter divide themselves into two basically different sorts. On the one hand, there are situations such as traveling to work, purchasing a book or an umbrella, meeting friends for luncheon, calling for information about train schedules, and so forth, which reduce to routine, which do not challenge or arrest us in any way, and which we do more or less habitually, regarding them as "normal" or "regular" parts of the business of living. On the other hand, there is another type of situation running through experience, and it calls for a different description. This type of situation has an insistence that arrests us and leads us to reflect on the seriousness and import of life as a whole. Such arresting situations are encountered in their most insistent form at the two boundaries of natural life—birth and death—but they are also to be encountered during the course of life in the form of certain "crucial" times that mark what may be called the "turning points" or times of decision, judgment, and risk in the life both of individuals and nations. In addition to birth and death, there is the time of marriage, the time of attaining adulthood, the time of serious illness and recovery, the time of war and of the concluding peace, the time of choosing a vocation and of launching a career, the time of setting out upon a long journey. Each of these times is marked off from the "ordinary" course of events, and in every case we frequently describe it as a time of "life and death," by which we mean to express our sense both of the power manifest and of its special bearing or import for our life as a whole. We are vaguely aware in such situations of something that is powerful and important, and our most universal response is that of "celebration." Such times, we feel, must not be allowed to sink to the level of ordinary routine; in some way they must be kept apart from all that is usual or taken for granted. On one side, these times set themselves apart from the ordinary because of their own arresting character; on the other side, there is our response or sense that these times must not be allowed to pass away unnoticed or to be reduced to the sphere of the ordinary. Celebration or ceremony is the attempt to preserve and inten- sify the importance of the crucial junctures of life.

The various forms of celebration which take place on these occasions are evidence both of their arresting character in themselves and of our human capacity to be arrested by them and to acknowledge their power. Everyone, even the most completely rationalistic person who regards himself as committed only to the pursuit of truth and objectivity without ceremony, experiences the seriousness and arresting character of wed- dings and funerals and the anxiety attaching inevitably to the birth of a new being. The philosophical task posed by such situations is to discover what there is about these events that evokes our response so that we come to identify them as times when the Holy is present. Assuming, as we may, that the cycle of human life contains such special and arresting times as we have indicated, we must attempt to discover wherein their special power resides and ultimately how they are related to the idea of God.

The most basic fact about the special events is their temporal position in life; most of them occur once and do not recur. Birth and death have an obvious "once-for-allness" about them, as do the attainment of manhood and the time of marriage. The latter, at the very least, is *meant* to be the establishment of a permanent relationship. What happens but once in life cannot be placed on the same level of importance with the endlessly repeated and repeatable events of the daily round. The unique temporal position of these events harbors in itself a special capacity, a capacity for calling attention to the being of the self and to life as a *whole*. This feature is, of course, most evident in the two boundary events of life. In birth and death we have to do with absolute beginnings and endings, with the coming into being or the passing away of an individual being who is unique. In both cases it is the total being who comes before us, the person as an indissoluble unit. The focus of attention on the person as such helps to direct attention to the *being* of the person and away from the parts and details of life. In the case of the crucial events falling between the boundaries of life and death, attention is also directed to the *course* of life viewed in its total quality or worth. Life as such and the purpose of living come into view at points where decision affects the direction and destiny of life in its entire cycle and not just in one aspect or part. We experience awe in the face of the crucial events because we see in them, at one extreme, the possibility of death and the destruction of our hopes or, in less serious situations, the possibility of a failure so basic that the purpose of living may seem to be destroyed. Conversely, the crucial events may prove to be occasions of creative self-realization and the laying of foundations for lasting achievement. A crucial event is said to be a time of "crisis" because it means a judgment upon life in the sense that a time of decision reveals the quality of a life and opens the possibility for success or failure with respect to that life as a whole.

The use of the term "crisis" to describe the crucial event expresses the dual sense of *choice* and of *judgment* appropriate to such situations. From the standpoint of the agent who contemplates marriage, for example, there is the responsibility of choice, commitment and the attendant risk that comes with realizing freedom at a specific point in life; an unwise or ill-considered choice at this point affects the course and quality of life as a whole and not only in some part or limited aspect. Choice in a crisis situation is "momentous" just because of the holistic nature of the consequences. In a trivial situation concerning a part of life, one can "experiment" and, through a process of trial and error, gradually arrive at the best method for achieving success without at the same time involving one's entire being in the process. But trivial situations are very different from the times of crisis; the latter involve our entire being, and the idea of "experimenting" with a marriage, for example, as if one could enter that relationship casually and sporadically, is inappropriate and severely damages the personal relations that must exist if the union is to be a success. The notion of experiment and trial is inappropriate at those points where the being of the person as a whole is in question.

On the other hand, a crisis situation brings with it more than the demand for decision on the part of the agent; a crisis brings us to a juncture where the direction and quality of life are judged or tested by the nature of the situation itself. The attempt to lead the quiet or sheltered life is generally the attempt to avoid becoming involved in situations that call for, i.e., demand or exact from us, a response that at once reveals the nature of our persons, our most intimate desires and values, our ultimate beliefs and commitments. The situation by itself, of course, exercises no "judgment," but its nature forces us to reveal ourselves, even if we try to avoid meeting the demands it makes upon us. In this sense the special events in life are literally the "times that try men's souls." The time of "crisis," as the Greek term from which the word is derived means, is a time of "judgment." The crucial times, moreover, reveal the precariousness of our existence and underline the truth that in existence no realization is absolutely guaranteed in advance. Precariousness is seen as affecting not only the details of life but life in its entire being. The crucial times make clear that we confront not only problems in life, but a fundamental problem *of* life, namely, the problem of finding the power upon which we depend for our being and our purpose The arresting character of the special times consists largely in their shocking us and thus forcing us out of the routine established within the framework of ordinary clock time into an awareness of our being and its purpose in a total scheme of things. Concern for details and the partial interests that make up so large a part of ordinary existence gradually deadens our sensitivity not only to our problematic being as selves in a precarious world but also to the ultimate questions about the world itself. Where all is "ordinary," open, manifest, and devoid of either depth or mystery, awe and reverence disappear and are replaced by boredom and indifference. But life has a structure of its own that works against the reduction of everything to the level of the profane. Life has its critical junctures, and these exert power over us, so that however completely the affairs described as the "ordinary business of living" prevent us from attending to what Socrates called the "care of the soul," the crucial times serve to bring us back to this concern and to a grasp of the problematic nature of our individual existence.

Thus far, the experience of the Holy through the crucial junctures of life has been understood entirely in terms of the *temporal* pattern of life, and we have referred exclusively to crucial *times* and *events*. But the whole of life is not exhausted in its temporal features; we are creatures of space as well as of time, and the question naturally arises: are there special or crucial *spaces* that have an arresting function, driving us out of the uniformity and the habitual routine of ordinary life and leading us to respond in awe to the Holy, to become aware of our own being and of the need to find a pattern and a purpose in life as a whole? Since space has its quality in itself and contemporaneously—a holy space does not possess its holy character in virtue of any *summing* of its parts, but immediately and at once—it will not intrude itself upon us as the temporal event does, but rather we shall have first to seek such a space and place ourselves in it in order to experience its power. When we are actually in such a space, it will have its own insistence and arresting force, but its effect can take place only when we have opened ourselves by going to the appropriate place. Here space differs from time and crucial events in that the latter descend upon us whether we will or not, whereas we must go to a special space or structure one for ourselves in order to realize its Holiness.

The best-known form of holy space is the sanctuary or physical enclosure clearly marked off from profane space and consecrated as a special place where the Holy is present in the form of the divine to be sought and worshiped. Once again, it is well to consider whether, instead of beginning with a readily acknowledged holy space, we can find features belonging to the spatial environment of life that would help to explain how it can be the mediator of the Holy in and through its own character. We may begin with the distinction evident in experience between the open, public, and neutral space in which the activities of ordinary life take place and shape, and those spaces where it is possible to break through routine and habitual responses in order to find ourselves confronted with the fact of existence and with the question of the purpose of our life as a whole. For example, a stadium filled with people waiting to see a football game is a singularly inappropriate space for discussing a matter of theological concern or for expressing thoughts most intimately expressive of our being and purpose. The space is too completely open and public; it has no arresting power to drive us back to a consideration of what is highest in importance or ultimate in being. On the contrary, such space is entirely extroverted and calls for self-forgetful expressions of enjoyment; the space of the stadium harbors no mystery within itself. Moreover, in such a space we are not elevated in either reverence or awe, and indeed it seems to prevent our withdrawal from the scene and makes it impossible for us to contemplate our being or the ultimate nature of things. For the consideration of what involves our lives as a whole and concerns us most intimately, we need a different kind of space. We must have a space that is not public in the sense that it is a scene where ordinary business is generally conducted, or where anyone may enter without warning or preparation. We must have a space different from one we normally pass through in the course of going to another place. A space that is able to express the sense of the Holy has three characteristics: first, it is set apart from ordinary or routine experience and thus cannot be universally accessible; second, it must have historic associations which remind us of the experiences of the Holy had by others in the past, as in the biblical example of Moses turning aside to see the burning bush, where a previously open and profane space became a holy space in virtue of the arresting experience associated with it; third, the holy space must be so structured as to direct our thoughts to ourselves and our own being and at the same time away from ourselves to an awareness of the Holy power upon which all existence depends.

The crucial times and the holy spaces may arrest us and bring us to a realization of the problematic character of our existence, of our dependence upon a power not ourselves, and of the need to find an object of supreme devotion. But by themselves these events and spaces do not solve our problem. The most they can do is arrest us and impel us to consider the question and the possibility of a form of Holy Life upon which our existence depends. There is no necessary, logical transition from an experience of the Holy, in encountering the crucial events and places, to the reality of God as understood in a specific, historical tradition such as the Judeo-Christian understanding of God represents. On the other hand, the experience of the Holy belongs to the structure of life and the world; it is not dependent on the assumption of certain traditional religious ideas, as if there were no experiential content in the crucial events themselves but only a "religious interpretation" in the form of a tissue of ideas. There is therefore a clear distinction to be drawn between the idea of God, specifically and historically understood, and the experience of the Holy. On the other hand, the two need not remain unrelated to each other. There is an ultimate connection between the experience of the Holy as a pervasive fact of human life and some idea of God or other, but there is no necessary transition from the experience to an historically specific conception of God. There is a missing link that remains to be supplied. The idea of God as the holy power in existence arises in our consciousness on occasions when we are arrested, taken out of our daily routine, and led to contemplate our being only if we have the belief that the power we sense is one upon which our ultimate destiny depends and is a reality that demands our worship and the devotion of our entire being. The sense of the Holy, with the awe we feel on the occasions when the Holy becomes manifest to us, is connected with the idea of God *only* if we identify that Holy with the controller of destiny and the supremely worshipful being.

It is, however, an error to identify the experience of the Holy, as it is open to any human being, with the apprehension of a definite Being as such, as if the approach to God through the Holy was a form of empirical confirmation of the divine existence so understood. Here there are too many possibilities for interpretation. We may hold that the structure of human life remains universal in character despite the undeniable differences that exist in the staggering variety of cultural forms and practices in religion, art, and morality. But just because there is such a plurality of religious traditions and cultural forms, we are not justified in identifying the experience of the Holy, taken as a phenomenon of universal scope, with the intuition of God as understood from the standpoint of any one religious tradition.

On the other hand, it is an error to suppose, as contemporary non-philosophical theologians do, that because there is no necessary logical transition from the experience of the Holy as a pervasive ingredient in experience to the God who is called "the God of Abraham, Isaac, and Jacob," there is no logical relation at all obtaining, between the two. Unless we are prepared to show that, for example, the sort of experience in which Abraham participated is absolutely discontinuous with human experience as known to us, there is no ground for denying an intelligible connection between our contemporary experience of the Holy and the God of the Judeo-Christian tradition. The way is left open for *interpreting* the power present in the crucial events and places encountered in living experience, in terms of the doctrine of God to be found in that tradition. Insofar as the power encountered in the experience of the Holy is regarded as that upon which our being, the purpose of our life as a whole, and our destiny depend, it is legitimate to introduce the idea of the biblical God at this point. That there is no logical necessity in the transition from the Holy to the God described in the Bible, such as might be based on an intuition of the individual Being of the Judeo-Christian tradition, does not preclude our interpreting the Holy in that sense.

The transition from the Holy to God, while not logically necessary, is nevertheless not without some ground; it is rooted in a mediating concept which we may call the general *concept* of God derived from reflective analysis of recurrent experience and presupposed as part of the meaning of every specific religious doctrine of God. The topic calls for more extended treatment, but one essential point can be elucidated. The term "God" need not be restricted to use as a name (although there are contexts in which it so functions) but stands as well for a concept that finds its basis in philosophical reflection on the world and ourselves. This concept embraces the idea of a supremely worshipful reality which gives being to and controls the final destiny of all finite realities. If the term "God" were merely a name, significant exclusively within the confines of a special religious tradition, there could be no intelligible connection between the experience of the Holy and God. But because there is a concept of God available for our use, it is possible to connect the concept of God with the experience of the Holy in which we become aware of the dependence of our being on a power that is at once the supremely worshipful being, and that upon which we depend for our final purpose and destiny.

The general concept of God as the object of supreme devotion, derived from reflective analysis of experience, including encounter with the environment and ourselves, mediates between the pervasive experience of the Holy and the specific idea of God existing within an historical religious community. The latter idea is itself dependent on experiences of the Holy, but those experiences are selected, historically specific encounters which have served as the foundation for an identifiable religious community. Thus the Hebraic community finds its unifying and identifying reference point in the historic encounters of the Patriarchs, Moses, and the prophetic figures with the Holy; likewise, the New Testament communities were rooted in the historic encounters of Jesus, Paul, and the disciples with the Holy, this time mediated through an historic personage. The historic encounters with the Holy, however, demanded in each instance an interpreter whose task was to set forth the specifically religious meaning of these encounters. At that point the generic concept of God comes into play. The experiences of the Holy come to be understood as encounters with God through the identification of these experiences as religion, i.e., as encounters with that reality which alone is worthy of absolute devotion. Once the transition from the Holy to God has been made via the generic concept of the supremely worshipful reality, the specific character of the historic encounters supplies the concrete content. For the Judeo-Christian tradition, for example, God is understood as Will and Righteousness, as Love and Mercy, because of the nature of the encounters had by Moses, the prophets, and Jesus with the Holy.

❖ MEROLD WESTPHAL ❖

Merold Westphal (1940–   ) is professor of philosophy at Fordham University and the author of many works on Continental philosophy. In the following excerpt from his book, *God, Guilt, and Death*, Westphal examines the meaning of guilt within religion. Distinguishing the experience of guilt from the fear of punishment, he then interrogates the phenomenon of guilt from the perspectives of the sociology of deviance, the literature of morbid awareness, and the psychology of false consciousness. As with the other selections in this section, Westphal skillfully uses the categories of existential-hermeneutical philosophy to carry out his phenomenological examination, and his results are both intriguing in their own right and call for comparison with the other existential-hermeneutical inquiries in this volume.

The Existential Meaning of Guilt

The Existential Meaning of Guilt

It may seem puzzling, or to some outright implausible, to say that guilt lies at the heart of religious concern and that religion is regularly a means of solving the problem of guilt. But let us stick to the methodology we have adopted and seek to understand what is being said before we evaluate it. Unless we know rather precisely what is meant by guilt in this context we will not be able to see for ourselves whether it in fact shapes a fundamental religious interest, just as we cannot tell whether the influence of snyks on the economy is rising or falling unless we know what snyks are.

We can, perhaps, best spell out the meaning of guilt, as it will be used from here on, by reflecting on the relation of guilt to punishment. To begin with, there is the objective sense of guilt. Here we are talking about being found guilty (as distinguished from feeling guilty) by a parent, teacher, court of law, or some such authority. To be guilty in this sense is to be liable to punishment. According to the dictionary, liable means, "subject, exposed, or open to something possible or likely, esp. something undesirable."

Naturally, a person can be guilty in this sense and be entirely unaware of it. In that case there might be objective guilt without any accompanying subjective guilt or guilt feeling. But the person who is aware of being liable to punishment will almost automatically, if the punishment amounts to anything, feel a fear or dread of it.

Since both punishment and the fear of punishment are painful, our natural desire is to avoid or eliminate both. Usually they come and go more or less together, but that is not essential. Fear of punishment can be a terrible ordeal, even if the punishment never actually comes. And a punishment which comes so unexpectedly as to permit no prior fears is scarcely for that reason less unpleasant.

But unless we get beyond punishment and the fear of punishment to a third dimension of the problem we will not fully understand the meaning of guilt as the believing soul experiences it. This third dimension is so fundamental that we should call it guilt proper. (In what follows I shall regularly refer to it simply as guilt.) For while the believing soul is as eager as anyone to be free from punishment and the fear of it, neither of these is the heart of the problem.

This third dimension is another subjective aspect, guilt in the sense of guilt feeling or guilt consciousness. We can perhaps get at it best through a concrete example. Consider the sixth grade lad who has gotten too big, as they say, for his britches. Looking forward to summer heroics in Little League, he and his buddies have found the school gym teacher's program somewhat beneath their professional dignity. So throughout the spring they have engaged in what we might euphemistically call systematic non-cooperation. The unexpected toleration of the gym teacher only serves to increase the shenanigans. But he is only biding his time; for he knows that the report cards call for two grades in every subject, one for achievement and one for "comportment." The latter is a pass-fail proposition. The student has either behaved satisfactorily or has not. And suddenly there it is, staring our lad in the face. Not one, but two check marks in the box marked unsatisfactory.

Up until this time he has not felt especially troubled about his behavior. Now, in the face of certain punishment, he feels terrible. He knows that lightning will strike quickly. It won't take his father long to find out what the two check marks signify and even less time to turn the son over his knee so as to continue their dialogue at the level of non-verbal, but ever so unambiguous communication.

The exigencies of the situation transform the boy into an instant presidential press secretary. To his father's inquiry about the double check mark he replies with as obfuscatory a half-truth as was ever served up to the White House press corps. To his utter disbelief and enormous relief, the topic is dropped. This cover-up has worked completely.

Is our hero suddenly at peace again with the world and himself? Hardly! As he gets a little distance from the immediate situation the sense of relief fades and is gradually replaced by a puzzled disappointment in his father. What was the matter with him anyway, that he had failed so conspicuously in his fatherly responsibility? Against the background of this disappointment there sounds the voice of the boy's guilty conscience. This voice is much quieter than the loud shouting which accompanied him home with the report card. Now that the fear of punishment is gone there remains only the pure sense of guilt, or guilt proper. No doubt it was present before, but we can only now see it clearly for what it is. In particular we can see as we reflect on this experience, which might have been our own, that the experience of guilt (guilt proper) is qualitatively different from the fear of punishment and is in no intelligible sense derived from that fear.

For, in the first place, fear looks forward toward what will or may happen, while guilt looks backward to what I have done or become. Furthermore, fear is object oriented while guilt is subject oriented. That is to say that in fear my awareness is directed outward to the source from which some unpleasant consequence is expected, while in guilt my awareness is directed toward myself. It is a mode of self-consciousness or self-knowledge in which, to use Buber's phrase, "the bearer of guilt is visited by the shudder of identity with himself" and comes to the "humble knowledge of the identity of the present person with the person of that time," that is, the time of the action in question. It will be objected by some that it is just this turning inward by which fear is transformed into guilt. Guilt is simply the fear of punishment which remains when no external threat is on the horizon. It can either be said to be an objectless fear or the fear of an internal punisher. But this familiar interpretation of the second difference between fear and guilt is entirely undermined when a third difference is noted. Put in Kantian language it is this: in fear I am concerned about my happiness, while in guilt I am concerned about my *worthiness* to be happy. The uneasiness which eats away the original sense of relief that our young friend experienced when his father let him off the hook is not the fear of an invisible or interiorized father. It is the gradual dawning of the awareness of himself as thoroughly *deserving* the punishment he did not receive. He is not so much afraid of anything as he is ashamed of himself.

Luther is a particularly clear example of this. Because he speaks so much about the wrath of God and because he believes in eternal punishment it is easy to make Scheler's mistake and assume that when he speaks of the terrors of conscience he simply expresses his fear of hell. What drove Luther, however, first to despair and then to grace was not a fear of suffering in hell, but the overwhelming sense that this is what he *deserved*. Not the mere fact of God's wrath, but its uncontestable rightness brought his existence to its crisis. For man can face enormous suffering with nobility and courage if with Job he is sure of his innocence or with Prometheus he is sure of God's guilt. What defines Luther's experience as that of guilt is precisely the absence of these comforts.

"I have often experienced," he writes, "and still do every day, how difficult it is to believe, especially amid struggles of conscience, that Christ was given, not for the holy, righteous, and deserving, or for those who were His friends, but for the godless, sinful, and undeserving, for those who were His enemies, who *deserved the wrath of God and eternal wrath.*"

These two examples, of Luther and our Little League friend, forbid us to equate guilt with the fear of punishment. But they also suggest a two-fold relation between the two. In the first place, fear of punishment can occasion the experience of guilt. Guilt essentially involves the awareness of myself as less worthy of happiness than I would like to be. Punishment presents itself as an unhappiness which I (allegedly) deserve, thereby raising the question of my worthiness. Where the answer to this question is patently unfavorable to my pride I am likely to deceive myself more successfully by avoiding the question altogether than by stubbornly affirming my innocence to myself. In that situation punishment tends to force the issue. I can defend myself from the *moral* pain of punishment only by consciously denying that I deserve it, thereby reducing it to misfortune or persecution. But even to consider that option is to raise the question which up to that time had been effectively tabled and which *ex hypothesi* has an obvious and unfavorable answer. This is clearly what happened to our schoolboy. He had managed to avoid feeling guilty by repressing any evaluation of his behavior whatever, until the defense mechanisms he had so diligently erected self-destructed in the face of impending punishment. Part of what he felt on his way home was guilt proper, though we were able to see it clearly only when it outlived the fear that originally was fused with it.

This fusion represents a second relation between guilt and the fear of punishment. In his discussion of defilement as a symbol of evil as fault Ricoeur calls this fusion dread. Reference is to the primitive understanding of taboo, prior to any conceptions of divine or social agents of retribution. Yet the violation of a taboo is a violation against an impersonal order which is effective and will certainly strike back in vengeance. Since this order is also prior to any division between the merely natural and the moral order, the offender does not merely anticipate an unpleasant response as inevitable, but also as somehow appropriate. In an inarticulate way he is already in possession of the Socratic wisdom that "to escape punishment is worse than to suffer it." In this case "fear of vengeance is not a simple passive fear; already it involves a demand, the demand for a just punishment."

The fear of punishment which demands precisely the punishment it fears is clearly not a simple fear. It is the radical ambivalence of desperately wanting to avoid just what we deeply want to happen. This was the state of mind which comes to light in the autobiographical elements of Luther's theology. Since this is a unified, if complex, mode of consciousness, it would be useful if there were a standard term for referring to it. Ricoeur's use of "dread" for this purpose runs the risk of introducing extraneous connotations from more firmly fixed existentialist usages, but this meaning is at least as close to pretechnical usage as the existentialist meanings.

This concept of dread serves two purposes. As already indicated, it enables us to acknowledge the close relationship between guilt proper and fear of punishment without identifying the two. Second, by preserving a clear distinction between the guilt and fear components, it provides us with a working definition of guilt. In this context guilt is an affirmative attitude toward the verdict which renders me liable to punishment. Since punishment is an unhappiness I (allegedly) deserve, it represents a negative judgment on my worth coming from outside me. Since in guilt I affirm this judgment, we can say that *in guilt I approve the other's disapproval of me*. To illuminate and confirm this initial result we shall take a closer look at the phenomenon of guilt from three quite different perspectives: the sociology of deviance, the literature of morbid inwardness, and the psychology of false consciousness.

Guilt and the Sociology of Deviance

It would appear from the foregoing that Nietzsche was mistaken in saying that punishment does not awaken the feeling of guilt. When he says that the sting of conscience is extremely rare among criminals and convicts, he confuses guilt with repentance. It may be that our correctional systems make men hard and cold; but this very hardness and coldness is more accurately seen as a defensive reaction to the dawning of an unpleasant awareness than as the calm assurance that all is quiet on the worthiness-to-be happy front. It may equally be true that the knowledge convicts gain of the cruelty and hypocrisy practiced in the name of justice helps to distract attention from their own guilt; but only those in whom guilty self-consciousness has dawned can find comfort in finding others to be just as bad or worse.

My own experience with those who have served time in prison does not suggest that they have come through the experience with an unscathed sense of personal worth. In their bitterness toward the system and its agents, as justified as it may be, they come through as willing, but never quite able, to justify themselves. From the point of view of public policy the problem is not that our penal system fails to awaken guilt, but rather that it fails to engender repentance. The law is simply a taskmaster when it should be a schoolmaster.

While it is mistaken, then, to think that the criminal has invincible defenses against guilt, it is nevertheless true that his avoidance mechanisms make up an awesome armory. For if it is true that punishment forces the question which gives rise to experienced guilt, those who live in the shadow of punishment will be able to sustain a viable self-image only by neutralizing most of the guilt they would normally feel. A closer look at the way they (and the rest of us, if we're honest about it) avoid being destroyed by the guilt that their deeds seem to call for may further illuminate the meaning of guilt. The soldier, too, has need of such "techniques of neutralization." These parallel those of the delinquent so strikingly that they can be presented together.

Does the juvenile delinquent live in an inverted world where all norms and values are the opposite from those prevailing in straight society? No, we are told. He shares the values of the larger society, at least abstractly, but is especially skillful at rendering them inoperative in relation to his own behavior. Five distinct techniques of neutralization can be specified. The first is *Denial of Responsibility*. The delinquent quickly learns to take the point of view of the social scientist and humane jurist who see him as a product of his environment. In the important sense that guilt requires, his deeds are not really his own. The soldier gets the same effect by viewing himself as merely part of a larger organic whole. Not only are thousands of others doing the same thing; it is others who are giving the orders and directing the show. His deeds are not really his, but those of this supra-personal entity known as The Army or My Country. Or he may submerge himself in a sub-personal entity, the machinery which immediately does the killing, and come to see himself more nearly as an extension of the weapons he uses than as their user. Once again his deeds cease to be his own and he can say, It wasn't really I who did it.

A second technique is called the *Denial of Injury*. The delinquent tells himself that vandalism is merely a prank which harms no one and that his stealing is from those who can afford it anyway. The soldier can hardly avail himself of these ploys, but in modern warfare he is often so spatially distant from his victims that it is easy for him not to notice that his shells and bombs will inevitably destroy children not unlike those who anxiously await his safe return home.

In this way no one gets hurt, except the Enemy, which brings us to a third technique, *Denial of the Victim*, or more precisely, the denial of the victims' innocence. In other words, they had it coming so why should I feel guilty about what happened. Delinquency and war depend heavily on our capacity to view the other as evil. Where the Enemy is to be found, there is war; and all is fair in war.

If we pause now and ask what self-awareness these devices are intended to ward off it would have to be expressed like this: I am responsible for injuring or harming an innocent victim. With this awareness there may or may not be a fear of anticipated unpleasant consequences. That is quite contingent. What is necessarily associated with this awareness is a depleted sense of personal worth that we call guilt or shame. In the likely event that the first three techniques are not totally effective, some further mitigating factor will be sought for. The required mitigation would have to be a supervening value which could drive a wedge between the awareness of myself as having harmed an innocent victim and the guilt which would otherwise be an inevitable part of that awareness.

This brings us to a fourth technique: *Appeal to Higher Loyalties*. The delinquent seeks to justify his assault on the larger society by reference to his loyalty to the smaller group to which he belongs, the gang, his buddies. The soldier does the same. Loyalty to his buddy or his unit or the Fatherland in its hour of need serves to transform acts that he could not normally perform at all, much less without guilt, into courageous deeds of valor. What was *prima facie* evil has now become justified, even obligatory. William Calley scarcely feels the guilt a healthy person would feel, not just because the women and children of My Lai are the Enemy, but also because he is there to protect his Friends.

The four defenses so far presented can be summed up colloquially as follows: I didn't do it, and anyway nobody got hurt. Besides, they had it coming, and you wouldn't want me to abandon my friends, would you? I had to do it! This is not a model of calm coherence, but of a desperate struggle against that diminution of self-esteem which might be expressed in a number of ways; I am worthy to be punished, I am not worthy to be loved, I am not worthy of happiness. The defense is all the more passionate because the confession would be so painful. But to whom is the defense offered in lieu of a confession?

The fifth, and for the present analysis, final protection from guilt indicates that the defendant has not been talking merely to himself, but to the Other. This technique can be called *Condemners* or *Rejection of the Rejectors*. "The delinquent shifts the focus of attention from his own deviant acts to the motives and behavior of those who disapprove of his violations." Once again, there is an Other who must be viewed as the Enemy if guilt is to be avoided. But this time it is not simply the victim who must be so conceived. It is the whole class of those who disapprove of the behavior in question. The attitude of veterans groups to war resisters indicates that this remains a necessity for soldiers, even decades after their war has ended.

It is worth stressing that this technique is not one of persuading the disapprovers, but of rejecting them. Persuasion would be nice, but it is not necessary. There is no need to eliminate the disapproval. All that is required, if the sense of guilt is to be avoided, is that I not find it necessary to approve the other's disapproval. For this purpose it is sufficient to discredit the other in my own eyes. This involves an element of persuasion, to be sure, since I must persuade myself that the other is the Enemy and can be disregarded. Under the circumstances I can probably persuade myself more easily than the other.

Although I end up talking to myself in order to persuade myself, this technique highlights the essential presence of the other in the experience of guilt. Where guilt is confused with fear of punishment its intersubjective nature is inescapable. But closer attention to the phenomena has led us to separate fear from guilt proper and to discover guilt as a form of self-consciousness. The other has gradually disappeared. We have seen conscience as the self saying to itself, Thou art the man (and trying to persuade itself that it is not). But this final aspect of the social scientific theory of delinquency confirms the suggestion of the two earlier examples that this is not the whole story, that the voice of conscience is not a soliloquy. If guilt essentially involves this reference to the other's disapproval, this aspect of the fear theory needs to be rescued in order to be faithful to the full concreteness of the phenomenon before us.

Yet there may be a lingering doubt whether the suggestion which has emerged from two examples and from social scientific theory can be confirmed by genuine eidetic insight. May it not be that the other seems to be essential to the experience of guilt only because in the cases before us external sanctions are actually at hand in the persons of the boy's father, Luther's God, and the penal system of the state? Since it has been argued that this element is only an occasion for guilt and not part of its essential structure and that guilt must be sharply distinguished from the fear of punishment, is it not possible that we have allowed punishment, which obviously involves the other, to play too large a role in our exploration? May there not after all be an experience of conscience as pure soliloquy, as unmediated self-consciousness? May it not be only the element of fear which brings the other on the scene?

Perhaps it is time to shift our focus briefly. Instead of trying to get at guilt from below, as it were, through specific cases or types of cases, we might approach it from above, from the general theory of self-consciousness. It seems to me that one of the most firmly established phenomenological insights into the nature of self-consciousness is the Hegelian and Sartrean discovery that self-consciousness is always mediated by consciousness of the other. I first come to see myself when I see you looking at me. In opposition to the abstract and unmediated self-consciousness of transcendental philosophy from Descartes to Fichte, any awareness rich enough to be described as self-esteem is never an act of unconditioned self-positing. It is always a response to the other's attitude toward me. Empirical psychology has increasingly come to recognize this fact, but for our purposes the point is that it is not simply a fact but part of the essential structure of the finite self-consciousness we are. If this be indeed the case for self-consciousness as such, then guilt, which we have come to see as a mode of self-consciousness, is but a special case of the same necessity. As self-consciousness, it remains distinct from fear, but like every self-consciousness it is mediated through the self's relation to the other. David needs Nathan after all. The voice which accusingly tells the self, Thou art the man, is in the first instance the other's voice. Guilt is a kind of echo effect; for when that voice resounds off the walls of the self's inner life it has been transformed into the self's own voice.

This fusion of voices is but another way of indicating that in guilt I recognize (even when I cannot bring myself to acknowledge) the justification of the other's judgment upon me. If we would keep guilt before us whole, we will have to preserve this unity of self-consciousness and other-consciousness.

Guilt and the Literature of Morbid Inwardness

What would be helpful at this point would be to return to the concrete to see anew the whole structure of guilt in both its complexity and its unity. It would be especially helpful if we could imagine or find an experience of guilt which, unlike Luther's, is thoroughly secular, and unlike all three cases considered to this point, is not staring punishment in the face. From among the candidates already worked out by the literary imagination of others, Dostoyevsky's Underground Man is perhaps best suited to our purpose. That his problem is guilt is indicated in numerous ways, among them the frequency with which he discusses the possibility of finding forgiveness for himself and the overt recollection that "at the very moment when I was most capable of recognizing every refinement of 'all the sublime and beautiful,' as we used to say at one time, I would, as though purposely, not only feel but do such hideous things. . . . The more conscious I was of goodness, and of all that 'sublime and beautiful'; the more deeply I sank into my mire and the more capable I became of sinking into it completely."

To begin with, it is clear that the ailment from which he suffers is not the fear of punishment, but a special form of self-awareness. Positively this is indicated by the name he gives to the morbid introspectiveness displayed in the opening monologue, hyper-consciousness. Negatively this is seen in the fact that far from fearing or seeking to avoid any humiliation overt enough to be considered a punishment, he positively longs for such and actively seeks it out. He would be delighted to be slapped in the face, to be thrown out of the tavern, or to be beaten up. Although he never succeeds in evoking anything physical, he does manage in each of the three episodes narrated in Part II to expose himself to extreme social humiliation, to which he is especially sensitive.

The one persistent feature of Underground Man's hyper-consciousness is the overwhelming sense of his own worthlessness. Symbolically this is expressed throughout the narrative by his description of himself as a mouse, a fly, a beetle, an eel, a spider, and a worm. But even this drastic symbolism is inadequate to the situation. Underground Man is thoroughly impotent. He cannot do anything, and the reason is that he cannot be anything. If only he could be something, he feels, his life would be saved. His demands are not inordinate. He once knew a man who was a connoisseur of Lafitte and who died triumphantly in the assurance that he was something. Underground Man would be more than happy if he could be sure he was a loafer, or someone spiteful, but he lacks what it takes. "Now I want to tell you gentlemen," he writes, " . . . why I could not even become an insect. I tell you solemnly that I wanted to become an insect many times. But I was not even worthy of that." After such a statement his repeated announcements that he is totally lacking in self-respect are a bit redundant.

In spite of an existence which he describes as "solitary to the point of savagery," Underground Man lives in the constant presence of others. They are, like Simonnet in the childhood experience of Sartre, "absent in the flesh." As such they are more oppressively present than anything physically present. "For forty years," he writes, "I have been listening to your words through a crack under the floor. I have invented them myself." It would be false to suppose that his guilt was first a self-contained self-relation which only came to involve others when he invented them and put words in their mouth. Rather, from the start he felt his existence to be under judgment by others and when, due to his own withdrawn style of life, the others were no longer empirically present he found it necessary to "invent" them, for they simply did not go away. The solitude of his existence is only the subsequently attempted ratification at the empirical level of what had come to be an existential fact for him—the total break with the other clue to a disapproval which he could only approve.

The three episodes of Part II show us this situation before he had actually taken up his underground life, though, as he tells us, he already had the underground in his soul. Throughout these three episodes three themes recur constantly. (1) While Part I recounts his lack of self-respect, the temporally prior Part II describes his desperate and unfulfilled longing for respect from others. (2) Beyond this he longs for a complete healing of the break between himself and others, and in each of the episodes he fantasizes a reconciliation which culminates in either friendship or love. (3) But it all remains at the level of desire and daydream, for the one all pervasive fact is his inability even to look anyone in the face. He not only feels their disdain; he feels it is justified. So much is this the case that when the prostitute Liza begins to respond to his compassion with what he rightly detects as love, he immediately withdraws. He lies to her cruelly and tells her he is nothing but a scoundrel who didn't really care for her for a moment, but was only laughing at her, using her psychologically after having used her physically.

All this confirms that the self-loathing to which Underground Man is addicted is his approval of the other's disapproval, his acknowledgment that others have the right, even the duty, to view him as worthless. His guilt separates him not only from himself, but from the rest of humanity as well. Like anyone who experiences guilt, he encounters the temptation to defend himself by somehow neutralizing the low esteem in which he and others see him. The intensity of his guilt indicates that he has failed to succumb to these temptations, two of which he recounts for us.

There is first of all the temptation to Reject the Rejectors. From start to finish this tendency emerges in the form of Underground Man's inner sense of infinite superiority to everyone else. Of course, he is visibly not very high on the socio-economic ladder, but he almost finds his hyper-consciousness to be an adequate remedy for this, giving him understanding of the whole scene which puts him in the know, leaving others out in the dark just as he is socially out in the cold. At the point where this comes to fullest expression, he suddenly screams at his readers, "Hurrah for underground! But immediately he takes it all back. He knows that there is something truly better than the complacency and stupidity around him, but that it is not underground. So he shouts again, "Damn underground!" The intellectual superiority that his hyper-consciousness gives him does nothing to invalidate the reproaches he feels from every direction. Even when these are social, rather than moral, he experiences them not just as embarrassment or social shame but, like Milton's Adam and Eve in their nakedness, as "guilty shame."

More prominent is the battle Underground Man wages against the

Denial of Responsibility which can be gained by seeing oneself as merely
the expression of a larger necessity. The stubborn refusal to bow to the
laws of nature and view himself as a piano key on which they play whatever tune they will is matched by an equally stubborn refusal to place his
hopes in the social utopias symbolized by the crystal palace. He is un-
willing to shift the blame for what he is to either natural or social necessity, and he is most explicitly articulate about this. Man's "most advan-
tageous advantage" is not reason, but the freedom to be responsible for
himself, even when unreasonable. No doubt it is the energy with which
Underground Man holds himself open to his guilt, refusing the comfort
to be found in rejecting his rejectors or in denying his own responsibility,
which makes him such an unforgettable character.

Guilt and the Psychology of False Consciousness

From the point of view of the preceding analyses one might seek to
discredit Freud and Nietzsche as phenomenologists of guilt. But a closer
look will show that in spite of their heavy investment in a model which
represents guilt quite differently from the foregoing, they provide still
further confirmation of our previous results.

The case against them would go like this. Both are too concerned to
explain guilt in terms of introverted aggression to notice that guilt is a
question of worth, of what I deserve. The aggression which is originally
directed outward on their theories is not valuational in this sense. For
Nietzsche it is a spontaneous cruelty and desire to dominate which entails
nothing whatever about the victim's merits. Similarly for Freud the impetus toward destruction is simply a biological instinct and wholly void
of moral judgment. In fact, Freud's metapsychology is nowhere more
thoroughly biological than in *Beyond the Pleasure Principle*, on which
his theory of guilt depends. The turning inward of this aggression is supposed to be guilt. But no account is given of the miracle (should we speak
here of transubstantiation or alchemy?) by which this non-judgmental
outward aggression is suddenly inseparable from questions of worth
when directed inward toward myself. The basic thesis of the aggression
theory systematically overlooks this aspect of guilt for the sake of causal
explanation, with the awkward consequence that whatever is explained,
if anything, is not guilt. At neither the descriptive nor the explanatory
level does the aggression theory survive close scrutiny.

Since few can claim to match Freud and Nietzsche when it comes to
powers of careful observation, we would be faced with an awkward di-
lemma if this were all there were to say on the subject. We would either

have the difficult task of explaining how they failed so completely as phenomenologists or we would have to begin doubting the results of our own investigation, which seem to be strongly confirmed. But neither Freud nor Nietzsche limited his interpretation of guilt to the mechanical model just summarized. Both present a theory of guilt from dammed up aggression in the fairly crude form in which I have presented it; but they also have a good deal more to say about the subject.

Let us consider Nietzsche first. He calls attention to all the essential elements of guilt according to the previous analysis, namely that it is a relation to oneself, that it involves the question of worth, and that it essentially involves relation to others.

That guilt is a relation to oneself is already implicit in the theory of introverted aggression, though the fact that the relation is one of self-consciousness is hidden. When Nietzsche describes it as "an animal soul turned against itself, taking sides against itself," it sounds as if something more than the interplay of biological forces may be involved, though this could be just a metaphor for the inward flooding of a cruelty whose outward flow has been dammed up. But when he goes on to speak of "a soul voluntarily at odds with itself," the previous ambiguity is surpassed. Only as self-consciousness can a soul be voluntarily at odds with itself.

The question of worth enters Nietzsche's account only when guilt has become guilt before God; but at least in this context it comes through loud and clear. In the face of the ideal of a holy God the individual comes "to feel the palpable certainty of his own unworthiness." This is the context in which nihilism and nausea are explicitly present as guilt phenomena, for "existence in general" comes to be "considered worthless as such." Although he has a rather different view from Luther's on how we are to be delivered from this dreadful disease, he is too acute an observer to let this aspect of the data pass unnoticed.

From a theological perspective, guilt is always in the final analysis guilt before God, and conscience is always in some sense the voice of God. That guilt involves relation to another is never in question. Just for this reason the suspicion may well arise that the attempt to find this relation as an essential part of guilt may stem less from careful observation of human experience than from theological assumptions. To the previous attempts to deal with this suspicion with help from Hegel, Sartre, and Dostoyevsky, we can now add the insights of Nietzsche. He is especially helpful in this respect, for while God comes on the guilt scene rather late in the day on his account, the other is there from the start, and ineluctably so.

"To breed an animal with the right to make promises"—it is this intersubjectivity of promise making that is the starting point for his analysis of guilt and bad conscience. Although he does not equate guilt with fear of punishment, he recognizes the close connection between guilt and punishment, since objectively guilt is the liability to punishment. Punishment he seeks to understand in terms of contract and the relation of creditor and debtor, a special sort of promise making. Hence the intimate connection between guilt and debt, embedded in German consciousness by the word *Schuld*, and not wholly missing from the English-speaking world, where many Christians continue to pray, "Forgive us our debts as we forgive our debtors."

Nietzsche seeks to derive guilt and justice in the moral sense from the realm of legal rights and contract by means of a "transfer." To those of us for whom moral and legal obligation have gone their separate ways this seems to introduce another miracle of transformation. For the knowledge that the other has the right to collect thirty dollars from me, since I have promised to pay it, does not necessarily involve any diminished self-esteem on my part, while the knowledge that the other has the right to punish me clearly does. But the fact remains that language retains a term we take to be pre-ethical for use in the ethical domain. Nietzsche calls our attention to an important symbolic usage whose significance needs to be explored. In what way is debt an appropriate symbol for guilt? The primary answer must be that both involve the violation of a relation to another. I become a debtor in a weak sense when I promise to pay someone for something; but in Nietzsche's strong sense, which involves liability to punishment, this occurs only when I break that promise and do not pay when I have promised to do so. In contract, the promise represents a bond of agreement between buyer and seller, making them in a specified respect one. The debtor (in the strong sense) breaks that bond (possibly through no personal fault) and creates a conflict between the two parties in place of harmony. Similarly, when guilty I see myself as moral debtor in having broken the promise implicit in my membership in the human community or explicit in some particular relationship. I know that this breaking of the bond between myself and the other is a wrong which confers on the other a right, possibly to punish, certainly to judge. Having failed to pay my neighbor the respect I owe, I confer on the neighbor the right to foreclose and collect what is due from the moral resources remaining to me, my own self-respect. Such is the essentially intersubjective nature of guilt from a Nietzschean perspective.

Freudian theory seems, if anything, more heavily laden with difficulty than Nietzschean. For not only does Freud have the problems inherent in the aggression theory; by consistently treating the super-ego as an internalized punisher, whose sadistic extravagances the most violent rhetoric can never quite adequately express, he regularly identifies guilt with fear of the super-ego. There is first the fear of external dangers such as the threat of castration. Even prior to internalization of any kind, Freud identifies this fear with guilt. It is, therefore, not surprising that when parental authority is introjected and (mysteriously) supplied with aggressive energy through blockage of the outward flow of aggression by social restraint, the resultant super-ego is not only portrayed as an internal aggressor, but guilt is said to coincide completely with the fear of it. In this equation of guilt with fear the question of worth seems to be completely subordinated to the question of happiness. Furthermore, the super-ego becomes as other to the self as the id and the external world, so that the moment of self-consciousness seems lost as well.

But again these aspects of the guilt phenomenon are too conspicuous to be overlooked even in the presence of metaphors unfriendly to their discovery. The picture of Freud presented so far is selectively abstract and incomplete. For example, the super-ego is not just presented as an aggressor, but as a judicial and critical agency and even as a faculty of self-judgment and self-criticism involving moral censorship and humility. And in spite of passages making guilt completely coincide with fear of punishment, Freud regularly speaks of guilt as the need of punishment, suggesting an approval of negative judgments against me, even if it is not fully conscious. In both cases Freud clearly sees guilt as a question of worth.

At the same time the complex unity of self-consciousness and other-consciousness previously described with the echo metaphor is present in Freud's account of the super-ego's origin through identification or introjection and in his original description of it as the ego ideal. Although the role of parents and other external authority figures is a powerful one and the voice which speaks within can sound as harsh and hostile as an external voice, the latter represents values with which I have identified and is undeniably my own voice. This interplay of self-consciousness and relation to the other is probably best expressed when Freud writes, "A child feels inferior if he notices that he is not loved, and so does an adult. . . . Altogether, it is hard to separate the sense of inferiority and the sense of guilt." In both cases we are dealing with a process in which I come to view myself as the other sees me, to adopt the other's sense of my worth.

Let us recapitulate. Objectively guilt is (1) liability to punishment. Subjectively it is (2) fear of punishment, and (3) approval of my own punishment, or, more carefully stated, approval of the other's disapproval of me which may render me liable to punishment. Even if it does not lead to punishment, the other's disapproval is a painful assault on my self-esteem made all the more so when I am compelled to approve of it, that is, to acknowledge its legitimacy. We have spent a lot of time exploring this third dimension of guilt, a focus made necessary because this aspect is both so easily overlooked and so central. It is just this element which leaves both our Little League friend and Underground Man with such big guilt problems in spite of their having no punishment nor fear of punishment to deal with.

Yet it would be a mistake to assume that the believing soul is only troubled by this final element we have called guilt proper. For the Sacred is experienced not just as judge, but also as punisher. This may seem most obvious in the context of a personal God or gods as enforcers of the moral law, but it is no less present in impersonal manifestations of the Sacred. As primitives fear the *mana* which punishes the violations of taboos and as the ancient Greeks feared the *Nemesis* which punished every human act of *hybris,* so devout Hindus and Buddhists fear the *Karma* which makes them pay for every wrong they have done, no matter how many lifetimes it may take them.

If guilt, then, is an experience, especially conducive to the manifestation of the Sacred as the *mysterium tremendum,* its meaning as *fascinans* will come to light as it helps us deal with guilt in all three of its dimensions. We remain with ambivalence. Religion will be repelling as it gives focus and new intensity to human guilt. But it will be attractive just to the degree that it (1) helps us to avoid the punishment we would otherwise be liable to, (2) gives us sufficient assurance of this to free us from the fear of punishment, and (3) heals the wounded self-consciousness which can only approve the other's disapproval, which knows how vastly its desire for happiness exceeds its worthiness.

❖ CAROLINE WALKER BYNUM ❖

In the following selection, which is taken from her introduction to a collection of essays, Professor Caroline Walker Bynum (1941–   ) of Columbia University explores the significance of the genderedness of human experience for understanding religious symbols. Attention to gender, or to the culturally created experience of being male or female, is necessary, she contends, to adequately comprehend human symbols. And religious symbols are one of the ways in which such cultural meanings are both taught and understood. Exploring the implications of the interpretive approaches to symbol of Clifford Geertz, Victor Turner, and Paul Ricoeur, Bynum emphasizes the complexity and significance of gender in unpacking the polysemic nature of religious symbols. Her essay contributes not only to the discussion of method in the phenomenology of religion, but also to substantive questions concerning an adequate phenomenology of women's religious experience.

❖

The Complexity of Symbols

Until recently the field of comparative religion dealt with *homo religious*—the religious experience of man. The fact that religious man often worshipped Mother Nature was considered an oddity, a stage he outgrew as he moved on to more transcendent (and frequently male) deities. When, under the impetus of feminist theory, "religious woman" began to be considered, scholars noted that she often worshipped a Father God or found the transcendent revealed in a male figure. Since societies in which women worshipped male deities tended to be societies in which men were dominant and since indeed the lack of interest in woman's religious experience seemed most acute among male scholars who studied patriarchal societies and patriarchal religions, some radical reformers began to suggest that male deities themselves were the problem. Recent feminist critiques of both Western and non-Western religious traditions have agreed that men gain authority from the fact that the source of ultimate value is often described in anthropomorphic images as Father or King. But feminist activists have been sharply divided between those who would respond by discarding male symbols in religion—often discarding much of the theological tradition in question as well—and those who would rewrite liturgies and reform language to insert female symbols and pronouns among male ones.

However the debate about current religious language and practice is finally resolved, the questions of feminists have changed the course of scholarship. It is no longer possible to study religious practice or religious symbols without taking gender—that is, the cultural experience of being male or female—into account. And we are just beginning to understand how complex the relationship between religion and gender is. . . .

Our Approach

In exploring the relationship between gender and religion, the authors of this volume insist upon two fundamental insights. First, they insist upon the feminist insight that all human beings are "gendered"—that is, that there is no such things as generic *homo religiosus*. No scholar studying religion, no participant in ritual, is ever neuter. Religious experience is the experience of men and women, and in no known society is this experience the same. Second, this volume assumes the phenomenological insight that religious symbols point men and women beyond their ordinary lives. As Paul Ricoeur explains it, there is no such thing as a religious symbol that is merely a sign of or statement about social structure. However religious symbols "mean," they never simply prescribe or transcribe social status. Rather they transmute it, even while referring to it. Religious symbols are, as the anthropologist Victor Turner puts it, "polysemic"; they have the quality of possessing manifold meanings.

The basic contribution of our collection of essays is to elaborate a theory of religious symbol as "polysemic" and a theory of experience as "gendered," and to elaborate these in such a way that each insight informs the other more fully than has previously been the case in American scholarship. It is to suggest that gender-related symbols—symbols that, at one level, signify maleness or femaleness (and symbols never merely signify)—do not simply determine the self-awareness of men and women as gendered nor do they simply reflect cultural assumptions about what it is to be male or female. Gender-related symbols, in their full complexity, may refer to gender in ways that affirm or reverse it, support or question it; or they may, in their basic meaning, have little at all to do with male and female roles. Thus our analysis admits that gender-related symbols are sometimes "about" values other than gender. But our analysis also assumes that all people are "gendered." It therefore suggests, at another level, that not only gender-related symbols but all symbols arise out of the experience of "gendered" users. It is not possible ever to ask How does a symbol—*any* symbol—mean? without asking For whom does it mean?

Some examples may make our method clearer. Let us take three cases of gender-related images from the chapters that follow. The Church of the Latter-day Saints, sometimes known as the Mormons, teaches that all spirits are created by a Heavenly Father and a Heavenly Mother and progress toward perfection in this life and beyond as members of human families. To Mormon adherents, the individual self has gender for all eternity, and this gender reflects a male/female division lodged at the heart of ultimate reality. To Christians in medieval Europe, on the other hand, God was sometimes seen as a bridegroom to whom all souls, no matter what sort of sexual body they inhabited, related as brides. But the "otherness" of God from creation meant that this God could also be seen as a whirlwind, a circle whose center is everywhere, or a nursing mother; it meant that all such epithets were finally valueless for evoking or explaining the essence of the divine. If we turn to the Chinese tradition, we find yet a third way in which gender symbols refer to the ultimately real. A beloved document of Confucianism says: "Heaven [Ch'ien] is my father and Earth [K'un] is my mother." But the Confucian tradition also teaches that wholeness is a feminine image and that wholeness transcends diversity. The ultimate, to a Chinese philosopher, is clearly not father or masculine; but if it is feminine, it is so only with an expanded meaning of feminine that leaves its referent in social experience far behind. Self and cosmos are thus not male and female for a Chinese philosopher or a Christian mystic in the same sense in which they are male and female for a Mormon. But do they have gender at all? And, if so, what does it mean to attribute gender to that ultimate Wholeness or Oneness that is beyond distinction or definition?

These three cases raise questions about the meaning of religious symbols. How do such symbols refer to and make use of gender? But the questions we ought to ask do not stop here. For it is also unclear, in the three cases described above, *whose* meaning we are analyzing. Neo-Confucian theories, which may be understood as feminizing the cosmos, were produced by men. Male mystics in medieval Europe venerated the Virgin Mary and wrote of Jesus as mother. Mormon theologians (all male by theological prescription) prohibit the priesthood to women because fatherhood means leadership. But what is the significance of Chinese men elaborating the idea of wholeness as feminine? Do female mystics in Christian Europe see God as mother and mean by *mother* what their male counterparts mean? Do Mormon women experience in the same way as Mormon men their church's theories of male and female roles lasting for all eternity?

Recent scholarship in the field of religion has been characterized by intensive and sophisticated discussion of the nature of symbol. I cannot enter here into the complexities of such discussion, but by treating three major theorists—Clifford Geertz (especially in his early writings), Victor Turner, and Paul Ricoeur—I can explain why we have opted for Ricoeur's more phenomenological approach. All three theorists see religious symbol as that which gives meaning to ordinary experience, not merely as a sign that points to it. All three are concerned with the believer or ritual participant as the one who receives or appropriates meaning. But of the three, Geertz relates symbol most closely to what it signifies. For this reason Geertz has been explicitly used (and misused) by some theorists who argue that female-referring symbols are especially attractive to women.

In his now-classic essay "Religion as a Cultural System," Geertz argues that symbol provides "model of" and "model for." In other words, to Geertz, religious symbols, which he defines as "historically created vehicles of reasoning, perception, feeling, and understanding," give meaning to existence by providing a model of the world as it is and a model for the world as it ought to be—a template that shapes ordinary experience by reflecting it and, in the process, imparts value from beyond it. In contrast to Geertz's concept of model, we might place Ricoeur's theory that symbols are opaque, oblique, and analogical. To Ricoeur, it is not the case that the symbol points out a meaning, that the meaning exists and the symbol names it. Rather the symbol itself in some sense precedes meaning; it "gives rise to thought." Water may signify (i.e., point to) cleanliness, but it will never "mean" cleanliness. For cleanliness itself will point to absence of or freedom from something else, something palpable and real but not communicable in a single word; it may even point beyond absence of whatever is "soiling" to another state of "purity" that not only transcends the opposites of clean/dirty, pure/sinful, good/evil but also expresses the subjective, human experience of such freedom. To Ricoeur, symbols point beyond ordinary experience, and *beyond* has a different meaning from Geertz's *beyond*. Although neither theorist thinks that symbol merely transcribes social structure, the beyond, for Geertz, is a set of ultimate values that, in a complicated but discoverable way, mirror the world. It is this "mirroring" that imparts meaning. For Ricoeur, in contrast, the beyond is open-ended—not really discoverable except by analogy. And meaning is not so much imparted as appropriated in a dialectical process whereby it becomes subjective reality for the one who uses the symbol. Therefore Ricoeur's model at least allows for the possibility that those with different gender experiences will appropriate symbols in different ways, whereas Geertz tends to suggest that *the* symbol system is *the* framework for all, no matter how complex its mirroring of reality may be. Moreover, Geertz's idea of "model of and for" inevitably suggests that gender-related symbols in some sense reinforce the experiences of men and women qua men and women.

The anthropologist Victor Turner does not really understand symbol in the same way as Ricoeur, but there are several similarities between them. Both see symbol as reflecting not just a multiplicity of meanings but a multiplicity of relationships between meanings. Both see symbol using as a process of appropriating meaning. To Turner, symbols reflect in some deep way a "likeness" between the orectic (sensory) and the abstract or normative poles of meaning; symbols unify or "condense" natural physiological facts (e.g., milk, food, breasts) and normative or social values (e.g., nurture, matriliny, etc.). The using of symbol takes the ritual participant through a process, from social integration through crisis to some sort of reversal or redress and finally to reintegration. Although Turner's approach is more functionalist than Ricoeur's, the two theorists agree in emphasizing two aspects of symbols: their capacity to refer simultaneously to many levels of human experience and their capacity to bring users to appropriate that to which the symbol points. Because of this agreement, we have adopted Turner's term *polysemic symbol* to signify an emphasis, first, on the multivalent quality of images and, second, on symbol using as an active process of appropriation. . . .

Like the idea of gender as culturally constructed and the idea of religious symbol as polysemic, the idea of genderedness has a scholarly context. It is a feminist insight, but feminist in a particular sense. For feminism is no more monolithic than is the recent discussion of symbol by anthropologists and students of comparative religion. Certain schools or emphases within feminism can, however, be identified, and two are relevant here. While all feminism arises from concern with the asymmetrical treatment of women in modern scholarship and modern life, it is safe to say very generally that American feminism in the early 1970s tended to emphasize the similarity of men and women; by the early 1980s it had begun to stress the differences between them. It is also safe to say that American feminism has tended to be empirical, inductive, and concerned with causal analysis, wrestling repeatedly with the question Why is the condition of women as it is today? Whereas French feminism has been more literary and phenomenological, wrestling with the question How can we talk about women's experience? . . .

. . . [I]f the conclusions of these final chapters are correct, the phenomenological theory of symbol discussed above may need modification. While retaining Turner's notion of symbol as polysemic and Ricoeur's idea that symbol is never merely sign, we may need to adapt for women the processual or dialectical elements in Turner and Ricoeur. That is, we may need to modify their models of how symbols mean by incorporating women's tendency to emphasize reconciliation and continuity. The symbolic reversals so important to Turner as a component of ritual may be less crucial for women than for men. The synthesis of objective referent and subjective meaning, which Ricoeur thinks is achieved in the user by the symbol, may be for women less a dialectical process than an acceptance of, a continuous living with, paradox. Thus attention to gender in the study of religion would lead not only to a questioning of Clifford Geertz's theory of symbol as "model of and model for" but also to an adjustment of even those more phenomenological insights that seem to allow for a greater complexity of relationship between social facts and symbolic meanings. In other words, the phenomenological emphasis of Ricoeur on the process by which the symbol is appropriated may need to be expanded by the phenomenological emphasis of French feminism on genderedness until we have a more varied and richer notion of the experiences of symbol users. By taking female symbol-users seriously, we might evolve an understanding of symbol itself in which paradox and synthesis take an important place beside dialectic, contradiction, and reversal. . . .

In conclusion, then, we make no arguments about the nature of "religious woman" or "religious man." We put forward no theory of the cross-cultural meaning of female or male symbols. We lend support to no current schemes of religious reform that involve the creation of new symbols or the exclusion of old ones. While sympathetic to the intention of those who would reshape the palpable inequities in society by providing new images, we find the meaning of symbols, myths, and rituals too multilayered, too complex in its relationship to social structure and social values, to feel confident either that new rituals are easily created or that radical excisions of traditional symbols will have predictable results.

And yet, radical suggestions lurk behind our cautious, academic conclusion that our subject is a complex one. One such radical conclusion has been drawn before: even traditional symbols can have revolutionary consequences. For, if symbols can invert as well as reinforce social values . . . , if traditional rituals can evolve to meet the needs of new participants . . . , then old symbols can acquire new meanings, and these new meanings might suggest a new society. If the images we explore in such detail in the chapters that follow—images of men becoming female cowherds for Krishna, for example, or of the marriage of Gnostic soul and spirit as escape from defilement—have not in the societies that produced them brought about the equality of the sexes, it is not, so to speak, the fault of the images.

A second radical conclusion lies behind our method as well. It is simply this: if we turn our attention not to what gender symbols signify (for they never merely signify) but rather to how men and women use them, we may find that the varied experiences of men and women have been there all along. To say this is in no way to suggest that we should maintain the religious status quo, for, as things are, women's voices in all their multiplicity are very hard to hear. But it is to argue that those who wish to effect the sort of changes that will let women's experiences speak may need to work, not to substitute female-referring symbols for male-referring symbols, but to open new symbolic modes. If we take as women's rituals and women's symbols the rituals and symbols women actually use, and ask how these symbols mean, we may discover that women have all along had certain modes of symbolic discourse different from those of men. Even where men and women have used the same symbols and rituals, they may have invested them with different meanings and different ways of meaning. To hear women's voices more clearly will be to see more fully the complexity of symbols. If this is so, an awareness of the genderedness of symbol users will enrich our understanding of both symbol and humanity.

❖ PAUL W. PRUYSER ❖

Paul Ricoeur's selection in this volume analyzes the language of hope in religious discourse. In this essay, Paul W. Pruyser (1916–1987), a long-time staff member of the Menninger Foundation and the author of such works as *The Vital Balance, A Dynamic Psychology of Religion,* and *Changing Views of the Human Condition,* examines the work of Ricoeur's teacher, Gabriel Marcel, applying phenomenological constructs to a psychological analysis of hope. Pruyser raises the question whether hope is grounded in the existential structure of humankind and seeks phenomenologically to discuss the relation of hope to the stances of wishing, fearing, anticipating, and waiting. Finally, he cites surprisingly relevant findings from animal studies and concludes by suggesting the importance of a phenomenology of hoping for the psychological field of personality theory.

❖

Phenomenology and Dynamics
of Hoping

Most psychological textbooks do not carry the words hope or hoping in their index or chapter headings. *Psychological Abstracts*, that great indexing journal of the psychological profession, has not had any entries or listings under hope for years.

The situation is hardly any better in the psychiatric journals and textbooks, but in that discipline the tide is turning. In French's monumental work on the integration of behavior hope is a key term, and Menninger's paper of 1959 has greatly helped to make hope an appropriate topic in psychiatry. Moreover, one can argue that the psychiatrists' long silence about hope was only a verbal and cognitive phenomenon. After all, as a professional healer the psychiatrist is by implication a hopeful, hoping, and hope-instilling person who works with hope, believing practically in its efficacy. Yet it must be said that more psychiatrists, like the psychologists, have thus far remained rather ignorant about hope's conditions and dynamics.

One may wonder what subtle reasons lie at the heart of the healer's ignorance and scientist's neglect of hope. Is it a tacit admission that hope's dynamics are so delicately equilibrated that every attempt to know it will make the phenomenon disappear? Is hope so ethereal that it cannot and should not be discussed? Is hope seen as the exclusive property of philosophers and theologians? Or as a myth?

Much the same situation prevailed only sixty years ago in relation to other subtle psychic realities, love and faith, once believed to be inappropriate objects for scientific study. But Freud's *Three Contributions to the Theory of Sex* which appeared in 1905 and James' *The Varieties of Religious Experience* published in 1902, were soon followed by a veritable cascade of further studies and discussion. Theories of love and faith are very much alive today showing that attitudes of wisdom and reverence towards them manage to coexist with attitudes of scientific exploration and theory building.

But this has been a slow gain, over many years. At first accusations were made that Freud did not really talk about love but "only" about sex, while James was not seen as discussing faith, but "only" religious experience. Ever since, there has been much bickering over the subtle differences between love, *agape, filia, eros*, sex and *koinonia*, while occasional battles rage over the differences between faith, religion, belief, *the* Faith, "true" faith, and so on. Anyone who tries to tackle a boundary concept which over the years has become communal property of several disciplines runs the risk of being disowned or kicked out of the commune. I acknowledge at the outset that hope is a boundary concept, that it is communal property of philosophers, theologians, poets, psychologists, psychiatrists, politicians and gamblers. And I know that I run the customary risk of being disowned of hope by somebody. As a psychologist I am interested chiefly in the phenomena of hope, its conditions and how it works, but I shall pursue these with explicit awareness of, and reference to, its many other interdisciplinary connotations.

Taking a long view it must be said that hoping has not always been evaluated as positively as it is by most contemporary Christianized and humanistic Westerners. Indeed, Greek and Roman attitudes towards hope were by and large negative, skeptical or cynical. Historically, it seems beyond question that man's common sense thought patterns about hope, at least in the Western hemisphere, owe a debt to Christian beginnings. Ever since its origins, Christianity as a movement has forced theological and philosophical thinkers to become explicit about hope, to inculcate hope, to assume hope, to extol hope, to help people towards hope. Not that it invented hope or suddenly discovered its existence, but cognitively and dynamically it called man's attention to the fact that he is a hoping being. It recognized hope explicitly, evaluated it positively, and made hope a theological and philosophical category. St. Paul's statement that hope should abide, Kant's question "What can I hope?," Kierkegaard's studies of "unhope" or despair, and the secular existentialists' descriptions of pathological hopelessness, emptiness and meaninglessness, are unthinkable without the Christian tradition.

It is quite astounding, therefore, to discover that even in such an explicit attempt at applying theologico-philosophical insights to psychiatric knowledge as the book *Existence* by May et al., the word hope does not occur in the elaborate index.

Marcel's View of Hope

It is within the sphere of non-psychiatric existentialism and phenomenology that one will find, to my best knowledge, the only scholarly contemporary work about hope as such. I refer to Marcel's *Homo Viator* with the subtitle "Prolegomena to a metaphysics of hope." The word "metaphysics" should not deter us here, for it is an elastic term which can cover many different loads, at times even psychology.

Marcel takes in his phenomenological study of hope perhaps unwittingly an important step. He often speaks of *hoping*, the verb, and not of hope, the noun. I think this is a first step in the psychological direction. Hoping is a process, a psychic activity of persons. It is not just an idea, but a real, live occurrence in a concrete and knowable setting. In what kind of settings does it occur?

Hoping occurs, according to Marcel, when a person is visited by a calamity. Only when a person feels caught can he hope. If everything goes perfectly well, hoping cannot enter the picture. Translating this into psychological language one might thus say hoping is a response to stress.

One form of stress is illness. Hence, illness, especially serious or terminal illness, is the stock example of a situation in which hoping may arise. Hoping is a response to the tragedy that is felt in illness. In order to hope one must first have a sense of captivity, of being caught by the human condition, in the Platonic sense of the word. The less life is felt as captivity, the less is a person susceptible to hoping.

But Marcel is at pains to make sure that we talk about hoping, and not about wishing or daydreaming or fooling oneself. Hoping is different from all these in the sense that it has only a global object. Wishes and dreams have specific objects and articulate contents; hoping is vaguer and more diffuse. There is a difference between "I hope" and "I hope that . . ." The more specific that "that" the more likely it is that a wish, an illusion or a delusion is at hand. What a person can truly hope for is very broad and global, such as deliverance, liberation, life.

Phenomenology thus seems to arrive at a position very different from Menninger's earlier position in *Love Against Hate*, which stresses the "essential identity of hoping, wishing, purposing, intending, attempting and doing," seeing all these as modifications of one great impulse. Phenomenology forces us to ask whether there is not a great difference between hoping and wishing at first, and at what conceptual level any similarity or identity between the two might be seen, after abstraction. From the point of view of drive or instinct theory, Menninger's definition of hope as a "consciousness of the realizable wish" seems quite pertinent, but when one works upwards, from pure description toward definition, one might object that when a wish is seen as realizable, one need not hope for its realization but can simply work toward it, in goal-directed fashion.

Marcel's ideas seem also opposed to the view of French, which lets the activity of hope concentrate on circumscribed goals, in marked contrast to the diffuse action which stems from needs. For French, hope is a motivating force which plays an important role in producing goal-directed behavior. In his system, the fundamental motivations consist of wishes, which fall into two classes; (1) needs or drives, with an essentially negative goal, namely the discharge or abolition of painful tension; (2) hopes, which are positive in the sense that they are wishes *for* something. Behavior is seen as polarized between needs and hopes, and integrated chiefly by the latter. Such discrepancies in the meaning of the term "hope" must mean that the word is a sort of wastebasket, which indicates all the more that phenomenological studies are needed to establish some essential distinctions before theorizing at higher levels will become fruitful.

In the psychoanalytic theory of thinking, as elaborated by Rapaport, it is assumed that in early developmental stages the presence of a strong drive in the absence of a suitable drive-object gives rise to hallucinatory images which form the elementary "stuff" of thoughts. Thus when French defines hopes as "wishes for something" one could argue with plausibility that hoping and hallucinating are closely related. This is further underscored by the popular meaning of the expressions "only a hope" or "false hopes" which stress the unreality of hope's content. But from Marcel's viewpoint this is not so; by stating that hope is essentially directed upon a global object he attempts to take it out of the sphere of wishful thinking.

There are observations which seem to support Marcel's view. A negative relation between hoping and hallucinating is indicated by [W.] Gibson's story "The Boat." Four persons out of 135 survived in a lifeboat in the Indian Ocean during World War II. When they lost hope, became thirsty, dehydrated, suffering severely from sunburn and exhaustion, they all started to hallucinate. Gibson himself, who said he survived chiefly because he had with him a woman who shared his feelings and convictions, regained his hope on the long run and with that the hallucinations disappeared.

Let us now try to look at the subject who hopes, at the "I" or "him" who does the hoping. Paraphrasing Marcel one might say that in hoping the ego feeling is different from states in which action or affect predominate. In hoping, the ego is less strongly cathected—it does not feel itself as an action or affect center. The psychologist is prone to think of the striking contrast with the studies on willing by the Wuerzburg school. In [N.] Ach's description of the will process the subjects had an enhanced ego feeling in the "Willensrück," the skeleto-muscular set of willing, the feeling of "I will" predominates. Hoping and willing, then, seem opposites in respect to ego feeling.

Marcel highlights this phenomenon from another angle, by contrasting hoping with doubt and certainty. He contends that in the phrases "I am sure" as well as in "I doubt" there is always an aggresssive undertone, by virtue of which the speaker sets himself apart as different from somebody else, whose opinion he cannot share for one reason or another. My certainty stands over and against someone else's doubt; my doubt over and against someone else's certainty. They are part of an argumentative dialogue, in which I assert my opinion against other opinions. But when a speaker says "I hope" he stands beyond argument. He does not take issue with others whose opinions have to be fought, although he may certainly depart from their viewpoint.

But hoping must also be delineated from optimism, and this too has a bearing upon ego feeling. Optimism, feels Marcel, is only possible when a person takes a position some distance from reality, enough distance so that certain obstacles which hitherto might have seemed insurmountable now seem attenuated. Optimism refers to externals, outside the intimacy of the self. The optimist as well as the pessimist accentuate aggressively the importance of "I," with distance and distinctness from others. The optimist reasons: "If you could only see things as clearly as I do . . ." or "If you could only adopt my viewpoint . . ." And similarly the pessimist, who also stresses the uniqueness and personal acumen of his viewpoint. The hoping person, in contrast to the optimist and the pessimist, remains part of the scheme of things. He is not distant from reality and from others; he appears to himself as being implied in a wider reality which transcends him. His attitude is one of modesty and humility before the nature of reality. Marcel says that there is an aspect of chastity in hope.

The chastity and humility of hoping can be seen from the relation between hoping and its global object. Hoping is not predicting that such and such will happen, nor is it claiming that such and such must happen. It is entirely outside the sphere of rights and certainties. If the things hoped for do not happen, there may be disappointment, but there is no urge to take revenge.

I believe that one can also highlight the difference between hoping and wishing by considering the role which urges or drives play in either of the two processes. Phenomenologically, hoping is connected with patience and forbearance. Hoping involves waiting, though with an added quality of awaiting. Wishing, on the contrary, is clearly associated with urges toward tension discharge. In its primordial form, wishing seeks immediate satisfaction, and while the maturation process may create possibilities for delay and postponement, the urge of the wish continues to make itself felt to the controlling ego which modifies the behavioral outcome.

In a paper by [W. C. M.] Scott one finds an interesting statement on the development of hoping out of other processes as part of a dynamic sequence. When a person's activities do not lead to satisfaction of his basic wishes, the following sequence may occur: (1) waiting; (2) anticipating; (3) pining; (4) hoping. Wishes in the absence of the gratifying object, give rise to hallucinations and the subject waits for the hallucinatory images to be transformed into sensations. In anticipating, one waits for the appearance of the sensory satisfaction to be obtained. In pining, one wishes for change, for sensory satisfaction, and for an object which will satisfy. In hoping, finally, there is also a belief that an object is forthcoming *which has itself the desire to satisfy the hoper*. In other words, hope presupposes a rather complex emotional relation between persons in which mutual desires for satisfaction occur. In this view, hoping is generated out of prior drive processes *via* waiting, anticipating and pining. It seems to me that Scott's continuum moves from primitive wishful thinking at one pole to reality-oriented thought at the other, and this important distinction may easily get lost in applying, as Scott does, the generic name "wishing" to all these processes. While wishing leads at first to magic, in hoping the magical elements are finally abandoned in favor of reality testing. I shall return to this aspect later.

Hope and Its Alternatives

Perhaps it is best to leave Marcel's descriptions at this point and consider a life situation of hoping. Suppose an adult person has been struggling for a while with certain symptoms of illness. He has consulted various physicians, who may have been able to give temporary relief and who may also have impressed upon him that his illness is serious and progressive. During a more recent visit to his doctor, the patient is told that his situation is quite precarious, and that it would be wise to prepare for the worst because the illness is considered terminal. No lasting cure can be effected, no technique can forestall the imminent collapse. Let us further assume that this patient is a realistic man, who has insight in the gravity of his situation and who is not likely to fool himself. He takes the diagnostic and prognostic statements of his physicians seriously, without altering them one iota. How will he react to this predicament?

Let us select from the many possible reactions to his imminent death two contrasting types. A first possibility is that the patient squarely faces his fate: he gives up all hope, he puts an end to all his plans and he yields to the forces of nature. Physicians would be quick to point out that such a reaction, though realistic from one point of view, would be very likely to hasten the process of dying. For where there is no hoping, the organism will not mobilize its resources to wage a valiant fight with the forces of illness.

A second reaction is to accept the doctor's prognosis, to see its inescapable implications, and to obey in reverence the scheme of nature, but yet to hope! Such a reaction is likely to enhance the use of the organism's resources and hence to prolong life, sometimes even to stave off the gloomy future that was prognosticated. Indeed, the medical literature is full of reports of this sort, even in such diseases as cancer.

For all their differences, both reactions bring up the difficult problem of reality and man's attitude towards it. Which of the two patients acted more realistically? Was it the best possible adaptation to reality to give up hope, as the first patient did? Was the hoping of the second patient, which one might describe popularly as a "hope against hope," flouting of reality, a maladaptation? To answer either question in the affirmative is justly felt as presumptuous, but one may not leave it at that. Why is it presumptuous to judge another man's attitude to reality in such a way as to justify or not justify his hoping? Obviously, because hoping is always in the sphere of reverence. But also because the boundaries of reality are fluid and uncertain.

It is precisely because reality as a whole cannot be exhaustively defined that hoping is a most intimate and private prerogative of persons. It is never possible to convince a hoping person that his hope is poorly based. The fact that he hopes where I would not hope means that his reality is different from mine or from his as I see it. He may see the point in all my objections and yet continue to hope. He may even distort reality less than I do and yet hope. Is his hoping then an act of unreality which can coexist with reality adaptation?

Now consider a third possibility, which shows also something of the sequence of events in hoping, and the difficulty in attaining hope: Pluegge's clinical account (quoted by [H. F.] Ellenberger) of the phase which some of his patients went through as they were afflicted with incurable diseases. After the patients became aware that they could not recover there was a first reaction of "spurious hope" based on denial, illusion and self-deceit. Then there came a second period in which anxiety, rebellion and despair were accentuated. But at long last, sometimes even in the very last stages of the illness, he observed a third period with new hope, quite different from the first one. Knowing full well that they were lost, the patients did not seem overwhelmed by their fate. An intense feeling of joyous hope swept away all anxiety and made it easier to tolerate the burden of physical sufferings and pain. Such hope was directed to a personal future, although the patients knew they would die. At the same time, marked positive changes in personality became apparent: patience, tolerance, humility. This was especially striking in one female patient, a spoiled and wealthy person who had always been very narcissistic. Such cases seem to indicate that hope is grounded in the existential structure of man.

Past and Future in Hoping

In regard to the relations between hoping and reality, Marcel suggests that arguments against hoping can only draw on past experience. An objector might say, "You better give up hope, because things have never turned out that way." But it does not convince the hoping person because in hoping he assumes an entirely different attitude toward time, and hence to reality. To the objector reality means "things as they are" and "things past," plus their logical extrapolations; to the hoping person, reality means "experience-in-formation." In hoping one sees the flow of time as a process in which novelty occurs and judges all knowledge, even the best, as only the distillate of past experience. To the hoper, reality is not fixed and crystallized, but open-ended. And with that, the hoping person assumes that reality has resources which are as yet undiscovered and untapped. In hoping, one lives life as an adventure.

On the other hand, it may well be asserted that the experience of time, life and reality as process is by no means in itself a guarantee for hoping. Past and present events may take away any tendency to hoping. To say that hoping requires living toward the future does not mean that the past can be ignored. Nothing is so inducive to hoping as one hope that was fulfilled. For hoping does not merely deal with possibilities, but also with the realization of possibilities. Tension between the actual and the possible is the climate in which hoping can thrive. From the point of view of knowledge and judgment, this tension is one between certainty and uncertainty. Both must be present, in a dialectic relation, for hoping to occur. In the third book of his *Ethics*, Spinoza describes hoping as "an uncertain (unsteady) joy which has been elicited in us by the representation of a future or past happening (event) of whose course we are still uncertain." And he adds in the discussion: "as long as he hopes he also fears that the event will not take a favorable course." In terms of Menninger's "consciousness of the realizable wish" this means that there is in hoping also a consciousness of the unrealizability of the wish.

Some element of uncertainty, then, is always present in hoping. In another publication, Marcel has pointed out that hoping is not a listless waiting, but that it is a psychic activity. Its affinity is not so much with desire and wishing as with willing, a view which was also expressed by W. Stern. But this is paradoxical when one recalls the phenomenal contrast in ego-feeling between willing and hoping, which I referred to earlier. Instead of activity, I would prefer to speak of participation and the determination to stick to the scheme of things. Hoping includes reality testing, perhaps with some sadness over the harshness of reality. It presupposes that a person have maximal orientation to all the aspects of his reality situation, including the barriers and obstacles he finds on his way toward wish fulfillment. But while willing is mobilized by heightened ego feeling, hoping requires some degree of surrender to the unconquerable power of nature outside of us, to the non-ego. This distinction is illustrated by the two famous phrases of the suffering Job: "Though he slay me, yet will I trust in him" shows the will of Job who tackles the formidable task of maintaining *his* trust in an undeserving God; the surrender and humility of the hoping Job is heard in "I have heard of thee by the hearing of the ear: but now my eye sees thee." Says Marcel: "Could not hope therefore be defined as the will when it is made to bear on what does not depend on itself?"

With the question the theologian is apt to enter the picture. He will say that man's contingency or his creatureliness is precisely the reason for subordinating the human will to the divine will and at the same time man's ground for hoping. All of human life has to be seen from the eschatological point of view; without it the image of man is not complete. While this point of view may have its theological validity, Marcel's distinctions between hoping and wishing may be usefully applied to the concrete eschatological pictures of religiously motivated thinkers, artists and dreamers in order to clear up some gross misunderstandings about eschatology. On the one hand there are the very specific imaginations of pearly gates and crystal lakes, harlots on beasts and laborious formulae for mass bloodshed that we are familiar with from the apocalyptic literature. These are obviously based on past experiences. They are arguments from the past, real or imagined delights and miseries projected into the future. Whatever eschatological surplus value these ideas might have, their fanciful promises and revenge themes are clearly within the realm of wishful thinking and should not be considered hopes at all in Marcel's sense of the word. True eschatology (in distinction to apocalypse), on the other hand, needs an optimal amount of globality, open-endedness and mysteriousness in order to be the kind of hoping which Marcel describes. Eschatology is the hope of things to come with a large margin of unheard-of novelty which transcends experience and imagination.

Dialectics of Hoping

Such considerations highlight some of the subtle dynamics of hoping. They imply that hoping is not a single force which runs a smooth course in human life, but a double-headed process which has contrasting qualities of experience. The experience of hoping presupposes the experience of doubting, fearing and despairing. Hoping is not an elegant drifting in leisure and comfort, as a tourist may do in a Venetian gondola. It is much more like steering a ship in a gale. Hoping is a singularly unsentimental and unromantic affair. It permits no departure from reality, otherwise it becomes illusion and delusion. In Marcel's words "Hope is a response to tragedy."

In some languages the words for hoping and its opposite share a common root French *espérer* and *désespérer*, Dutch *hopen* and *wanhopen*. The etymological meaning of our English word despair is "un-hope." Only against the background of "un-hope," or despair, is hoping possible. And in hoping, this background remains dynamically active. If reality does not first give us reasons for despairing, it cannot give us grounds for hoping. If hoping is a response to tragedy, the individual must have a tragic sense of life out of which hope may be generated. A cold-blooded appraisal of reality leads neither to despair nor to hope. To the extent that a person's ties with reality are exclusively rational and to the extent that the knower knows himself to be on a par with the world he is still on the hitherside of despairing and hoping. A tragic sense of life demands a different relationship between the knower and the known; it requires a felt difference in scale, so that the world is apprehended in its grandeur over and against the smallness of the knowing individual. Perhaps this experience lies in the borderland of reason or beyond it, as Pascal reminds us: "the last step of reason is to acknowledge that there are infinitely many things which surpass it."

I would hold then, that the forces of despairing co-determine the dynamics of hoping. And indeed, since despairing is a form of appraising reality in relation to ourselves, its continued activity in hoping is one safeguard against falling into illusions and other forms of reality distortion. For hoping is not denial of reality, but a continued re-evaluation of its content in contrast to other possible evaluations. From a structural point of view one might also say that at the moment hoping sets in, the hoper begins to perceive reality as of larger scope than the one he has

hitherto dealt with. He can faithfully take all that he himself and man-
kind has ever known about reality, acknowledge it without abrogation,
and yet envisage it as only a part of a larger reality which contains, because of its wider scope, also certain unknowns. This need not be a view
of two worlds—it is more likely to be two views of one world. When one
sees the world with oneself in it as an open-ended process, finiteness refers only to the crystallized things of the past, and all knowledge becomes
only a knowledge of parts. But the summation of knowledges of parts
does not yield the knowledge of the whole, which still thrusts toward
novelty.

Light from Animal Studies

Menninger has called attention to one of the most fascinating experimental studies on hoping, which has come from the animal laboratory as
a byproduct of certain physiological endurance tests done by [C. P.] Richter. They are worth repeating here. Immersing domesticated rats in a water jar into which from above a temperature-controlled stream of water
came down, Richter first noticed that at all temperatures a small number
of rats died within a few minutes after immersion, while others would
swim for many hours, some as long as 81 hours, without any apparent
difference in health between the two groups. Recalling a peculiar effect
of trimming the whiskers and facial hairs off rats, as demonstrated in
previous experiments, Richter then applied this deprivation technique to
another group of domesticated rats of the same variety and found a substantial increase in the number of rats which would die within a few
minutes after immersion. But a sizeable number of such curtailed rats
kept swimming from 40 to 60 hours. In a later stage of the experiments
the same procedure was used with wild rats which had all been recently
trapped. After clipping and immersion, *all* these rats died within the span
of a few minutes, without exception.

Not content with the immediate inference that the trimming of whiskers is the cause of rapid or sudden death in rats under these circumstances, especially for wild rats, Richter then carefully traced the various
steps in handling the rats throughout the process of capturing, keeping,
handling and immersing them. He inferred that the most important factor in producing rapid dying consisted in the restraint involved in holding
the wild rats. This is a situation which suddenly and finally abolished all
hope of escape! In other words, these rats die on account of hopelessness.

Although this experimental report may seem unbelievable, the next observation of Richter is even more startling. Careful electrocardiograph recordings and autopsies showed that the physiological mechanism of such sudden deaths consists of overstimulation of the parasympathetic rather than of the sympathicoadrenal system, which suggests an intense emotional reaction. The same phenomena could be observed in other forms of restraint, not in the water jar, such as holding the rats in a situation from which there was no escape, and no possibility of either fight or flight. But the *experimentum crucis* for the correctness of Richter's assumption that this sudden death is a response to felt hopelessness lies in the next dramatic observation. If such rats are being held briefly and then freed for short times, and immersed in water for brief periods on several occasions, there is a quick learning effect. The signs of "giving up" disappear and valiant swimming ensues for many long hours. Richter interprets this to mean that the brief moments of relief from the experimenter's grip or from the jar convinced the rats that escape was not impossible. It seemed as if this brief experience instilled new hope in an organism that would otherwise consider itself as being caught. And with the hope, there is a new utilization of the organism's resources.

I believe that even with the most judicious extrapolations from these animal studies, Richter's observations that one moment of escape from the water jar brought about hope illustrates a common experience in human hoping. One little ray of hope in a world of darkness is enough to invigorate some people. One moment of release from unbearable stress makes the world appear in a different image. Are there prototypes of joyful experience on which hoping feeds?

Grounds of Hoping

In the course of life there are all sorts of situations in which a person finds release from tension. Every time a wish is fulfilled there is a pleasure-laden relaxation which convinces us, at least for the moment, of an essential goodness of life. But such situations are far too specific in content and object to be the wellsprings of hoping. They may help a person to become optimistic, to expect something from life, or to assume a demandingly masterful attitude toward life. If Marcel's descriptions are correct hoping relates not to specific objects but to "ontic" states, such as deliverance, freedom, joy. It is interesting to note that Kierkegaard says the same thing about despair: "Despair over something is not yet properly despair." But while Marcel holds that hoping is an unnarcissistic act, Kierkegaard asserts the opposite about despair: "No despair is entirely without defiance." This is common psychiatric knowledge. Intensive psychosomatic despair, such as is seen in the syndrome of severe depression, is full defiance and highly narcissistic.

If despairing co-determines the dynamics of hope, then, hoping implies an internal battle with one's self-love, in the direction of reduced narcissism. Fear, doubt and despair accentuate one's sense of self-importance; hoping arises in a monaltruistic atmosphere. Yet it would be absurd to say that hoping requires self-denial or a low self-esteem. It means surrender, not only to reality-up-till-now but also to reality-from-now-on, including unknown novelties.

And at this point we encounter again the penetrating insights of Kierkegaard who held that hoping is an attempt at solving some basic contradictions in life that it is the effort to arrive at a synthesis of possibility and necessity. Kierkegaard also makes much of a particular form of despair which he describes as "not to be willing to hope." I think that this phrase highlights the dynamics of narcissism and their overcoming in hoping with extreme lucidity. Hoping is forever tenuous, because of the narcissistic pull of doubting. It is no easy job to hope. If hoping is an urge toward deliverance, does this not mean that deliverance is sought not only from "the situation" (the external conditions) but also from a too much loved self (the internal conditions)? If this is so, the invigorating influence of hoping on the sick organism loses some of its mystery. For the reorganization of the narcissistic self towards a more modest self-regard will liberate energies which can now be used for other purposes, such as defense against illness, better adaptation and the maintenance of love relations which were hitherto impossible. And many secondary effects may follow once the chain has been set in motion, leading to a gross alteration of the total circumstances. Prototypes of hoping, then, must be sought in situations which lead to altruism and reduced self-love.

At this point one might raise the question: can one hope if one is alone, in loneliness? I am sure that one can continue to wish, to daydream and to have longings. And as a consequence, if the wish is strong and contact with reality weak, one can hallucinate. The literature on isolation, accidental and experimental, is full of such examples. But can the lone man hope? Marcel stresses that true hoping requires an inter-personal context. Our construction that hoping occurs in situations of reduced narcissism would also emphasize this point. Isolation leads to hopelessness and to disintegration of personality functioning. When communication between persons fails, the isolated individual goes to pieces. Remember the ill-famed experiment of Frederick II Hofenstaufen of Sicily in the thirteenth century. He ordered some newborn babies to be nursed by a wet-nurse without speaking, singing, humming, lulling, etc., in order to study which was the original language of man: Greek, Latin or Hebrew. These children did not only fail to speak, they all died! Similarly with the children about whom Spitz has reported, who had hospitalism, marasmus, and an extremely high death rate. All these situations are well described by the words "hopelessness" and "absence of human communication."

Hoping, Wishing, and Longing

Now let us return to phenomenology and once more delineate wishing, longing and the search for pleasure from hoping. I believe that pleasure is obtained by an active search. One *seeks* pleasure, one *aims* for it, one *tries* to obtain it. One *strives* for it. Every wish is linked with an urge, which is felt as restlessness leading to action of some sort, internal (as in hallucinating) or external (as in motor behavior), until the wish is fulfilled. The language of hoping does not accentuate action verbs, but verbs of relationships and receptivity. A hope is *found*, it is *given*, it is *received*. One hopes with, through and sometimes for someone else. Hoping is basically a shared experience. Hence also the contagiousness of hoping. What William James said about courage and faith is pertinent here: "Just as our courage is so often a reflex of another's courage, so our faith is apt to be . . . a faith in someone else's faith." So it is with hoping.

I think this has some profound implications for the nature of the doctor-patient relation. Hoping is of its essence. Who gives hope to whom is an irrelevant question; the point is that hoping is generated *in* the relation. In addition to the processes of transference and counter-transference, which are products of derailed wishing, there is the process of hoping, shared by patient and doctor. Through it the relation has that quality of modesty, humility and chastity which Marcel detected at the heart of hoping. In it, also, is realized the experience of life as part of a creative process which produces novelty, even if the novelty is only the awakening of dormant potentialities. The dynamics of hoping may well be related to the placebo effect also, about which there is a growing literature.

Research in the nature and conditions of hoping is badly needed. The present report falls short of generating testable hypotheses. It states only some prolegomena for theoretical formulations. But the writer hopes that hoping will soon find its due place in personality theory.

Selected Bibliography

The following bibliography lists works dealing with both philosophical phenomenology and the phenomenology of religion. These studies should be consulted in conjunction with those of the phenomenologists of religion featured in this book.

I. PHILOSOPHICAL PHENOMENOLOGY

Michael Hammond, Jane Howarth, and Russell Keat, *Understanding Phenomenology* (Oxford, 1991)
Martin Heidegger, *Being and Time* (New York, 1962)
———, *The Piety of Thinking* (Bloomington, 1976)
Edmund Husserl, *Cartesian Meditations* (The Hague, 1973)
———, *The Paris Lectures* (The Hague, 1975)
Maurice Merleau-Ponty, *The Phenomenology of Perception* (London, 1962)
Maurice Natanson, *Edmund Husserl* (Evanston, 1973)
Paul Ricoeur, *Husserl: An Analysis of His Phenomenology* (Evanston, 1967)
Robert C. Solomon, ed., *Phenomenoloqy and Existentialism* (New York, 1972)
Herbert Speigelberg, *The Phenomenological Movement*, 2 vols. (The Hague, 1971)

II. PHENOMENOLOGICAL METHOD AND THE STUDY OF RELIGION

Ugo Bianchi, et al., eds., *Problems and Methods of the History of Religions* (Leiden, 1972)
Julius Bixler, "German Phenomenology and Its Implications for Religion," *Journal of Religion*, 9 (1929) 589–606
Hsueh-Li Cheng, "Phenomenology in T'ien-T'ai and Hua-yen Buddhism," *Analecta Husserliana*, 17 (1984) 215–227
Edward Farley, "Phenomenological Theology and the Problem of Metaphysics," *Man and World*, 12 (1979) 498–508
Inguild Gilhus, "The Phenomenology of Religion and Theories of Interpretation," *Temenos*, 20 (1984) 26–39
Eva Hirschmann, *Phänomenologie der Religion* (Würzburg, 1940)
L. Honko, ed., *Science of Religion: Studies in Methodology* (The Hague, 1979)

Åke Hultkrantz, "The Phenomenology of Religion: Aims and Methods," *Temenos*, 6 (1970) 68–88

Emefie Ikenga-Metuh, "Implications of a Phenomenological Approach to the Study of African Religions," *Religious Studies Bulletin*, 4 (1984) 142–153

George A. James, "Phenomenology and the Study of Religion: The Archaeology of an Approach," *Journal of Religion*, 65 (1985) 311–335

Ursula King, "Historical and Phenomenological Approaches to the Study of Religion," in Frank Whaling, ed., *Contemporary Approaches to Study of Religion*, 2 vols. (Berlin 1985) I: 29–163

Peter Koestenbaum, "Religion in the Tradition of Phenomenology," in J. Clayton Feaver and William Horosz, eds., *Religion in Philosophical and Cultural Perspective* (Princeton: 1967) 174–214

Sanford Krolick, "Through a Glass Darkly: What Is the Phenomenology of Religion?" *International Journal for the Philosophy of Religion*, 17 (1985) 193–199

Fillippo Liverziani, "The Phenomenology of Religion as a Science and as a Philosophy," *Analecta Husserliana*, 11 (1981) 321–334

R. J. Merkel, "Zur Geschichte der Religionsphanomenologie," in Christel Schroder, ed., *In Deo Omnia Unum* (Munich, 1942), 38–61

Hans Penner, "Is Phenomenology a Method for the Study of Religion?" *Bucknell Review*, 18 (1970) 29–54

Kurt Rudolph, *Historical Fundamentals and the Study of Religions* (New York, 1985)

Thomas Ryba, *The Essence of Phenomenology and Its Meaning for the Scientific Study of Religion* (New York, 1991)

Arvind Sharma, "An Inquiry into the Nature of the Distinction Between the History of Religion and the Phenomenology of Religion," *Numen*, 23 (1976) 81–95

Stephan Strasser, "History, Teleology and God in the Philosophy of Husserl," *Analecta Husserliana*, 9 (1979) 317–333

Linda Tober, "Husserl's Contribution to a Phenomenology of Religion," *Journal of Religious Studies*, 11 (1983) 85–96

Harold W. Turner, "The Way Forward in the Religious Study of African Primal Religions," *Journal of Religion in Africa*, 12 (1981) 1–15

Jacques Waardenburg, *Reflections on the Study of Religion* (The Hague, 1978)

Geo Widengren, "Some Remarks on the Methods of the Phenomenology of Religion," in Walter Capps, ed., *Ways of Understanding Religion* (New York, 1972)

Evan Zuesse, "The Role of Intentionality in the Phenomenology of Religion," *Journal of the American Academy of Religion*, 53 (1985) 51–73

III. ESSENTIAL PHENOMENOLOGY OF RELIGION

Joseph Geyser, *Max Schelers Phänomenologie der Religion* (Freiburg, 1924)

Daniel Guerriere, ed., *Phenomenology of the Truth Proper to Religion* (Albany, 1989)

Friedrich Heiler, *Prayer* (New York, 1932)

Steven Laycock and James G. Hart, eds., *Essays in Phenomenological Theology* (Albany, 1986)

Paul Mertens, *Zur Phänomenologie des Glaubens* (Fulda, 1927)

Clyde Pax, "Truth in Religious Experience," *Analecta Husserliana*, 22 (1987) 443–456

Simon Silverman Phenomenology Center, ed., *Phenomenology and the Numinous*, (Pittsburgh, 1988)

Kurt Stavenhagen, *Absolute Stellungnahmen* (Erlangen, 1925)

Gerda Walther, *Phänomenologie der Mystik* (Olten, 1955)

IV. HISTORICAL-TYPOLOGICAL PHENOMENOLOGY OF RELIGION

C. J. Bleeker, *The Sacred Bridge* (Leiden, 1963).

————, *The Rainbow* (Leiden 1975)

Douglas Brear, "A Unique Hindu Festival in England and India, 1985: A Phenomenological Analysis," *Temenos*, 22, (1986) 21–40

Mariasusai Dhavamony, *Phenomenology of Religion* (Rome, 1973)

Hans-Jurgen Greschat, "Essen und Trinken: Religionsphänomenologisch," in Manfred Josuttis and Gerhard Martin, eds., *Das Heilige Essen* (Stuttgart, 1980), 29–39

Antoine Guillaumont, "Esquisse d'une phenomenologie du monachisme," *Numen*, 25 (1978) 40–51

Martin Kämpchen, "Der Heilige im Hinduismus: Skizze einer religionsphänomenologische vergleichenden Studie, *Zeitschrift für Missionswissenschaft und Religionswissenschaft*, 67 (1983) 191–205

Gunter Lanczkowski, "Different Types of Redemption in Ancient Mexican Religion," in R. Zwi Werblowsky and C. J. Bleeker, eds., *Types of Redemption* (Leiden, 1970) 120–129

————, *Einfuhrüng in die Religionsphänomenologie* (Darmstadt, 1978)

Charles H. Long, *Alpha: The Myths of Creation* (New York,1963)

————, *Significations*, (Philadelphia, 1986)

Gustav Mensching, *Structures and Patterns of Religion* (Delhi, 1976)

Jacob Olupona, *Kingship and Religion in a Nigerian Community: A Phenomenological Study of Ondo Yoruba Festivals* (Stockholm, 1990)

Ivar Paulson, *Die primitive Seelenvorstellungen der nordeurasischen Volker: eine religionsethnographische und religionsphänomenologische Untersuchung* (Stockholm,1958)

————, "Zur Phänomenologie des Schmanismus," *Zeitschrift für Religions- und Geistesgeschichte*, 16, (1964) 121–141

Raffaele Pettazoni, *Essays on the History of Religions* (Leiden, 1954)

Olof Pettersson and Hans Akerberg, *Interpreting Religious Phenomena—Studies with Reference to the Phenomenology of Religion* (Stockholm, 1981)

James E. Royster, "The Study of Muhmad: A Survey of the Approaches From the Perspective of the History and Phenomenology of Religion," *The Muslim World*, 62 (1972) 49–70

Arvind Sharma, ed., *Women in World Religions* (Albany, 1987)

Ninian Smart, *The Phenomenon of Religion* (New York, 1973)

————, *The Science of Religion and the Sociology of Knowledge* (Princeton, 1973)

————, *Concept and Empathy—Collected Essays of Ninian Smart* (New York, 1986)

Theophus H. Smith, "A Phenomenological Note: Black Religion as Christian

Conjuration," *The Journal of the Interdenominational Theological Center*, 11 (Fall 1983–Spring 1984) 1–18
Nathan Soderblom, *The Living God* (London, 1933)
Harold W. Turner, *From Temple to Meetinghouse—the Phenomenology and Theology of Places of Worship* (The Hague, 1979)
Gerardus van der Leeuw, *Religion in Essence and Manifestation* (London, 1938)
———, *Sacred and Profane Beauty* (New York, 1963)
Jacques Waardenburg, *Religionen und Religion* (Berlin, 1986)
Joachim Wach, *Types of Religious Experience* (Chicago, 1951)
———, *The Comparative Study of Religion* (New York, 1958)
Geo Widengren, *Religionsphänomenologie* (Berlin, 1969)

V. EXISTENTIAL-HERMENEUTICAL PHENOMENOLOGY OF RELIGION

Carl B. Becker, "Hermeneutics and Buddhist Myths: Bringing Paul Ricoeur to Mahayana Buddhism," *Soundings*, 67 (1984) 325–335
Walter Brenneman, Stanley Yarian, and Alan Olson, *The Seeing Eye: Hermeneutical Phenomenology in the Study of Religion* (University Park, 1987)
Henry Duméry, *The Problem of God in Philosophy of Religion* (Evanston, 1964)
———, *Phenomenology and Religion* (Berkeley, 1975)
Charles Wei-hsun Fu, "Chinese Buddhism as an Existential Phenomenology," *Analecta Husserliana*, 17 (1984) 229–252
Cyriac Kanichai, "Being and Non-being: a Phenomenological Analysis of Limitation and Liberation from Indian and Western Points of View," in Zacharias Thundy, et al., eds., *Religions in Dialogue* (Lanham, 1985), 89–99
Gabriel Marcel, *The Mystery of Being*, 2 vols. (London, 1950–51)
———, *Creative Fidelity* (New York, 1982)
J. N. Mohanty, "Phenomenology of Religion and Human Purpose," in William Horosz and Tad Clements, eds., *Religion and Human Purpose* (Dordrecht, 1987), 31–47
Nel Noddings, *Women and Evil* (Berkeley, 1989)
Thomas Oden, *The Structure of Awareness* (Philadelphia, 1969)
Clarence Shute, "A Phenomenological Study of Providence," in Amiya Mazumder, ed., *The Bases of Indian Culture* (Calcutta, 1971)
Sten H. Stenson, *Sense and Nonsense in Religion: An Essay on the Language and Phenomenology of Religion* (Philadelphia, 1969)
Anna-Teresa Tymieniecka, *Logos and Life: Three Moments of the Soul* (Dordrecht, 1988)
John Wild, *Existence and the World of Freedom* (Englewood Cliffs, 1963)

Acknowledgments

RUDOLF OTTO, "On Numinous Experience as *Mysterium Tremendum et Fascinans*." Reprinted from *The Idea of the Holy: An Inquiry into the Non-rational Factor in the Idea of the Divine and Its Relation to the Rational* by Rudolf Otto, translated by John W. Harvey (2nd ed. 1950), by permission of Oxford University Press.

MAX SCHELER, "Basic Character of the Divine" (beginning on p. 87 above), from *On the Eternal in Man* by Max Scheler, translated by Bernard Noble. Copyright © 1960 by SCM Press. Reprinted by permission of Harper & Row, Publishers, Inc., and SCM Press.

WILLIAM EARLE, "Phenomenology of Mysticism," from *The Monist* 59 (1976): 519–531. Reprinted by permission of *The Monist*.

KATSUKI SEKIDA, "Samadhi," from *Zen Training: Methods and Philosophy* by Katsuki Sekida, ed. A. V. Grimstone (New York & Tokyo: Weatherhill, Inc., 1975), pp. 29–30, 91–97. Reprinted by permission of Weatherhill, Inc. Business address: Nibancho Onuma Building, 8-3 Nibancho, Chiyoda-ku, Tokyo, Japan.

CAROL P. CHRIST, "Nothingness, Awakening, Insight, New Naming." From *Diving Deep and Surfacing* by Carol P. Christ. Copyright © 1980 by Carol P. Christ. Reprinted by permission of Beacon Press.

LOUIS DUPRÉ, "Philosophy of Religion and Revelation: Antonomous Reflection vs. Theophany," from *International Philosophical Quarterly* 4 (1964): 499–513. Reprinted by permission of *International Philosophical Quarterly*.

C. J. ARTHUR, "Phenomenology of Religion and the Art of Story-telling: The Relevance of William Golding's 'The Inheritors' to Religious Studies," from *Religious Studies* 23 (1987): 57–79. Copyright © Cambridge University Press 1987. Reprinted with the permission of Cambridge University Press and the author.

W. BREDE KRISTENSEN, "Prayer," from *Meaning of Religion: Lectures in the Phenomenology of Religion* by W. Brede Kristensen, trans. John Carman (The Hague: Martinus Nijhoff, 1960), pp. 417–426. Reprinted by permission of Kluwer Academic Publishers, P. O. Box 17, 3300 AA Dordrecht, Holland.

J. M. KITAGAWA, "Three Types of Pilgrimage in Japan," from *Studies in Mysticism and Religion Presented to Gershom G. Scholem*, ed. E. E. Urbach, R. J. Zwi Weblowsky, and Ch. Wirszubski (Jerusalem: Magnes Press, Hebrew University, 1967), pp. 154–65. Reprinted by permission of Magnes Press.

MIRCEA ELIADE, "The World, the City, the House," from *Occultism, Witchcraft, and Cultural Fashions: Essays in Comparative Religions* (Chicago: University of Chicago Press, 1976), pp. 18–31. © 1976 by The University of Chicago Press. Reprinted by permission of University of Chicago Press.

ÅKE HULTKRANTZ, "The Cult of the Dead among North American Indians," from *Temenos* 14 (1978): 97–126. Reprinted by permission of *Temenos*.

PAUL RICOEUR, "Guilt, Ethics and Religion," from *Talk of God*, ed. G. N. A. Vesey, Royal Institute of Philosophy Lectures, vol. 2, 1967–68 (London and New York: Macmillan and St. Martins, 1969), pp. 100–117. Reprinted by permission of the Royal Institute of Philosophy and the author.

JOHN E. SMITH, "The Experience of the Holy and the Idea of God," from *Phenomenology in America: Studies in the Philosophy of Experience*, ed. James M. Edie (Chicago: Quadrangle Books, 1967), pp. 295–306. Reprinted by permission of The New York Times Company and the author.

MEROLD WESTPHAL, "The Existential Meaning of Guilt," from *God, Guilt, and Death: An Existential Phenomenology of Religion* (Bloomington: Indiana University Press, 1984), pp. 73–89. Reprinted by permission of Indiana University Press.

CAROLINE WALKER BYNUM, "The Complexity of Symbols," from *Gender and Religion*, edited by Caroline W. Bynum, et al. Copyright © 1986 by Beacon Press. Reprinted by permission of Beacon Press.

PAUL W. PRUYSER, "Phenomenology and Dynamics of Hoping," from *Journal for the Scientific Study of Religion* 3 (1963): 86–96. Reprinted by permission of *Journal for the Scientific Study of Religion* and Society for the Scientific Study of Religion.

UNIVERSITY PRESS OF NEW ENGLAND
publishes books under its own imprint and is the publisher for Brandeis University Press, Brown University Press, University of Connecticut, Dartmouth College, Middlebury College Press, University of New Hampshire, University of Rhode Island, Tufts University, University of Vermont, and Wesleyan University Press.

Library of Congress Cataloging-in-Publication Data

Experience of the sacred : readings in the phenomenology of religion /
edited by Sumner B. Twiss, Walter H. Conser, Jr.
    p.   cm.
Includes bibliographical references.
ISBN 0-87451-530-0 (pbk.)
    1. Religion—Philosophy.   2. Phenomenology.   I. Twiss, Sumner B.
II. Conser, Walter H.
BL51.E954   1992
291—dc20   92-53867